'Do I Not Like That!'

One-liners, wise words, gaffes and blunders from the world's greatest football managers

Geoff Tibballs

Virgin

First published in Great Britain by
Virgin Publishing Ltd
Thames Wharf Studios
Rainville Road
London W6 9HT

A catalogue record for this book is available from the British Library.

ISBN 0 7535 0371 9

Typeset by TW Typesetting, Plymouth, Devon

Printed and bound by Mackays of Chatham PLC

Contents

Acknowledgements

Apart from the books listed at the end of the relevant entries, most of the quotes featured here have been culled from *The Times*, *Sunday Times*, *Daily Telegraph*, *Daily Mail*, *Express*, *Mail on Sunday*, *Observer*, *Daily Record*, *Guardian*, *Sun*, *World Soccer*, *Total Football*, *Matchday*, *Match of the Day*, *When Saturday Comes*, *Football Monthly* and *FourFour Two*, plus assorted TV and radio interviews, match-day programmes and back copies of the fondly remembered *Football League Review*. My thanks to all of these publications for reporting the words of wisdom (and otherwise) of the world's soccer managers, and to Nottinghamshire Library Services for allowing me to sift through back copies of newspapers. Thanks also to Rod Green and Lorna Russell at Virgin Publishing for having faith in the project, and to Carol, Nicky and Lindsey for maintaining total silence during *Football Focus*. And, lastly, thanks to the managers themselves, without whom this book would be . . . very thin.

Introduction

The time was when football managers talked only in clichés, about games of two halves and taking each match as it comes. But as an increasingly hungry media hangs on their every word, many have smartened up their act to incorporate witty, readily quotable one-liners and pithy put-downs reminiscent of Bernie Clifton at his peak, along with philosophical statements worthy of a latter-day Descartes, whose mathematical genius would surely have been tested by the relative merits of 4–4–2, 4–5–1 and 4–2–4. Now that Kenny Dalglish, whose friends assure us that his wit is as dry (and indeed as productive) as the Sahara, has left Newcastle, taking with him press conferences not unlike the 'Yes, No' interlude on *Take Your Pick*, the monosyllabic managers have all but become extinct. The trend now is for snappy soundbites. So maybe when King Kenny returns to gainful employment (as he may already have done by the time you read this), he will have hired Paul Whitehouse as his scriptwriter and will be forbidden from saying 'at the end of the day' unless it's actually midnight.

The improvement in managerial responses over the years is partly due to the superior quality of the questions they are now asked. Whereas a question from Garth Crooks can go on for several pages and be phrased with an earnestness befitting the outbreak of war, thirty years ago post-match interrogation amounted to little more than 'How does it feel?' On the subject of which, I was intrigued to discover that Alf Ramsey, of all people, is reputed to be the first manager to use the phrase 'over the moon', after Ipswich had won the First Division Championship in 1962. I had always assumed Ramsey was a kindred spirit to C.J. in *The Fall and Rise of Reginald Perrin*, for whom a cliché was like a red rag to a bull. Ramsey's interviews were always singularly unrevealing, but worth listening to just to hear him add his aitches in the wrong places – like Parker in *Thunderbirds* – or drop the last letter of present participles (runnin', shootin', kickin' and headin'). Or there would be the joy of counting how many times he said 'most certainly' (the forerunner of Ron Atkinson's 'very much so'), or mentioned Martin Peters. Similarly, thirty years on, Glenn Hoddle interviews are to be cherished, not only to marvel at how one who used to be so artistic on the pitch (if not on *Top of the Pops*) can be so clumsy with the English language – the need for 'them three points' being a prime example – but also to wait for the next time he uses the word 'situation'. The wait rarely lasts more than a few sentences since it is clearly his favourite word, one which he is able to slip into any, er, situation.

While Ramsey almost never knowingly came out with a merry quip – I only managed to unearth one example, er, and Hoddle rarely does, there were a select band of managers in the 1970s who did. Men such as Bill Shankly, Tommy Docherty, Brian Clough and Malcolm Allison were experts at giving the media what they wanted, and their good work has been carried on by the likes of Ron Atkinson, Kevin Keegan, Dave Bassett and Joe Kinnear. From this list, it might be deduced that there are fewer jesters in the lower divisions. Not true. If you're a manager at, say, Hartlepool, you'd have to laugh or you'd go mad, but in this Premiership-obsessed age your comments are reported less frequently. As a long-suffering Millwall supporter (is there any other kind?), I have endeavoured to make sure that the smaller clubs – managed by the likes of Barry Fry, Neil Warnock and Colin Murphy – are well represented in this book.

That the title should mirror Graham Taylor's remark on the Channel 4 documentary *An Impossible Job* is natural in as much as the phrase 'do I not like that' has since virtually become an acceptable part of the English language, but is perhaps a little unfair on the man himself. In an age where some of his colleagues think erudite is an adhesive, Taylor, for all he has been subjected to, continues to be eloquent, honest and sensible. And maybe subsequent events at England level and also at Wolves under the unlamented Mark McGhee – not to mention his own achievements at Watford – have shown that Taylor is a better manager than a lot of people ever gave him credit for. That'll be a fiver please, Graham.

Geoff Tibballs
November 1998

1 The Job

My life is my work. My work is my life.

Liverpool's Bill Shankly, 1968

I was the best manager in Britain because I was never devious or cheated anyone. I'd break my wife's legs if I played against her, but I'd never cheat her.

Bill Shankly, 1974

Liverpool was made for me and I was made for Liverpool.

Bill Shankly, 1960s

I met Mick Jagger when I was playing for Oxford United and the Rolling Stones played a concert there. Little did I know that one day he'd be almost as famous as me.

Manchester United's Ron Atkinson, 1984

It's bloody tough being a legend.

Ron Atkinson, 1983

No, I always thought I was good.

Ron Atkinson when asked whether he thought he was a better manager for his unhappy experiences in Spain with Atlético Madrid, 1990

I know I am better than the five hundred or so managers who have been sacked since the war. If they had known anything about the game, they wouldn't have lost their jobs.

Brian Clough on landing his first management job, at Hartlepool United, 1965

Arrogant is a fair word – and conceited. I'm conceited that I've got them this far, having worked so hard with them. I think conceit and arrogance are part of a man's make-up. Perhaps I've got too much.

Brian Clough, a year before he won the First Division title with Derby County, 1971

I do not think we [me and Peter Taylor] could get Aston Villa into the First Division, I *know* we could.

Brian Clough on rumours linking him with the Villa job, 1974

I'd want to be number one in my industry for management rather than just motivation. I couldn't motivate a bee to sting you if it didn't have the equipment. I couldn't motivate a snake to bite you if it didn't have the teeth. You can only bring out of people what they are capable of giving. Two of the great myths circulating now are that Heinz beans are the best and that I can get more out of men than they have inside them.

Brian Clough, 1975

It's easy enough to get to Ireland. It's just a straight walk across the Irish Sea as far as I'm concerned.

Brian Clough announcing his interest in becoming manager of the Republic of Ireland, 1985

I can't promise to give the team talk in Welsh, but from now on I shall be taking my holidays in Porthcawl and I've bought a complete set of Harry Secombe albums.

Brian Clough nurturing hopes of becoming the new manager of Wales, 1988

I could manage England part-time – and still walk the dog.

Brian Clough, 1993

You drink to celebrate a victory – and I had more to celebrate than most.

Brian Clough on stories about his drinking, 1994

2

I call myself 'Big 'Ead' to remind myself not to be one.

Brian Clough as manager of Nottingham Forest, 1980s

My missus could keep this lot up.

Clough's former sidekick, Peter Taylor, on taking over Derby County when they were bottom of the Second Division, 1982. They rallied to finish a respectable thirteenth

Give me nine games. If I've not turned it round by then you can write me off for all time, string me up and call me a fake.

Peter Taylor, as Derby made an awful start to the following season, 1983. Six months later, the noose was in place

My electricians' exam was much tougher than this.

Jimmy Case on taking over at Brighton, 1995. He soon received a nasty shock

Failure is not on my agenda.

Hibernian's Alex McLeish, 1998

I'm convinced managers don't sign me because they think I would be after their job in a couple of months.

Chris Waddle, puzzled by the lack of offers after making Burnley fans yearn for the good old days of John Bond, 1998

I was just as disappointed as Mandela.

Chelsea's Ruud Gullit on a cancelled meeting between the two men, 1997

There's so many clubs been ruined by people's ego. The day after we won our first European Cup, we were back at this club at 9.45 in the morning, talking about how we would do it again, working from that moment, because nobody has the right to win anything they haven't earned.

Liverpool's Bob Paisley, 1982

Bob Paisley said it took him twenty years to get his European experience with Liverpool. I am taking the short-cut.

Terry Venables on joining Barcelona, 1985

What my name has really been built on is a reputation not only for winning but for leaving every club I manage in a better condition than when I arrive.

George Graham, during his last days at Leeds, 1998

I've made my career by getting players nobody else wanted and getting them to believe that they are the bollocks.

Birmingham City's Barry Fry, 1994

I built up a reputation as something of a repair man at struggling clubs.

Former Colchester United boss Dick Graham, 1973

I honestly believe I could go into the jungle and find a winning side.

Tranmere Rovers' John King, 1994

I've been at this game a long time and I've got a lot of it right. But I've never mastered the trick of pleasing the eight lads I have to leave out every Saturday.

Manchester United's Alex Ferguson, 1998

I still had my L-plates on when I was down at QPR. The L-plates have gone now. I feel as though I have passed my test.

Birmingham City's Trevor Francis, 1998

People keep telling me how old I am, so my motivation in the job is to prove I'm still as good as the younger ones.

Derby County's Jim Smith celebrating 26 years as a League manager, 1998

I don't have many other talents. I am just a football person. You get these people, and I am one of them.

Aldershot's Ian McDonald, soldiering on, 1992

I'm uncomfortable with all this fame and adulation. Before this, I think I was just seen by most people as a little twat!

Barnsley's Danny Wilson, 1997

If UEFA want to send me an award as manager of the week, I will accept it gratefully.

Wales manager Bobby Gould after restoring national pride with wins over Denmark and Belarus, 1998

Managers are like players. A player might think he is George Best when he is not, and similarly I could go on for ever thinking I was someone like Don Revie when I know I am not.

Unassuming Sheffield Wednesday boss Derek Dooley overcoming an identity crisis, 1971

At my stage in life, I don't have an ego and I'm not out to make a fantastic name for myself. I just enjoy football. I live it, I eat it, I sleep it.

Southampton's fifty-year-old Dave Merrington, 1995

We cheat, we tell lies, we con people. Any manager who says we don't do that isn't being honest. That's the only way to survive. It's the law of the land.

Tommy Docherty, two years after his exit from Manchester United, 1979

We are the Cinderellas of the World Cup. Our mission is to postpone midnight for as long as possible.

Jamaica coach Rene Simoes, 1998

Success for this club will be a position in mid-table and still being in existence in twelve months' time.

Exeter City's Peter Fox, 1995

If we are in the same position come May, then we'll all be doing laps of honour around the pitch.

Alan Curbishley, with Charlton twelfth in the Premiership, 1998

We've had three Wembley appearances and three promotions, but it gets difficult when you have to keep selling your best players. You have to try to pull another rabbit out of the hat.

John Rudge on his fifteen years in charge at Port Vale, 1998

When I came here, I honestly thought that the club wasn't called Southampton. I thought it was called Struggling Southampton, because that was all that was ever said about them.

David Jones, 1998

I look at myself every night and wonder if, perhaps, I've run over a black cat or knocked down a nun.

David Jones seeking an explanation for Southampton's poor start to the season, 1998

I must have broken a job lot of mirrors and run over a few black cats.

Everton's Mike Walker, 1994

All you need is a team of eleven very good players that are also very lucky.

Herbert Chapman revealing the secret of his success with Huddersfield and Arsenal, 1930s

For too long, people have talked of this being an unlucky place. They even added a second magpie outside the ground to stop people thinking 'one for sorrow'.

Kevin Keegan changing Newcastle's fortunes, 1992

I'm a lucky bastard.

Birmingham City's Barry Fry, 1996

I'm not a believer in luck, although I do believe you need it.

Manchester City's Alan Ball, 1996

With our luck, one of our players must be bonking a witch.

Norwich City's Ken Brown, 1987

Right now, if I robbed a bank I'd get mugged on the way out.

Manchester City's Brian Horton, 1994

Napoleon wanted his generals to be lucky. I don't think he would have wanted me.

Graham Taylor mulling over England's World Cup exit, 1993

This is a bloody awful job, but it's not going to turn me into a bloody awful person.

Graham Taylor on managing the national team, 1993

For the first ten days after I resigned as England manager, I would wake up every morning feeling as though I'd gone ten rounds with Frank Bruno.

Graham Taylor, 1994

People say it got to me and, given that I'm not used to waking up in the morning and screwing the sweat out of my pyjamas, it probably did.

Graham Taylor reflecting on the pressures of the England job, 1997

I think I have the best job in the country.

England's Bobby Robson, 1985

I just feel I am an honest, straightforward guy. I have found some of the criticism quite hard to take. I know I did a good job at Ipswich – it was what got me the England job. Will anyone come into the England job, after me or instead of me, with my track record? They will need to have their club in the top four or five in the First Division for getting on for ten years.

Bobby Robson, 1988

The job was bringing too much heartache to those nearest to us. It was rough on my son and daughter, and it's not very nice to hear your father constantly attacked. Nearly everyone in the country seems to want me out. So I'm giving them what they want.

Don Revie on walking out on England, 1977

This is a great job – until a ball is kicked.

England coach Terry Venables, 1995

The more I find out about the job, the more I realise that club managership is no apprenticeship for it.

Glenn Hoddle on the England experience, 1997

You've got to be joking. Even the Pope would have second thoughts about taking the job.

Swiss national team manager Roy Hodgson on why he wouldn't be applying for the England job, 1993

I don't want the job and I don't envy whoever gets it.

Steve Coppell ruling himself out of the England post, 1993

I wanted to be the England manager, but I swear too much.

Barry Fry settling for Southend United instead, 1993

I made the first move. They did not contact me. I fancied being England manager.

Don Revie, 1974

As manager of the national team you know that, apart from the Chancellor, you'll probably be the most hated person in the country.

Spurs' Ossie Ardiles on speculation that he was in line for the England job, 1993

With a national team, you have to be a coach and a politician.

Nigeria's French coach Phillipe Troussier, 1998

Who will the FA pick next? Probably Walt Disney.

**Sheffield United's Dave Bassett considering the next
England manager, 1993**

When the FA get into their stride, they make the Mafia look like kindergarten material.

Brian Clough, 1970s

They do not judge Pavarotti by how he sings in the shower. They wait until he is on stage.

**Holland's Leo Beenhakker, criticised after losing to
Austria in the build-up to the World Cup, 1990**

What is the pleasure of being in international management? You never see the players, you have to win – and then afterwards you don't see them again. There is pressure all the time. If you have a good generation of players, the manager can do well. If you don't, you do badly. Only a masochist would want the job.

Arsenal's Arsène Wenger, 1998

I've never been attracted to a club which was at the top of their division or even close to it. Perhaps that's down to the fact that when you inherit success, so much more is expected of you.

Jack Charlton, from *Jack Charlton: The Autobiography*
(Partridge Press, 1996)

It's always a problem, being right at the top of the League every season. People just expect you to be there, and if you slip up, they're not going to forgive you.

Rangers' Walter Smith, from *I Think I'll Manage* by George Sik
(Headline, 1996)

If Barça come second, that's failure.

Barcelona coach Louis Van Gaal, 1998

You can have the best collection of footballers ever, but if there is no one driving the bus, you'll not get there.

Manchester United's Alex Ferguson, 1990s

Being manager of Barnet was like living with a double-decker bus on your head. When I left, it was like it had been driven off.

Barry Fry, 1993

There's a queue of people a mile long waiting for me to fail. I know that. If they found me in a gutter, they wouldn't help me up. I'd be smashed over the head with a cricket bat to make sure I stayed down.

Birmingham City's Barry Fry under no illusions about his popularity, 1994

Even if you are the worst manager in the world, you should win at least once in three months.

Barry Fry lamenting Birmingham's relegation to the Second Division, 1994

You're only as good as your last result.

Spurs' Bill Nicholson resigning, 1974

Football is a capricious taskmaster.

Sutton United's Barrie Williams, 1989

Once you are going to be a manager, you accept the rules of the game. And the rule of the game is that if you win, you will be regarded as a good, successful manager. If you lose, you will be regarded as a failure.

Roy Hodgson, ten days before being sacked by Blackburn, 1998

The problems were Friday nights and Sunday mornings – knowing we were going to lose on a Saturday and then reading about it the next day.

Roy Hodgson on his stint as assistant manager to Bobby Houghton at Bristol City, 1982

We looked bright all week in training, but the problem with football is that Saturday always comes along.

Spurs' Keith Burkinshaw, 1983

It's a great job, apart from Saturday afternoons.

Jocky Scott, boss of bottom-of-the-table Dunfermline Athletic, 1991

Southampton is a very well-run outfit from Monday to Friday. It's Saturday we've got a problem with.

Ex-Saints boss Lawrie McMenemy, 1995

The image I had at Wimbledon was of an ebullient cheeky fellow, and I wasn't the Archbishop of Canterbury that Watford needed.

Dave Bassett on becoming Sheffield United manager after an unhappy spell at Watford, 1988

If Dave Bassett is going to resign, I don't threaten to resign, it happens.

Bassett dismissing rumours of his impending departure from Sheffield United, 1991

The more I thought about it, the more I realised that Paul Daniels would have been a better choice as Manchester City manager.

Dave Bassett declining to sit in the Maine Road hot-seat, 1996

It's a massive club. It's just a little bit sickly.

Joe Royle accepting the Manchester City job, 1998

I would think about it if asked, but it has taken me a year to get my golf handicap down to single figures and I'm not going to give that up easily.

West Bromwich Albion caretaker boss Richie Barker considering the possibility of taking the job on a permanent basis, 1997

I want to be here a long time.

Steve Coppell taking over at Manchester City, 1996. He resigned after six matches

They say Steve Coppell showed courage to leave. It takes more courage to stay!

Phil Neal, caretaker boss of struggling Manchester City, 1996. Coppell had quit, claiming the job was affecting his health

I've got the orchestra baton now, although there are not many singers about. But if we dig deep, we can get a male voice choir.

Phil Neal admitting the size of his task at Maine Road, 1996

I can't teach lame ducks to fly any more.

United States coach Bob Gansler announcing his resignation, 1991

It was a surprise, but a very pleasant one. I had not planned to become a football manager.

46-year-old club physiotherapist Bertie Mee becoming manager of Arsenal, 1966. Five years later, he led them to the Double

I never wanted the job in the first place.

Liverpool's Bob Paisley, 1980s

We would never put him in the position of having to cope with the senior team. That isn't what he's happy at.

Scotland's Jock Stein on his eventual successor Andy Roxburgh, 1985

Well, I didn't ask for the job, you know.

Andy Roxburgh after Scotland's 4–1 defeat in Belgium, 1987

When I'm managing Maidenhead in two years' time, I'm quite sure that I'll know I have made the wrong decision.

Martin O'Neill on his decision to turn down Nottingham Forest and stay at Wycombe, 1993

In 1993, when the opportunity of managing Forest came up, I lived a mile and a half from the City Ground, I still had a house up there and I was living in rented accommodation down in High Wycombe. The decision was so simple it was untrue. Only an Irishman would have turned it down.

Martin O'Neill, 1998

I thought about Leeds, agonised, soul-searched, and even lost a bit of weight.

Leicester City's Martin O'Neill deciding to stay at Filbert Street, 1998

Potential in a club is nothing until it has been realised. The shadow of that earlier era at Leeds has been cast too long. You can't pay the mortgage on memories.

Howard Wilkinson, aware of the challenge ahead at Elland Road, 1988

I'm not afraid of the challenge. Someone who's afraid doesn't leave home in the morning.

Vanderley Luxemburgo, the new coach of Brazil, 1998

Manchester United and its supporters were living in a fool's paradise, and had been doing so for some considerable time. Manchester United were simply not good enough to contemplate a tilt at any of the major prizes in the game.

Ron Atkinson taking over at Old Trafford, from *United to Win* (Sidgwick & Jackson, 1984)

I knew it was a hell of a challenge. You don't get these jobs if a club is successful, do you?

Eddie May trying to keep Torquay United afloat, 1996

I found myself with two players and no backroom staff.

Mike Pejic taking charge at Chester City, 1994

I used to come in some mornings and think, what can I do with this lot?

Harry Redknapp remembering the lack of good players when he took over at West Ham, 1998

The club put on a trial match for me to see what talent I had available. At half-time my wife turned to me and said, 'Let's go home.'

Sir Alf Ramsey recalling his first impressions of the 1955 Ipswich Town playing staff, 1970s

I like being manager of Wimbledon. I don't think there's any challenge in being manager of AC Milan.

Joe Kinnear, 1993

This is my first job as manager and I picked the most difficult time in the club's history.

Shane Westley, boss of impoverished Lincoln City, a week before his dismissal, 1998

The whole place is a shambles. It has to be sorted out and discipline restored. It's my job to manage and the players have to play. There are too many who talk a good game. I will do the talking. They will do the playing.

Graham Taylor on his first day in charge at Aston Villa, 1987

There is no doubt I have taken on a far more difficult job here than I had at Chelsea. It was never going to be easy but I came into it with my eyes open.

Newcastle United's Ruud Gullit, 1998

Preparing the side is just like the matador dressing up to go in the ring. The adrenalin is flowing and he feels ready. The only problem is, he has to face the bull. We will have to face the bull next season, and I don't intend to go jumping behind any barriers.

Rochdale's Uruguayan-born manager Danny Bergara, 1988

Everybody wants to take on the best, and I do too. I want to pit my wits against all of them – Manchester United, Real Madrid, Juventus and Fray Bentos.

Barry Fry, 1993

I want to be a great manager. I want to be known as a great manager. That's in there screaming.

Southampton's Alan Ball, ever the dreamer, 1994

I'd be barmy to leave. I could not, in the final analysis, turn my back on people who had been so good to me.

Ron Atkinson turning down Aston Villa to stay at Sheffield Wednesday, 1991

The biggest single reason is my home life. Wednesday's board were prepared to bend over backward to accommodate me, but it still meant a four-hour journey every day to work and back.

Ron Atkinson changing his mind about the Villa job a few days later, 1991

Regarding the recent speculation concerning myself and Aston Villa FC, I wish to make it clear that I will not be the next manager of Aston Villa FC.

Brian Little's resignation letter to Leicester City, 1994. Four days later, he became the manager of Aston Villa FC

I would be very flattered to be offered the job at Anfield, but I would never contemplate leaving Rangers. I see my short-term and my long-term future here. We are building something which will last a very long time.

Graeme Souness at Rangers, 1991

I feel I have gone as far as I am allowed to go in trying to achieve success at this football club. Certain things happened at Rangers or in Scottish football that made me think seriously about my future there.

Graeme Souness, two months later, taking over at Liverpool, 1991

I love challenges. I like the aggravation that goes with football management.

Graeme Souness inheriting the Anfield kingdom, 1991

I daren't play in a five-a-side at Anfield, because if I collapsed, no one would give me the kiss of life!

Graeme Souness, recovering from open-heart surgery, encountering plenty of aggravation at Liverpool in 1993, from *Liverpool from the Inside* by Stan Liversedge (Mainstream, 1995)

The strain of trying to win promotion has proved too much.

Liverpool's Phil Taylor announcing his resignation, 1959. The board chose Bill Shankly as his successor

I'm just not up to the job.

Doug Livermore resigning after a month in charge at Swansea City, during which time they failed to gain a single point, 1983

At least I'll be able to sleep tonight.

Everton's Howard Kendall after a welcome 1–0 win over Southampton, 1993. An hour later he resigned.

Pressure is ten times greater when you are bottom of the table.

Millwall's Benny Fenton, 1972

It's tough at the top – it's hell anywhere else.

Birmingham City's Freddie Goodwin, 1969

Believe me, the pressure is greater when you're at the top because people expect more of you.

Colchester United's Jim Smith, 1974

Managing at the top is a million miles more difficult. These are hard jobs – you have restrictions – but it's nowhere near as hard as managing in the Premiership.

Stoke City's Brian Little, formerly with Aston Villa, 1998

The pressure is such that some coaches would love it if there were no matches.

Cameroon coach Claude Le Roy, 1998

The pressure at Anderlecht is great. But it appears that my presence put more pressure on the players. We have reached the point where the only way I can take the pressure off is by leaving.

Anderlecht coach Arie Haan tendering his resignation, 1998

If a fox is completely brilliant, he finds himself a hole and hides. If his position is discovered, he is dug up and thrown to the hounds. But a football manager hasn't even got a hole to hide in.

Brian Clough, 1970s

I'm not the worrying type. But the pressures of football management are still wearing, even for a chap like me. To an emotional, highly-strung individual, the job must be very exacting. Very exacting indeed.

Sheffield United's Arthur Rowley, 1968

To me, pressure is being homeless or unemployed, not trying to win a football match.

Scotland coach Andy Roxburgh, 1980s

I've a saying that if you don't like the heat in the kitchen you should get out. I can put up with the heat.

Aston Villa's Ron Saunders, 1979

I look at the hype of the Premiership and realise it is quite a pleasure to work in the Second Division.

Graham Taylor at Watford, 1997

It's a great ship. There's plenty of room, plenty of rations and nobody wants to leave. But sometimes we've got to row like hell.

Tranmere's John King likening the season to a voyage and the club to a Viking longboat, 1994

Each season is like a woman having a baby. Winning the Cup was a nice baby. At the moment, our baby is the stand. It's a bit of a jumbo and there is a hell of a problem with the delivery.

Chelsea's Dave Sexton on the burden of Chelsea's new West Stand, 1973

At a club like Barnsley, you have to take the fear away.

Danny Wilson preparing for the unknown country of the Premiership, 1997

I never think we are going to win before a match. It is not until the game is under way that I can start to grow in confidence.

Notts County's Jimmy Sirrel, 1971

I enjoy it when we're not playing or when there's ten minutes to go and we're leading 5–0. Otherwise I don't enjoy it at all.

Bertie Mee echoing the views of many fans of the day who enjoyed soccer when Arsenal weren't playing, 1972

I never enjoy watching my own team play.

Howard Wilkinson of Leeds United, 1989

One thing I have learned from being at Spurs is the word 'crisis'.

Gerry Francis at Tottenham, 1997

A man must find some way to make himself jerk out of his hectic round one way or another. He must do this, or go potty.

Queens Park Rangers' Alec Stock, 1968

When you are a manager, there are so many more people you have to try to get away from.

Coventry City's Noel Cantwell, 1968

A manager is never free of football. At the ground, at the theatre, in the streets, there's no respite.

Middlesbrough's Peter McWilliam, who became the League's first four-figure manager, 1932

In management, make sure you don't live in the town. If you're in the place where you work, you can't get rid of it. It sticks to your clothes.

Alan Durban, ex-Sunderland manager, 1990

You can never leave this job behind. Even when you're sitting at home watching television on a Sunday afternoon, you'll be thinking about the game. There's no getting away from it.

Norwich City boss Ron Saunders, 1973

I never let football people come to my home. Football always has been, and always will be, of secondary importance to me.

West Ham's Billy Bonds, 1990

I woke up this morning for the first time without a headache.

Billy Bonds after resigning from West Ham, 1994

I asked my five-year-old son Adam if he wanted his daddy to go back to being a football manager. He said he didn't, and I asked him why. He replied: 'Because I won't see you any more.'

Gerry Francis returning to Queens Park Rangers, 1998

You'd come in after a bad result and wait for a bit of sympathy and you'd get slaughtered. Cathy would say: 'What a bloody day I've had with these weans. You'll need to do something about it!'

Alex Ferguson on the receiving end of a tongue-lashing from his wife, 1989

My wife thinks I've been too greedy, wanting to win the League every year. She's maybe right. But you try telling players and supporters that.

Alex Ferguson, 1998

You need a thick skin at times, a sense of humour and a good wife behind you.

Hull City's Terry Neill, 1974

I don't need a thick skin. I've not been caught in bed with any strange women.

West Ham's Harry Redknapp responding to David Mellor's comment that football managers need to be thick-skinned to cope with criticism, 1997

At times there were problems with the travelling. A chance came that was going to be better geographically.

Ray Harford explaining why he was resigning from West Bromwich Albion to take over at Queens Park Rangers, 1997. He had previously worked at Blackburn

I told him that even though they're building the Channel Tunnel, it just wouldn't be possible for me to drive back from Marseilles every night.

Ron Atkinson revealing that he had turned down an approach from the president of Marseilles before joining Aston Villa, 1991

Women should be in the kitchen, the discotheque and the boutique, but not in football.

'New Man' Ron Atkinson, 1989

Football's not a place for wives. If a player can't take care of himself, you've got to look at his character and ask yourself, can he look after himself on a Saturday afternoon?

West Ham's Harry Redknapp, 1998

When I'd agreed to join, I told my wife that I'd had another offer from abroad. You should have seen her reaction.

Hereford-based Colin Addison joining Welsh club Merthyr Tydfil after spells in Spain, South Africa, Kuwait and Qatar, 1996

It wasn't her wedding anniversary, it was her birthday, because there's no way I'd have got married in the football season. And it wasn't Rochdale. It was Rochdale reserves.

Liverpool's Bill Shankly refuting stories that he had taken his wife Nessie to watch Rochdale on their wedding anniversary, 1960s

Whenever my family came to watch me in my Sunderland days, we always seemed to lose. It's got beyond a joke, so from now on they're all banned – in my own interest.

Reading boss Charlie Hurley, 1972

I'm too old and tired. It's a job for a young man's brains and energy. It's not an eight-hours-a-day job, it's twenty-four hours a day. And there's no way you can get away from that.

64-year-old Joe Fagan stepping down from Liverpool, 1985

To be honest, I suppose I wasn't sane. I was raving and creating hell with everyone. Why us? Was it some human error, or had this been decreed from above? If so, why hadn't I died with them? What was so special about me that I'd survived?

Manchester United's Matt Busby reflecting on the 1958 Munich air crash, 1960s

People shouldn't use the words 'catastrophe' and 'disaster' when they talk about football. A catastrophe is when a mine closes down and a community is put out of work. A disaster is when a plane comes down and kills hundreds. Football is a pressure situation, but believe me there are bigger pressures in life.

Oldham Athletic's Joe Royle putting things into perspective, 1994

I've never had any sleepless nights in this game and I don't aim to start now.

Jack Charlton in his first managerial post, at Middlesbrough, 1974

Then and there I said to myself that I wasn't going to die in the dugout. There are more important things in life than football. If I can choose the way I will leave this world, it will be clutching a rod, with a 40lb salmon on the other end of the line dragging me down the river!

Jack Charlton on the death of Jock Stein during the Wales v. Scotland international in 1985, from *Jack Charlton: The Autobiography* (Partridge Press, 1996)

At least it proves to everyone that I do have a brain.

Jack Charlton after a brain scan, 1994

Football is not a matter of life and death. It's much more important than that.

Liverpool's Bill Shankly, 1960s

I had to say I was retiring, though I believe you retire when you're in a coffin and the lid is nailed down and your name is on it.

Bill Shankly 'retiring' from Liverpool, 1974

I have decided to quit as a full-time soccer manager four years from now. That statement is not meant to shock people, to stir them up or to frighten them. It is a fact.

Nottingham Forest's Brian Clough, 1978

I didn't expect today to be so emotional, but I ain't going to miss the job at all.

Brian Clough retiring after Nottingham Forest's relegation, 1993

For eighteen years I have been devoted to United. Now I must find a future away from Old Trafford.

Wilf McGuinness resigning from Manchester United after being demoted to reserve-team trainer, 1970

If I do lose, with all the costs, I'll be on the streets selling the *Big Issue*.

Lou Macari resigning from Stoke to fight a court case against Celtic, 1997

I'm proud of my profession, but it worries me that it is turning into a circus act.

Blackburn Rovers' Roy Hodgson, 1998

I am not just a coach, I am a scientist. My training is brilliant and, like all scientists, I can make things work.

Malcolm Allison beginning his second spell in charge at Manchester City, 1979. Einstein was sacked a year later

Sometimes I feel like Red Adair. People only call me when things get out of control.

There are two types of people who succeed in coaching: the con man and confidence trickster, or the intelligent man who builds your confidence and belief. I'm the con man.

There are a lot of genuine and dedicated people making a living out of the game, but there are con men too, and they are guys who don't have real ambition. They drift within the game. I want to be the best, at anything I do. If I ran a pub, it would be the best pub in the district.

A coach is like a winemaker: he must produce the best wine with the grapes available.

You have to be able to say nice things to people you don't like and nasty things to people you do. If you can manage that, you're on the right lines. All you have to worry about then is results, finding new players, keeping supporters happy, finding Barnet's ground on a wet Wednesday night, keeping the chairman happy and picking the right team.

I wrote out my best eleven players and Liz said, 'Where's Crossley?' I'd forgotten the goalkeeper.

The secret of being a manager is to keep the six players who hate you away from the five who are undecided.

In my opinion the two most important attributes for a manager are a knowledge of the game and the ability to judge players.

Birmingham City's Freddie Goodwin stating the blindingly obvious, 1971

The big thing is determination, the desire to succeed. We can usually respond to any challenge. I can't define the whole thing, but I know what drives us on. It has to be the hunger to be a winner.

Manchester United's Alex Ferguson on why Scottish managers have always been so successful, 1994

If you went for a meal with me at night, you'd find me the most charming person you'll ever meet. But when I get down to work, I work.

Spurs' George Graham, 1998

I don't pretend to know the truth about football, but I am prepared to bear the consequences of my choices.

Juventus coach Marcello Lippi, 1997

A strong manager is vital. But it's better if he's a decent bloke as well.

Ipswich Town's Bobby Robson, 1979

The three toughest jobs are football management, lion taming and mountain rescue – in that order.

Former Leeds boss Jimmy Armfield, 1990s

Being in football management is like being in a mental asylum.

Welsh national manager Bobby Gould, from *The Boss* by Charles Lambert (Vista, 1997)

People will think I'm crackers. I'm voluntarily going back into the madhouse.

Trevor Francis taking charge at Birmingham City, 1996

Like a nitro-glycerine juggler.

Joe Royle when asked what it felt like to be manager of Oldham, 1994

It's like strapping yourself into the electric chair for a while.

Wycombe Wanderers' Neil Smillie sitting in the dugout watching his Second Division strugglers, 1998

Sundays are obliterated when there's no result. The family tend to suffer.

Neil Smillie, 1998

The hardest job I've got is going home to be a good husband and father. When you get a result like this, it can affect your home life, and I don't want that to happen.

Southampton's Graeme Souness after a 2–1 home defeat at the hands of Stockport in the quarter-finals of the Coca-Cola Cup, 1997

I love winning games of football. It makes your weekend. Losing makes you want to get back on Monday to start all over again.

Newcastle's Kevin Keegan, 1993

I'm taking a vow of chastity until we win a game.

John Lambie, as he and his Hamilton Academicals team suffered a barren spell at the start of the season, 1986. It was not until November that a 3–1 victory over Hibernian restored relations with his wife Mary

People ask me, 'How do you keep smiling?' I just know if I didn't I'd go doolally flip. I've been a bit of a headcase.

Barnet co-manager Gary Phillips, 1994

If you keep moping about, you'll win nowt.

Portsmouth's Alan Ball with a saying which has helped him win precisely that, 1998

Sometimes I wish I was a gardener.

Walsall's Kenny Hibbitt digging for victory, 1993

I'm almost afraid to look in the mirror in case my face is contorted. The fear of failure unsettles your life.

Sheffield Wednesday's David Pleat, 1997

Football and management are precarious professions. There is so much fear in the game, it spreads like the plague.

Johnny Giles resigning from West Bromwich Albion, 1977

I thought, why not bring Christmas forward? The players thought I had totally lost it. I ordered them all to turn up in Christmas gear. We had a turkey, a visit from Father Christmas, the lot.

Dave Bassett on bringing Christmas forward to August to inspire his Sheffield United team (he had noticed that they only seemed to start playing in the second half of the season), 1992

Sometimes you have to accept there's nothing you can do: extra training, psychology, getting strippers in – none of it will help.

Sheffield United's Dave Bassett despairing at his inability to improve results, 1993

If a player is not a good player, no amount of kidding or psychology will make him one.

Tottenham's Bill Nicholson, 1973

My experience shows me that there are things which are out of my control in football. There's always a banana skin waiting round the corner.

Graham Taylor at Watford, 1997

I could be a bit more philosophical, but it would try the patience of a saint, and I'm no saint.

Blackburn's Roy Hodgson in confessional mood after the club's exit from Europe, 1998

The despair when you lose in football goes very very deep. There is no such deep emotion when you win.

Sheffield Wednesday's Peter Eustace, 1988

Victory never compensates for losing.

Ron Atkinson, 1995

Things are never as good as they seem when you are winning, and never as bad as they seem when you are losing.

Spurs' Terry Venables, 1990

Winners can laugh. Losers have to make their own arrangements.

Newcastle's Kevin Keegan, 1995

Today, everyone is more demanding, be they press, players or spectators. There is nothing in this game for losers.

Barnsley's Johnny Steele, 1971

In England, you accept defeat as part of the game. But here it is a tragedy.

Yugoslavia coach Slobodan Santrac, 1997

I'm a gritty northern fighter. When I have my back to the wall, I come out with all guns blazing.

Southampton's David Jones, 1998

I'm one of those twenty-year, hard-graft, overnight successes.

Howard Wilkinson on Leeds United's run-in to the title, 1992

I've never been top of the First Division before. But I don't suppose it will stop it from raining tomorrow, will it?

Leeds' Howard Wilkinson, 1991

The missus has said once or twice, why can't I get a secure job – be a binman or something.

Long-suffering Chester City boss Kevin Ratcliffe, 1998

Management is a seven-days-a-week job. The intensity of it takes its toll on your health. Some people want to go on for ever, and I obviously don't.

Kenny Dalglish after walking out on Liverpool, 1991

The worst part of it is that you don't have a day off.

Kenny Dalglish on semi-retirement, 1991

I've been part and parcel of football since I was sixteen. I didn't have much of an academic education. If you are going to make yourself a life you have to do it in the industry in which you are best equipped. Football is the one most suited to Kenny Dalglish. Anyhow, the wife wanted me out of the house.

Kenny Dalglish returning to football with Blackburn, 1991

I don't want to continue as manager. I don't want the team responsibility or heavy day-to-day involvement.

Kenny Dalglish becoming Director of Football at Blackburn, 1995. Eighteen months later he was back as a manager, at Newcastle

I can't see West Ham going for a Director of Football. Director of Traffic, maybe.

Harry Redknapp, 1995

You never really get used to being out of it. Football is something you can't get out of your system.

Former Swindon and Sheffield Wednesday boss Danny Williams returning to management at Mansfield, 1971

When you get a free from Rochdale, you know you've got to seriously consider your future.

Hull City's Terry Dolan on why he went into management, 1993

I wanted to become a manager so badly that I used to have nightmares of not making the grade. I was so determined to make a success of the job that when I took my first step into the managerial ranks with Yeovil I even took a drop in money – for the first and last time.

Aston Villa's Ron Saunders, 1979

This is a million times better than going out shopping with the wife on a Saturday afternoon.

Ray Harford returning to management at West Bromwich Albion, despite a home defeat by Swindon, 1997

Driving from home, from Worksop, takes an hour and a half, depending on the taxi driver. I've got to want the job fairly badly.

David Hodgson, second time around at Darlington, 1996

I have no regrets. There are only 92 managers' jobs and we cannot all wait for the big one.

Former Liverpool player Jan Molby starting management at the bottom with Swansea City, 1996

I remember coming here with Wimbledon and telling the players if they didn't behave, they'd end up here.

Crewe Alexandra's Dario Gradi, 1989

If I was asked to go somewhere else, I wouldn't. Preston is the most exciting place in the Football League to be.

North End boss Gary Peters on the Las Vegas of Lancashire, 1995

I would have come in and helped make the tea if necessary.

Terry McDermott eagerly accepting Kevin Keegan's offer to be his assistant at Newcastle, 1992

I don't want to be anyone's assistant, but I'd go to Manchester United as the kit manager.

Macclesfield boss Sammy McIlroy, a former United player, 1997

I would have loved to have gone and worked with one of the top European clubs, but unfortunately I'm crap at languages.

Nottingham Forest's Dave Bassett, 1998. English included?

I've been on this planet for 45 years, and have supported Liverpool for 42 of them.

Roy Evans landing the job of his dreams, 1994

To be manager of a Third Division club and find yourself on a plane to Barcelona on a scouting mission is the stuff dreams are made of.

Wigan Athletic's Graham Barrow signing a trio of Spaniards, 1995

We're a club on top of a hill in a small village. It has to be seen to be believed.

Forest Green Rovers' Frank Gregan as the club headed for the Conference, 1998

I'll just hold the reins for a few weeks. I'll tell the players to go out and enjoy themselves.

Genial Joe Mercer providing a welcome breath of fresh air as England's caretaker manager, 1974

I have to be with the players all the time. Managers become father, mother, sociologist, social worker, everything. I tell them: 'Just play with the smile on your face.' It may sound funny. I like to be romantic.

Spurs' Osvaldo Ardiles, 1994

I'm finally starting to enjoy this management lark.

Barnsley's John Hendrie after a draw at Wolves, 1998

Who'd want to be a football manager? People like me, who are too old to be a player, too poor to be a director and too much in love with the game to be an agent.

Steve Coppell, following his departure from Crystal Palace, 1993

We lost at home to Woking and I was in bed at half-past six. That's how passionate I am about this club.

Doncaster Rovers' Ian Snodin, 1998

I have been here for four years, but there still seem to be those who can't understand a word I say.

Yorkshireman Danny Williams encountering a language barrier at Swindon, 1968

I had no language problem. I'd grown up with the music of the Kinks, Stones, Who, Troggs and Small Faces.

The biggest problem at first was understanding each other.

I don't know what had gone on but you could feel that apathy had got a real grip on the place.

When I went there, they had no hope, no ground, no nothing.

When I went there, they didn't think they could win. When I left them, they didn't think they could lose.

I knew the financial situation before I arrived. But how many managers have been forced to sell three million pounds' worth of players, and spend less than a million on five different players from lower divisions, and still be expected to be successful?

It might be better to let someone else come in and spend a million pounds. I certainly can't go out and spend a million like other managers. I have a conscience about spending such money. You grow up with values in your life and there comes a time when you can't change.

I can spend and do what I like and I am very excited.

Former Crystal Palace chairman Ron Noades embarking on a career in management with Brentford, 1998

We haven't the money to buy skill so we do the best with what we have. We got promotion with a team that literally cost nothing and a 39-year-old centre-half.

Port Vale's Gordon Lee, 1972. The centre-half with the bus pass was Roy Sproson

I only signed players who were knackered. They had to be cheap because we couldn't afford anything else.

Former Southampton boss Lawrie McMenemy on the old folks' home he formed at The Dell in the late 1970s, 1995

What did our team cost? Around three to three-and-a-half million, I suppose. That is about the same as one of Tottenham's players.

Southampton's Dave Merrington after a narrow defeat at White Hart Lane, 1996

The only market I might go into would be Billingsgate.

Lennie Lawrence, boss of impoverished Charlton, denying that he intended going into the transfer market, 1989

I've never had so much money to spend – well, apart from perhaps in a previous life.

Lennie Lawrence, the Buddha of Middlesbrough, 1991

People might say I'm tight with the money, but it's the fans' money and I'm going to spend it carefully.

Sunderland's Peter Reid, 1998

There is a tremendous team spirit and character and you can't buy that on the transfer market.

Peter Reid, 1998

The people who come to watch us play, who love the team and regard it as part of their lives, would never appreciate Liverpool having a huge balance in the bank. They want every asset we possess to be wearing a red shirt.

Kenny Dalglish, 1988

Money in the bank is no use to a football team. You have to put your money on the field where the public can see it.

Manchester United boss Matt Busby, 1960s

United will no longer be a football club. It will be a giant Old Trafford fruit machine.

Tommy Docherty on the proposed BSkyB takeover of Manchester United, 1998

City had horrendous debts in the wake of their halcyon spending sprees on players. We could hardly buy a fish supper.

Billy McNeill on his three years in charge of Manchester City, 1988

I'd hang myself, but we can't afford the rope.

Hamilton Academicals' Iain Munro, 1995

I'm going to have to listen to offers for all my players – and the club cat Benny, who's pissed off because all the mice have died of starvation.

Halifax Town boss John McGrath, 1993

It would be nice to introduce some new faces to give everyone a lift, including me.

Queens Park Rangers' Gerry Francis longing to move into the transfer market, 1994

I've got a player I can't put in my team because if he plays another game, we'll have to pay the club we bought him from another £20,000.

Cambridge United's Gary Johnson, 1994

I went through a list of one thousand free transfers. Thing was, we had no money to buy anybody or even pay travel expenses, so I pretty much restricted myself to players who lived round the M25.

Barnet's Gary Phillips, 1994

Blokes like George Graham and Graeme Souness, they have their problems too. It's just that their problems are different – a lot bloody different.

Theo Foley, boss of hard-up Northampton Town, 1991

If I had one-and-a-half million to spend, I would have to buy a grandstand.

Notts County's Neil Warnock on the decrepit state of Meadow Lane, 1991

I've been racing Formula One in a Mini Metro.

Bobby Gould citing lack of funds as the reason for his resignation from Coventry City, 1993

It's like going into a nuclear war with bows and arrows.

Joe Kinnear on Wimbledon's lack of spending power, 1997

That's the story of my managerial life. Buy in Woolworth's, sell in Harrods.

Joe Kinnear at the pick 'n' mix counter, 1994

I spent the first year on a good horse, but I was like an apprentice riding the Derby favourite. I was cautious and went too wide round the bends. We should have won the Championship.

Bob Paisley looking back nine years to his first season in charge at Liverpool, 1983

Bill Shankly set such a high standard. Liverpool have been geared to this sort of thing for fifteen years. I have just helped things along.

A modest Bob Paisley picking up his first Championship, 1976

Anfield without European football is like a banquet without wine.

**Roy Evans declaring his ambition to bring the heady
days back to Liverpool, 1994**

Europe is still on. I also believe Israel will win the Eurovision
Song Contest.

**West Ham's Harry Redknapp, 1998. One out of two isn't
bad . . .**

The only time we've been to Europe before was to stock up on
duty-free.

**Wimbledon's Joe Kinnear considering the prospects of
European competition, 1997**

I still believe we have an outside chance of reaching the
play-offs, but then again, I believe in Father Christmas.

Birmingham City's Trevor Francis, 1998

I would be treading dangerously if I predicted I could become
anywhere near as successful as Dad, but I have sought his
advice and he was very positive.

**Nigel Clough, son of Brian, stepping into management
with Dr Martens League team Burton Albion, 1998**

I stepped out of line at St Mirren and somebody trampled all
over me. I was 38 at the time and full of it. We had just won
five games in a row and I was asked about promotion. I boasted
we would win the League, no bother. We lost the next four
games and I was cut off at the knees.

**Alex Ferguson refusing to predict Manchester United's
future with the Double in sight, 1994**

Any new manager who promises to win such and such in so
long is a fool.

Bobby Charlton taking charge at Preston, 1973

Retain it!

**Super-confident Scotland boss Ally MacLeod when
asked what he planned to do after the World Cup, 1978**

There is a serious advantage in putting myself out front to shout the odds a bit. It takes the pressure off the players. If things go wrong, everybody's going to blame me. I have been the big mouth and I will take the rap.

Scotland's Ally MacLeod before the World Cup, 1978

We will win the European Cup. European football is full of cowards and we will terrorise them with our power and attacking football.

Malcolm Allison after Manchester City won the League title, 1968. They went out of the following season's European Cup in the first round

I think we will be the first team to play on Mars.

Malcolm Allison preparing to conquer Europe, the world and the solar system, 1968

I know that with Crystal Palace I can enjoy far more and prolonged success than I have had with any other club.

Malcolm Allison, 1973. Three years later, having taken Palace down to Division Three, he left

Wales's football is improving quite dramatically. Within two or three years, I am certain that it is going to be one of the strongholds of the game in Britain.

Cardiff City's Jimmy Andrews, 1976. They're still waiting

I believe Doncaster will reach the First Division by 1999.

Sammy Chung, 1994. He didn't say he meant Division One of the Unibond League

The men who got us into the First Division will prove themselves good enough to keep us there.

Ipswich Town's Alf Ramsey, 1961. That season they repaid Ramsey's faith by winning the First Division title

England *will* win the 1966 World Cup.

Alf Ramsey on succeeding Walter Winterbottom in the England job, 1963

England will not only beat West Germany but will also go on to win the Championship.

Gypsy Rose Ramsey before defeat against the Germans in the quarter-final of the European Championships, 1972

I think for years Germany will not be beaten. I'm sorry but, for a time to come, we will be invincible.

Franz Beckenbauer after World Cup success, 1990

Look at Jesus. He was an ordinary, run-of-the-mill sort of guy who had a genuine gift, just as Eileen has.

England coach Glenn Hoddle singing the praises of faith healer Eileen Drewery, from *My 1998 World Cup Story* (André Deutsch, 1998)

Why is it wacko when the Brazil, Italian and German teams have been doing that for twenty years? We have been trying to beat the Germans for many years, but we were playing on beer and steak for twenty years. Why do the Germans come back in games when they are losing? It's not luck. If you're finely tuned to physical and mental strength, you have some team.

Glenn Hoddle defending his use of vitamin injections and Ms Drewery, 1998

The German mentality is stronger than that of other nations. I can assure you Germany does not have better players, but even when they are under pressure, they seem to maintain a winning mentality.

Franz Beckenbauer, 1995

Ninety-five per cent of management is psychology. The other five per cent is coaching and team preparation.

Port Vale's Roy Sproson, 1974

Players these days are stronger, run faster and jump higher than ever before. But we're not nearly so professional at sorting out the mental side of the game. We don't use psychiatrists. We should, though, and eventually we will. It'll come, I'm sure of that.

Terry Butcher was a big one for self-hypnosis. He used to sit on the toilet for about 25 minutes before the game with his Walkman on, listening to the tapes, and if anybody banged the door or tried to get into the toilet, he'd come out and throttle them.

Northampton Town manager Ian Atkins (a former Ipswich player with Butcher) employing a coach in positive thinking at the Sixfields Stadium, 1998

In a way, I quite like this situation. I get a certain pleasure out of being down and knowing that I've got to get this right and that right. That's what I'm here for.

Malcolm Allison on Manchester City's sluggish start to the season, 1972

Any fool could have turned them round to a limited extent.

John Bond outlining his credentials for the Manchester City job, 1981

If Mickey Mouse had taken charge, it would have given the place a lift.

Everton's Mike Walker, 1994

Two months ago, I changed the players' pre-match meal to two meat and potato pies. That day we beat Huddersfield so I kept the order with our catering manager. And we haven't lost at home since.

Stockport County's Gary Megson on the club's upturn in fortunes, 1997

When I took over Dunstable in the 1970s they had finished bottom of the League eight years running and had an average crowd of 34. I decided I had to put the club on the map, so I rang up George Best. He came down and played a couple of pre-season friendlies. We had crowds of 12,000 and 14,000. I then signed Jeff Astle. We went on to win the League that season, scored more than a hundred goals and had an average crowd of 892.

Birmingham City's Barry Fry recalling life at Dunstable Town, 1996

A lot of the players had been here a long time and had got used to losing.

Tony Pulis winning Gillingham's first manager of the month award for ten years, 1995

I've introduced something new to the training. It's called running.

Gerry Francis on the improvement in Tottenham's fortunes, 1994

The secret? I'm not quite sure. If I knew, I would can it and sell it.

Glenn Roeder on the sudden improvement in results since he took charge at Watford, 1995

If we don't have some sort of measurable success in three years, I'll consider myself a failure. Too many managers hang on to the security of long contracts rather than try to achieve success in a short time. Football just won't wait.

Nottingham Forest's Dave Mackay, 1972

I'm always suspicious of instant success. A truly solid foundation takes time to build.

Spurs' George Graham, 1998

The thing is: when you're young and you've done it all, what do you do for an encore? If you're Jack Nicklaus or Lee Trevino you go on and do it again. It's easy enough, perhaps, for one man to capture that sort of drive, but how do you instil it into eleven men?

Arsenal's Bertie Mee on his team's post-Double hangover, 1972

Who are we playing today? Arsenal? Oh, we'll piss that lot.

Sunderland's Johnny Cochrane, famed for his laid-back approach and concise pre-match team-talks, 1930s

People say to me that I look as if I don't care, but I do, immensely.

Queens Park Rangers' Ray Wilkins, 1996

When the players come in, they call me Harry. I don't ask them to call me boss. But they know that if they're not performing, then my tongue can be sharp. Some people think I'm easy-going, and I am – until people start taking liberties.

West Ham's Harry Redknapp, 1998

All managers have their own ways of letting out their frustration. But I won't jump up and down if things are going wrong. I just sit there, because it really means I haven't done my homework right. I can't scream and shout from the touchline, and anyway, I don't see the point because you can't make yourself heard with all the noise from the crowd.

Chelsea's Ruud Gullit, 1996

I could not be a sergeant-major manager, the one that throws teacups. There is another kind of manager, one who is more subtle, who is trying to understand how the players feel and trying to put his message through. I could not take them by the throat. They are bigger than me anyway.

Spurs' Osvaldo Ardiles, 1994

I don't go along with copying other people's styles completely. I want to be my own man and I don't think you will find me hurling teacups around.

Sheffield United's Steve Bruce adopting a more relaxed approach to management than his old Manchester United boss, Alex Ferguson, 1998

I was determined to manage the team as I felt players wanted to be managed. I wanted a more humane approach than there was when I was playing ... There never seemed to be enough interest taken in the players. The manager was at his desk and you saw him once a week. From the start I tried to make even the smallest member think he was part of the club.

Sir Matt Busby, 1970s

Some players you can whip, some players you can tickle.

Ron Atkinson, 1998

The first thing I learnt was that those in the dressing-room had so little talent. Poor lads – I couldn't give them a hard time because they had a big enough problem with their inability to play.

Brian Clough recalling his first managerial job, at Hartlepool, from *Clough: The Autobiography* (Partridge Press, 1994)

In the old days, when I was manager at Bradford or Swansea, I would play holy shit with players who got things wrong. Now I can't see the point of giving myself a heart attack over other people's incompetence.

Cardiff City's Terry Yorath, 1994

I've had to take a step back this season otherwise my head will explode.

Charlton Athletic's Alan Curbishley leaving the ranting and raving to assistant Mervyn Day, 1998

I haven't got an ability to be able to relax at the end of it all. I would love to be able to do it and I do envy other managers who, once they step into their car to go home, the game no longer counts for them. Well, I am not one of those, unfortunately.

Leicester City's Martin O'Neill, 1997

My two daughters and my wife have to listen to me persistently about this and about that, about the game. And when they come in and put a point of view and I don't agree with that point of view, then it's bedlam and it goes on for ever. I can't let go.

Martin O'Neill, 1997

I don't suppose I will ever be Mr Valium. If I did not do what I do during games, then I would probably keel over.

Coventry City's Gordon Strachan on his animated touchline displays, 1998

I could relax and put my feet up if I had Alex Ferguson's team.

Gordon Strachan, 1998

People used to say I was too nice to be a manager, but I think that's been forgotten about now!

Bristol Rovers' John Ward, from *A Passion for the Game* (Mainstream, 1995)

I'm not as soft as people think. I never was on the field, but some seem to think I am here.

Liverpool's Bob Paisley, 1982

I am very strong-willed. People don't understand that. They think that with that touch and flair, I'd have to be soft.

Glenn Hoddle at Chelsea, 1993

I do not get mad. I get even.

Glenn Hoddle after Robbie Fowler and Steve McManaman were withdrawn by Liverpool from the England squad for Le Tournoi, 1997

I will not become a bastard. I don't think you have to swear and scream to get results.

Jimmy Dickinson taking over at Portsmouth, 1977

Rules apply to everyone. I let a few swearwords go at half-time and the players fined me a tenner.

Walsall's Ray Graydon breaking the clubs code of conduct, 1998

I will be a hard man to play under. I will be a taskmaster. I like standards. If you dress smart, you'll play smart.

Hull City's Mark Hateley, 1997

I have to rebuild in the players' minds the facility to win. And I'm nae a very good panicker.

Scottish hard man Jock Wallace assuming control at Colchester United, 1989

One player called us a monster with two heads.

Leyton Orient's John Sitton on his management partnership with Chris Turner, 1994

People look at me and think, 'Oh, he must be hard to handle', and they don't realise what they get for their money: dedication and a will to win second to none. If I had been a Mr Nice Guy, I'm sure I'd have been offered something by now.

Altrincham's John King (not to be confused with the Tranmere manager of the same name) on being overlooked for a job with a League club, 1995

I have come to accept that my only friend in the world is myself.

Brighton & Hove Albion's Pat Saward, 1973

It's very tough. The team bus is more like a school outing, full of kids eating crisps.

Hartlepool's John MacPhail on life at the bottom, 1993

You're reconciled to competing with the big clubs so you've just got to make sure you're a better talker.

Doncaster Rovers' Maurice Setters on the secret of persuading young players to go to Belle Vue, 1972

There are so many problems here, you don't know where to start.

Barrow's Jack Crompton, 1972

When the ball was kicked into the river we had to hail passing rowers to retrieve the ball for us as our financial constraints were such that we could not just shrug our shoulders and wave the ball goodbye.

Craig Brown on the hazards of training with Clyde at Glasgow's Richmond Park, from *Craig Brown: The Autobiography* (Virgin, 1998)

There are people about when we train at Southend, but they are more likely to be taking a jog in the park or walking the dog.

Southend's Ronnie Whelan comparing life with Anfield, 1995

When I arrived everything was a mess. There were no training facilities, and for the first few months we had to use public parks. Do you have any idea of how hard it is to coach players when you've got dogs chasing after the ball?

More parklife from Gillingham's Tony Pulis, 1996

At training the other night we were up to our knees in snow and the water in the cabins was frozen. Players from as far away as Glasgow and Dundee had to get into the car wet and freezing and drive home before they could get a bath.

Cowdenbeath's John Reilly on the club's Portakabin dressing-rooms, 1993

At the end of my first season there, I concreted the car park, dug the drains for the pitch and decorated the boardroom. I went back twelve years later and it was my wallpaper still hanging there, so I must have done a good job!

Jim Smith reflecting on his first managerial job at Boston United in 1970, from *Bald Eagle: The Jim Smith Story* (Mainstream, 1990)

I got arrested driving the tractor on Christmas Day, trying to flatten the pitch. When I said I was the manager, the policeman replied, 'Yeah, and I'm George Best!'

Barry Fry remembering life at Barnet, 1993

The chairman cuts the grass and volunteers raise money to keep the club alive. Last season the players went unpaid for fourteen weeks.

Former England international Garry Birtles in charge at Gresley Rovers, 1998

The directors do what they can, but a lot of what goes on behind the scenes, they think the fairies do it! I'm the manager, but I'm the cleaner, the kitman, the barman and the groundsman too.

Former Arsenal Double winner John Radford on life as manager at Bishops Stortford, from *A Passion for the Game* (Mainstream, 1995)

English managers have to do too much. When I was at Ipswich I was first in and last out. I did everything except buy the toilet rolls.

Bobby Robson revealing why nobody used the loos at Portman Road, 1992

The managers didn't manage, they signed the cheques. It was player power. The older players decided the tactics.

Former England manager Walter Winterbottom on the game in the 1930s, 1989

I was never a desk manager, like many were at that time. I would tell the directors that they could get me in the office before a quarter to ten. After that, I would be out with the team, coaching.

Spurs' Bill Nicholson, 1970s

Some people might think we are lazy, but that's fine. What's the point of tearing players to pieces in the first few days? We never bothered with sand dunes and hills and roads; we trained on grass, where football is played.

Bill Shankly on Liverpool's pre-season training routine, 1970s

In the League they have always threatened, never delivered.

Kevin Keegan on taking charge at Newcastle, 1992. When he left nearly five years later, delivery was still expected any day

I don't think Ossie was a million miles away. You can see how his problems arose and I'm left to pick up the bits, but the bits aren't as bad as I thought they'd be.

Kevin Keegan after his first win in charge at St James's Park, 1992

It's not like the brochures.

Kevin Keegan discovering the harsh facts of management life at Newcastle, 1992

Newcastle United are going to be the biggest football club on the planet.

Kevin Keegan signing a new ten-year contract, 1994

There are days when I think there are better jobs around and there are days when I think it's the greatest thing you could do. The mood swings are unbelievable at times.

Kevin Keegan at Newcastle shortly before his departure, 1996

It was the expression on the face of Gerry Francis, a man I like and respect a great deal. The elation of winning suddenly meant nothing when I looked at him and thought, 'Oh no, how must he be feeling deep inside?' I wanted to go up and give him a cuddle. I went straight home. And I knew that was it . . . that when you feel like that, you have to get out.

Kevin Keegan explaining how a crushing 7–1 victory over Tottenham played a major part in his decision to quit Newcastle, 1997

I once said I would never go into management, so you can't believe anything I say.

Kevin Keegan refusing to rule out a return to management, 1997

A manager can never say always and can never say never.
England's Graham Taylor, 1991

I'll definitely be getting rid of my Arsenal memorabilia at home.
George Graham making his pledge to the fans of his new club Tottenham, 1998

There is one golden rule: no matter how good the team may be, there should always be an attempt to improve it.
Arsenal's Herbert Chapman, 1930s

You have to make changes just to stand still.
Spurs' Peter Shreeves, 1992

I always tell young managers to pick their best team at the start of the season, write it on a piece of paper and tuck it away in a drawer. Halfway through the season, if things are going wrong, look at those names again ... because the first team you pick each season is always your best team.
Former Spurs chief Arthur Rowe, 1993

It's very easy to demolish a car, but it takes a lot longer to build one.
Chelsea's Ruud Gullit, still coming to terms with the one-way system around Stamford Bridge, 1997

It is easier to knock down a house than it is to build one.
Bournemouth's John Bond, 1973

It does give me great satisfaction, spotting something, anything, in a footballer, bringing it out and seeing him go on upward. The thrill is finding it.
Dario Gradi, renowned for bringing on young players at Crewe, 1997

You find a lad, coach him, have to let him go. And then you start all over again with someone else. It can be a bit frustrating.
Shrewsbury Town's Maurice Evans, 1993

The job at this level is all about balancing the books, selling players to make ends meet. I get satisfaction from bringing players on, getting them to the standard that's required of them so that people want to buy them.

York City's Alan Little, 1998

This was a First Division club – but, to be frank, in name only.

Matt Busby on the state of Manchester United, 1945

I did not set out to build a team; the task ahead was much bigger than that. What I really embarked upon was the building of a system which would produce not one but four or five teams, each occupying a vital rung in the ladder, the summit of which was the first XI.

Matt Busby recalling his mission at Manchester United twelve years earlier when he became manager, 1957

I am going to make the move which will make or break Manchester United.

Matt Busby telling his board that he was about to replace the club's old faithfuls with a crop of youngsters – the future 'Busby Babes', 1952

With a railway timetable my constant companion, I travelled the length and breadth of the British Isles to watch school teams, youth teams, works teams and even water board teams. As soon as a tip arrived from one of my scouts, I followed it up regardless of the distance involved or the inconvenience suffered ... I was first in the field, knowing that before long the competition would become fiercer, and well aware that you cannot discover footballers if you sit in the manager's chair all day.

Matt Busby on the creation of the 'Busby Babes', 1957

My aim has always been to be the best manager in football. At Old Trafford I will get the best chance of proving I have what it takes.

Tommy Docherty becoming manager of Manchester United, 1972

It's just the sort of job I've been looking for. Altrincham are the Manchester United of non-League soccer.

Tommy Docherty taking up the managerial reins at Altrincham, 1987. He stayed four months

I regard Maidstone as the Manchester United of non-League football.

Barry Fry in Kent, 1985

We know we are no Real Madrid.

Port Vale's John Rudge knows his place, 1998

We think big. We may be a Third Division team but we all think in terms of being a First Division outfit. If you don't think big in football, you'll never win anything.

Brighton & Hove Albion's Pat Saward, 1972

I have tried to kid everyone that this is hard work. Sometimes players get on my wick, and sometimes I must get on their wick. But when you consider that all of us are being paid handsomely for something we'd probably do for nothing, it can't be bad, can it?

Ron Atkinson savouring life at Aston Villa, 1993. Within a year, he had been sacked

I haven't given up my job, pastime and hobby. I've just given up my life. But I can't do the job and I couldn't con a living.

Arthur Cox resigning from Derby County after six weeks on his back with a prolapsed disc, 1993. Seven months later he was back in football on the coaching staff at Newcastle

I'm going to be as natural as I can – a right miserable bastard.

Ray Harford taking up the reins at West Brom, 1997. He had once been sacked by Luton for not smiling enough

I cannot help the face God has given me. People just look at my expression and categorise me as a bit of a miserable sod.

Leeds' Howard Wilkinson, 1996

When I was a player, I was completely out of control and even my best friends believed I was heading for prison. I was involved in drugs, and once I threatened supporters with a shotgun because they were barracking me at a training session. I came very close to throwing my life away. These days I am a disciplinarian, and if any of my players behaved like I used to I would show them the door immediately.

Mario Sergio, manager of Corinthians of Brazil, 1994

Being a manager is second to being a player. There's nothing better than to be a player – fourteen or fifteen lads in that dressing-room, having a laugh. I miss that.

Rochdale's Graham Barrow, from *The Boss* (Vista, 1997)

I longed for Saturday afternoon so I could leave the desk and telephone and move outside to play.

Terry Neill remembering his early days at Hull as player/manager, 1974

Being a little bit older, I was more or less a father figure to them anyway.

Rangers' John Greig overcoming the problems of switching from player to manager with the same club – poacher turned gamekeeper, 1978

Every Thursday night, I sack myself as manager and become just a player so that I can prepare properly for Saturday's match. There is no job on my desk that cannot be put off from Friday morning until Monday.

Manchester City player/manager Peter Reid, 1990

Player management is violent exercise on top of a pile of worries.

Yeovil's Alec Stock, 1949

Initially I found it difficult. I was like a bull in a china shop. I was trying to change the course of the game immediately. When I was playing, I was trying to play and manage. It was impossible.

Swindon Town's Steve McMahon, 1996

I think I'm in the side on merit. I wouldn't pick myself otherwise.

Reading player/manager Jimmy Quinn, 1997

I'm not afraid to drop myself. I know better than anyone when the time comes to call it a day. I will never be a burden to any team. It's just that I can't stop playing.

Swindon Town player/manager Dave Mackay finding it hard to hang up his boots, 1972

I'm far more nervous as a manager than as a player.

Dave Mackay, having moved to Nottingham Forest, 1972

The legs won't go any more.

Bolton player/manager Phil Neal packing in the playing side after taking the club down to the Fourth Division for the first time in their history, 1987

I've been sub a couple of times this season but not had to come on yet. I reckon I'm probably good for twenty minutes.

54-year-old former Welsh international Brian Godfrey, coach of Cinderford Town, 1995

It's so much more frustrating when you lose as a manager because the buck stops with you. You have to sort it out. No one else will.

Barnsley player/manager Viv Anderson, 1993

Even on the pitch you want to kick every ball. If you're not careful, your own game suffers.

Viv Anderson, 1993

How long will I stay as a player? After today, about a week.

Viv Anderson after Barnsley went down to Millwall, 1993

As a player, I didn't realise what an easy life I had compared with a manager. As a player, everything is done for you. As a player, you can hide behind people. As a manager, you cannot hide behind anyone.

Kevin Keegan at Newcastle, 1993

As a player you only have to worry about yourself. As a manager you have to worry about everyone. You're carrying the can for the whole of the club.

Former Motherwell boss Ian St John, 1980s

As a player, you only had to worry about yourself. If you'd had a good game and the team had lost, it was on the bus and 'Who's for a game of cards?' If you lose as a manager, it's your fault. You pick the team, you decide the tactics.

Mansfield Town's Andy King, 1994

As a player, I could find consolation in a defeat if I'd had a good game. For a manager, there's no consolation. You just lose.

Steve Coppell of Crystal Palace, 1993

This job comes a close second to playing – when you win.

Glenn Hoddle, 1997

All managers are frustrated players.

Joe Mercer, 1960s

I had three months in Majorca and there are only so many times you can ride a motorbike round the island before you want to do something else.

Stoke City's Brian Little on recharging his batteries after leaving Aston Villa, 1998

I'm aiming for automatic promotion, not the play-offs. I like to take my holidays early.

Sunderland's Peter Reid, 1998

I find between seasons the worst time of the year, when you're talking to players' agents about their contracts. But once pre-season training starts, and you're out there and you've got the banter and the camaraderie, it's just a special feeling.

Derby County's Jim Smith, from *I Think I'll Manage* (Headline, 1996)

When I was a player with Barnsley it was a small-town club with a chip on its shoulder. Later I went to Millwall, a club with a chip on both shoulders.

Mick McCarthy taking the Republic of Ireland job, 1996

I met a pal who'd lost track of me after I'd played at Celtic, and he asked me what I was doing. I said I was player/manager at Millwall. His wife immediately said: 'How embarrassing.'

Mick McCarthy, 1996

It was a bit of a culture shock.

George Graham on joining Millwall, 1982

If you're a doctor or an aircraft pilot or a chartered accountant, people know that not everybody can do it. With football management, you can ask practically everyone in the country, and they all think they can do the job.

Wycombe Wanderers' Alan Smith, from *I Think I'll Manage* (Headline, 1996)

What we have got now is just a hit-and-miss affair . . . there are no courses in management and people can get a job simply on their reputation as a player or on the strength of wide publicity. The situation is very different on the Continent. In France, Italy and West Germany, for instance, you cannot manage a football club unless you have a licence in football management – and those licences are very difficult to get.

England's Ron Greenwood, 1979

A lot of managers are too young. They've been great players, but they've got no grounding. They've never started down with, say, Bournemouth or Doncaster so they go straight into a big club and find it very difficult.

West Ham's Harry Redknapp (formerly in charge at Bournemouth), 1998

A young manager learns his values in the Third and Fourth Divisions. There, he is mainly dealing with players who are not quite good enough for First Division football or are past their best. He learns to improvise. There are problems all along the line, but there can be no better training.

Everton's Harry Catterick, 1969

The experience you gain by managing a club like Halifax must stand you in good stead for the future. If you can make a success of the job at this level, then you are on your way.

George Mulhall, 1974

What better way is there for a new manager to start in a job than at the bottom? After all, there is only one way to go from there, and that is up.

Bradford Park Avenue's Laurie Brown, little realising that the club would go out of business and out of the League at the end of the season, 1969

The crazy thing about football that makes it different from any other walk of life is the fact that if you have been a successful player, clubs automatically think you're going to be a successful manager.

Celtic's Tommy Burns, from *I Think I'll Manage* (Headline, 1996)

It seems the in-thing is to stop playing one day and become a manager the next.

Notts County's Colin Murphy, 1996

You don't have to have been a horse to be a jockey.

Arrigo Sacchi, the former manager of Italy, who never played professional football himself, 1996

The Protestant, because I know Rangers would never sign the Catholic.

Celtic's Jock Stein when asked who he would sign if offered a choice between two players of equal ability, one Catholic, the other Protestant, 1970s

It is not a thorny question as far as I am concerned. How could I possibly have taken on this if I could not have signed Catholics? I am married to one.

Graeme Souness declaring his intention to sign Catholics for Rangers, 1986

Rangers are the biggest club in Scotland, but they had an attitude that seemed to be against change and against progress. When I came to Rangers, I knew I'd have to change those attitudes.

Graeme Souness announcing the signing of the club's first Catholic, Mo Johnston, 1989

The Premier League in Scotland is the most physical, cynical and brutal league in the world.

Dundee United's Jim McLean, 1987

Everyone is always talking about the Mickey Mouse competition in Scotland.

Rangers' Dick Advocaat hoping for European success, 1998

I suppose that while accepting the pats on the back, we have to accept the hoots. However discombobulating we have been made to appear, we shall genuinely endeavour to discoidulate the cleavage.

Colin Murphy's highly individual programme notes at Lincoln City, 1988

It's a funny old game. And it's a great leveller.

West Ham's Billy Bonds offering two clichés for the price of one, 1993

At the end of the day, it's not the end of the world.

Jim McLean repeating the offer as Dundee United lose in the UEFA Cup final, 1987

At the end of the day, it's all about what's on the shelf at the end of the year.

A crafty variation from Crystal Palace's Steve Coppell, 1984

2 The Match

It was a typical English game with so many foreigners.

Arsenal's Arsène Wenger on his club's encounter with Leeds, 1997

You cannot accept that every time people turn their Christmas trees on you cannot have a football match.

Arsène Wenger after Arsenal's festive fixture at Wimbledon was abandoned due to floodlight failure, 1997

One train disnae make a railway.

Notts County's Jimmy Sirrel refusing to get carried away after a welcome victory over neighbours Nottingham Forest, 1970s

For five or six minutes, Wales were a threat.

Holland's Guus Hiddink after his country crushed the Welsh 7–1 in a World Cup qualifier, 1996

We had a good spell – between the 50th and 58th minutes.

Luton's David Pleat offers a terse assessment of defeat at Leeds, 1992

When we were 3–0 up I looked over at [Rangers coach] Dick Advocaat and he had his face in his hands. That was worth the admission price alone.

Shelbourne's Dermot Keely as his team of humble part-timers gave Rangers a European scare before going down 5–3, 1998

I'm an advocate of attacking football – but that was carrying it to extremes.

Ron Greenwood after England's 4–3 European Championships qualifying win in Denmark, 1978

I'm like a dog with two dicks.

Joe Royle unearths an old northern saying to describe his feelings after Everton's win at Chelsea, 1994

It's nice for a bluenose to come here and win. I'm going to have a pint now and a gloat.

Southampton's David Jones (a former Everton player) making the most of a win at Anfield, 1998

This would bring a tear to a glass eye.

Emotional Raith Rovers boss Jimmy Nicholl after his minnows beat mighty Celtic to lift the Scottish League Cup, 1994

It was the worst and best day of my life.

Burnley's Brian Miller on the club's last-day escape from relegation out of the Football League, 1987

Really good . . . magnificent . . . brilliant . . . absolutely brilliant . . . fantastic . . . excellent . . . terrific . . . absolutely magnificent . . . I was ecstatic.

Leicester's Martin O'Neill flicking through *Roget's Thesaurus* after an emphatic 3–0 victory over Spurs, 1997

We were absolutely fantastic. We pulverised a championship-chasing team. We blitzed them. If our supporters live to be a hundred, they won't see a Leicester team put in that much effort again.

Martin O'Neill in equally ecstatic mood, despite the fact that Leicester had actually lost 4–2 at home to Chelsea, 1998

For most of the players, being in the position we are now is completely new. They've never known what it's been like having other sides chasing you.

John Newman, manager of Fourth Division high-flyers Exeter City, 1973

We are so high in the table our noses are bleeding.

Queens Park Rangers' Gerry Francis, 1992

That's the big problem with our players – they're not used to winning.

Dunfermline Athletic manager Iain Munro on hearing that Mark Smith, named man of the match for the Scottish Cup defeat of Rangers, was unable to collect his award after the game because he had fainted, 1988

Beating Argentina is the greatest moment for our people since the revolution.

Romania coach Anghel Iordanescu, 1994

The last time Nottingham were five ahead of anybody was in a cricket match.

Brian Clough as Forest emerged from the Christmas programme with a five-point lead at the top of Division One, 1977

I thought it was 19–0. I must have lost count.

Stirling Albion manager Alex Smith after the 20–0 Scottish Cup thrashing of Selkirk, 1984

If we go on like this, I shall be a very happy man.

Tottenham's Bill Nicholson as his first game in charge brought a remarkable 10–4 victory over Everton, 1958

It was almost frightening at times.

Bob Paisley as his Liverpool team hit Spurs for seven, 1978

If I could give them more than ten points out of ten, I would.

Terry Venables as nine-man Spurs beat Luton, 1990

We were half decent.

Ron Atkinson as his players were photographed coming out of the shower following a 2–2 draw at Southampton, 1990

That will make Blackburn tremble – they'll be looking over their shoulders at us now!

Ron Atkinson after his first match in charge had seen Coventry beat West Ham and jump five places to thirteenth, only 28 points behind leaders Blackburn, 1995

Yes, there's some money available. But we're just going to spend that on drinks.

Ron Atkinson celebrating Coventry's win over West Ham, 1995

We've got a strong squad and everyone's playing well. That gives me a headache, but it's a pleasant headache to have.

St Johnstone's Sandy Clark after a win at Aberdeen, 1998

I've just put a sign on my door, saying GONE TO LUNCH. BACK MONDAY. If we win, it will probably be Wednesday.

Bashley manager Frank Whitman (he ran a building company) before the Cup tie with Swansea, 1994. He was back in the office for Monday

It's not the usual George Graham style, but I'll accept that.

Spurs' George Graham after a 2–0 win over Newcastle in a game of many chances, 1998

I went to church this morning and it clearly worked.

Bournemouth's Mel Machin after a welcome victory over Brighton, 1995

I told my players that Alex Ferguson was here, that they could do themselves a bit of good. He was actually here to watch his son Darren playing for Wolves, but my lot wouldn't know that, would they?

Luton's David Pleat resorts to underhand methods to secure a 3–2 win at Molineux, 1994

He rose high enough to see the Blackpool Tower.

Millwall's Bruce Rioch on defender David Thompson's header from a corner in the 4–1 win at Bristol City, 1991

We were showboating.

Carlisle United's Mick Wadsworth as the Cumbrians took it easy to beat Guiseley 4–1 in the FA Cup, 1994

I just sat there rubbing my eyes to make sure it was true.

Oxford United's Arthur Turner after his Fourth Division minnows had beaten Blackburn, second in Division One at the time, 3–1 in the fifth round of the FA Cup, 1964

After the game, Maurice Goodall was holding up the boot that brought the goal and he was so thrilled he was shaking like a leaf.

Corby Town manager Tommy Hadden after his team's 1–0 FA Cup win at Luton, 1965

After we had drawn up there, Macdonald said in the papers that Hereford had had their moment of glory and that he would score ten in the replay. I simply pinned that article on our dressing-room wall.

Hereford United player/manager Colin Addison ramming Malcolm Macdonald's words down his throat with the non-Leaguers' famous 2–1 FA Cup victory over Newcastle, 1972

Scoring that second goal was about the worst thing Halifax could have done. Until then my players had been very nervous. But they suddenly seemed to realise there was nothing they could do but have a go.

Whitby Town manager Tony Lee celebrating a 3–2 win at Halifax in the FA Cup, 1983

I should have been going to Portugal for a seven-day break with my wife this week. I'll try to postpone it until after the replay tomorrow, but if not I'll just have to cancel it.

Worcester City manager Nobby Clark despairing of his side's 1–1 Cup draw at Aldershot, 1983. His holiday was further delayed when Worcester won the replay

It's a few bob and a day out.

**Hendon's Frank Murphy looking forward to a Cup replay
at Notts County, 1998**

If you'd gone to the ground not knowing who the teams were, you'd never have guessed we were the non-League side. They were the ones who looked nervous, and I fancied us after ten minutes. Even the Preston supporters were cheering us towards the end.

**Telford United's Stan Storton following a 4–1 Cup romp
at Preston, 1984**

It was like the Alamo out there. We had one shot, but we shot the chief.

**Enfield's Eddie McCluskey on his team's 1–0 Cup win at
Leyton Orient, 1988**

It was like the battle of the Alamo out there.

**Slough's Graham Roberts shows that imitation is the
sincerest form of flattery after a hard-earned FA Cup
draw at Macclesfield, 1998**

When West Brom scored, I think our boys felt they might as well start making a game of it. Buzaglo is a very laid-back man who just decides to do these things now and again.

**Woking manager Geoff Chapple after his side's 4–2 Cup
win at West Brom in which Tim Buzaglo scored a
hat-trick, 1991**

We'll be tired by the time we reach Wembley.

**Worthing manager John Robson before his team's
first-round FA Cup tie at Bournemouth, their sixth game
in the competition that season, 1994. His players were
soon able to put their feet up as Bournemouth won 3–1**

The Chinese say it's the Year of the Dog. It isn't, it's the Year of the Underdog.

**David Pleat writing the tabloids' intros after Luton's
surprise victory over Newcastle in the FA Cup, 1994**

I've had two parrots on my shoulder this week – one saying that we would get slaughtered and one saying that we would win.

The parrot saying we would get slaughtered has been getting dimmer, and the parrot that said we could do something has been getting brighter.

Stevenage Borough boss Paul Fairclough going off his perch after the battling 1–1 Cup draw with Newcastle, 1998

For Barnet to be taken away now would be a tragedy. I just hope the judge isn't a Chelsea supporter.

Barnet's Gary Phillips after a battling draw at Chelsea in the FA Cup, two days before the club was due to be wound up in the High Court, 1994

It's the best competition in the country . . . in the world.

Hednesford Town's John Baldwin after his team's Cup defeat of Barnet, 1998

I haven't the slightest bit of interest in the Cup but I have told my players as long as they don't lose League matches while we're in it, I don't mind.

Big-hearted Brentford chief Ron Noades after a 5–0 win over Camberley Town, 1998

Winning the Welsh Cup is more of a priority.

Wrexham's Brian Flynn before a second-round FA Cup tie with Telford United, 1991

The boys have worked very, very hard for this. It's the sort of result that is going to give the lads a lift. Who knows, we may even be able to get a win this season.

Poole Town's Keith Miller after his Beazer Homes League team had ended a 39-game losing run with a goalless draw against Bashley, 1996

That's a good fisherman, isn't it?

Arsenal's Don Howe comparing a 1–0 win over QPR to a fisherman who tries all day for a catch before finally pulling one out, 1984

I have never been kissed so much in my life – especially by men!

Wilf McGuinness after guiding Greek club Aris Salonika to their first away win in over a year, 1971

Only the British can unleash such a battle on a football field without falling into excess.

Anderlecht coach Raymond Goethals going over the top about the European Cup tie between Liverpool and Nottingham Forest, 1978

We had struck such a great blow for English football. I did not even bring on a substitute when Eddie Stuart was injured. I was determined to play the game the good old British way.

Stan Cullis on Wolverhampton Wanderers' floodlit friendly victory over Moscow Spartak, part of a series of experimental matches played under lights, 1954

Floodlit soccer has come to stay.

Southampton's Sid Cann after the FA lifted its long-standing ban on competitive floodlit matches to allow Southampton Reserves to play Spurs Reserves in a Football Combination fixture at The Dell, 1951

Those lights were something special. It was as if an electric fuse went all the way round the ground. The atmosphere was unique.

Stan Cullis on Wolves' memorable 3–2 floodlit friendly win over Hungarian champions Honved, 1954

You tell me a better way to spend a Wednesday night – under the floodlights at a cracking stadium, big game, plenty at stake. Not even *Coronation Street* is that good.

Ron Atkinson deriving pleasure from the evening despite Coventry's defeat at Wolves, 1996

If we had to lose our record, I'd sooner it be against Liverpool than anyone else.

Kevin Keegan as Liverpool became the first team that season to take a point off Newcastle at St James's Park, 1994

I have never been so proud of you in victory as I am in defeat.

Tom Whittaker to his gallant Arsenal team after losing in the Cup final to Newcastle, 1952

After this, Wembley could be something of an anti-climax.

Stoke City's Tony Waddington after a dramatic League Cup semi-final victory over West Ham, 1972

It's like having your main course as a starter.

Terry Venables discovering that his first game in charge at Barcelona was away to Real Madrid, 1984

This was a massive game for us.

Ross County's Neale Cooper talking up a win at Stenhousemuir, 1998

It took me days to get over it. Although I train with the team, I haven't played since I was fifty.

Mel Gingell, 53-year-old manager of Screwfix Direct Western Leaguers Calne Town, who, with his team losing 8–1 to Bridgwater Town with twenty minutes still to go, brought himself on to play in midfield with his fifteen-year-old son Craig, 1998. To Gingell's delight, Calne didn't concede another goal

The missus was going on at me to play and I had a good training session in mid-week, so I thought I'd give it a go.

38-year-old Tranmere Rovers player/manager John Aldridge making a rare appearance to score the winner at Bradford, 1997

I don't know how old I was at the start of that game, but I'm 93 now!

Martin O'Neill after a nail-biting second-leg draw with Wimbledon took Leicester City to the Coca-Cola Cup final on away goals, 1997

I didn't spend the afternoon biting my nails by the telephone because I gave the Albanians no chance. Instead, I've been getting my garden in order.

Northern Ireland's Billy Bingham as Albania lost 2–1 to

Watching Manchester City is probably the best laxative you can take.

Caretaker boss Phil Neal, 1996

I have kicked every ball and headed twice as many as anyone else.

Bobby Robson after Ipswich's UEFA Cup victory over AZ67 Alkmaar, 1981

We did win, didn't we? I think we finished ahead, but it was all happening so fast.

Stoke's Lou Macari after a nail-biting 4–3 win over West Brom, 1992

I'm off to buy a bottle of Grecian 2000.

Kenny Dalglish after Newcastle fought back from 3–1 down to beat Leicester 4–3, 1997

It's bad for the heart but good for the revenue.

Reading's Ian Porterfield after a 3–3 draw earned an FA Cup replay at Newcastle, 1990

I'm just glad we are still here. At half-time I had to ask myself who the part-timers were.

Rotherham's Ronnie Moore getting a second bite of the cherry against Emley, 1998

If the stories I was told were true, there were dozens of people rushing about with fivers in their hands during the interval trying to put money on us. It seems I was the only one in the stadium who thought we would lose.

Alec Stock after his Third Division Queens Park Rangers had come back from 2–0 down at half-time to beat First Division West Bromwich Albion 3–2 in the 1967 League Cup final, 1970s

At half-time I would have settled for us just getting a corner.

Martin O'Neill watching Leicester recover from 2–0 down at the interval to force an FA Cup replay with Chelsea, 1997

We got a result which came from nowhere.

Martin O'Neill as an outplayed Leicester scored twice in the last two minutes to overhaul Leeds in the Worthington Cup, 1998

It will be nice to enjoy Sunday for a change.

Martin O'Neill after Leicester's first win in six games, against Northampton in the Cup, 1998

These moments, you might as well cherish – you might not get another.

Martin O'Neill celebrating Leicester's victory at Aston Villa, 1996

We've won a lot of friends this season, but not enough points.

Charlton's Alan Curbishley picking up three with a 4–2 victory over West Ham, 1998

Fair play is an English word – it is not a French word – and it has been copied all over the world. Unfortunately, it does not function any more here.

Arsène Wenger after a perceived lack of sportsmanship by Blackburn's Chris Sutton cost Arsenal a precious win, 1997

Chris Sutton was wrong to do what he did because it is not in the spirit of the game. He is a very silly lad at times, a very simple lad.

Blackburn caretaker boss Tony Parkes on the throw-in incident at Highbury, 1997

He gets arrested for bawling and shouting. I don't suppose Gerry Francis or anyone else in a dugout has ever shouted before! There were thousands of people swearing out there.

Sheffield United's Steve Bruce after his assistant, John Deehan, had been arrested for alleged swearing during the match with QPR, 1998

All I heard was a couple of hello, hellos from the police.

QPR's Gerry Francis on the same incident, 1998

I don't think the contact was as severe as the player made out. That part of the pitch was uneven, but it won't need any rolling now.

Everton's Howard Kendall after Duncan Ferguson had been sent off for swinging an arm at Derby County's Paulo Wanchope, 1998

You'd roll about too if your Adam's apple had been pushed halfway down your throat.

Derby's Jim Smith giving his view of the same incident, 1998

Lloyd McGrath is lucky he's not running in a gelding plate now. That tackle was so high it was very nearly a squeaky-voice job.

Coventry's John Sillett, horrified by a tackle from Everton's Dave Watson, 1987

It was a brawl, not an exhibition of football.

Austrian manager Hugo Meisl after a tempestuous World Cup quarter-final against Hungary, 1934

Great game? You know what that was? Two Third Division teams trying to kick each other to death, that's what it was.

Bill Shankly, unimpressed by the Scotland–Brazil match at the World Cup, 1974

If that's what football is about, then I'll have to look for another job. We expected a physical game, and we certainly got one.

Liverpool's Graeme Souness after a bruising Coca-Cola Cup draw with Crystal Palace, 1992

I don't remember Souness being a wallflower in his playing days. The side we had out couldn't maul a church choir.

Palace assistant manager Alan Smith on the same match, 1992

If a team can come here and play like that and a referee can allow it, then the game has gone to pot.

Liverpool's Graeme Souness moaning again, this time about over-physical Southampton, 1992

I thought you exchanged shirts after games, not during them.

Newcastle's Kevin Keegan protesting at Arsenal shirt-pulling which resulted in the sending-off of David Ginola, 1996

There's always a bit of an atmosphere between League and non-League, but the general spirit throughout this match was bad. It was a game I didn't particularly enjoy. My players won't be joining theirs for a drink.

Torquay United's Mike Green after a bruising FA Cup draw at St Albans City, 1980

It was more of a scrap than a football match.

QPR's Don Howe following a draw at Derby, 1990

We have been eliminated brutally – I would say, scientifically.

France's Michel Hildago after defeat against West Germany in the World Cup, a game marred by German keeper Harald Schumacher's cynical aerial assault which flattened France's Patrick Battiston and denied the French a goal, 1982

I don't believe players go out of their way to break each other's legs, although they can be a bit careless.

Torquay United's Dave Smith taking a detached view after losing defender Phil Lloyd with a broken leg at Maidstone, 1990

Confrontation? My missus belts me harder than that.

Nottingham Forest's Dave Bassett dismissing suggestions of an on-field vendetta between Pierre Van Hooijdonk and Charlton's Eddie Youds, 1998

Let's not lose our dignity. Whatever the result, we must keep our dignity.

Jock Stein to his assistant Alex Ferguson during the second half of the crucial World Cup qualifier against Wales in Cardiff, 1985. Stein died at the end of the match

Most roads are paved with good intentions, but this one was littered with obstacles.

Jock Stein as injury-hit Scotland were eliminated from the World Cup qualifiers, 1966

I'm as baffled as Adam on Mother's Day.

Bolivia coach Xabier Azkargorta (presumably with a little help from an interpreter) expressing his disappointment that clubs had refused to release players for the country's World Cup warm-up games, 1994

We didn't relish the challenge until it went to 2–0. We were like somebody going to the dentist's, taking painkillers and waiting until it was all over.

Coventry's Gordon Strachan after the 2–0 defeat at Old Trafford, 1998

Defeat at Bournemouth was a horrible experience. Funnily enough, we beat Barcelona not long after in the Cup Winners' Cup, and I told Maradona he could think himself lucky he hadn't been playing Bournemouth.

Ron Atkinson recalling Manchester United's FA Cup defeat at Dean Court, 1984

Watford are the worst team that's ever beaten us.

Bill Shankly after Liverpool's Cup exit at Watford, 1970

It was men against boys – and we were the boys.

Wimbledon's Dave Bassett on the Third Division club's 4–1 FA Cup defeat against Enfield, 1981

Alastair Robertson pulled a thigh muscle in the first ten minutes and was still our best player. That says a lot.

Wolverhampton Wanderers' Graham Turner after his side's ignominious FA Cup defeat at the hands of Chorley, 1986

The FA Cup can be very romantic – but not for us.

Bruce Rioch after his Middlesbrough team went out to Fourth Division Grimsby, 1989

The Cup is the icing on the cake, but at the moment we haven't got any cake.

Grimsby Town's Kenny Swain after crashing 7–1 at Sheffield Wednesday, 1997

A third-round replay would be a Cup run for us.

Oldham's Joe Royle before the tie with Spurs, 1988. Oldham lost 4–2

I don't know whether to go out and get drunk or throw myself in the nearest canal.

Shrewsbury Town's Ian McNeill after going out of the FA Cup to the League's bottom club, Colchester, 1989

It won't be the end of the world if we lose, but it will be close to that.

Manchester City's Malcolm Allison before the shock FA Cup defeat at Halifax, 1980

The final indignity came when our team coach got stuck in the mud when we tried to leave the bloody place. In vain, twenty strong men tried to shift it, and we were forced to stand there, red-faced, until a replacement coach arrived.

Jack Charlton recalling Sheffield Wednesday's FA Cup defeat at non-League Wigan Athletic in 1977, from *Jack Charlton: The Autobiography* (Partridge Press, 1996)

It's a very thin dividing line between success and failure.

Arsenal's George Graham, following his team's FA Cup exit at Wrexham, 1992

Never mind, boys, these things do happen.

Arsenal's Herbert Chapman in philosophical vein after the Gunners' sensational FA Cup defeat at the hands of Third Division Walsall, 1933

We weren't going to win the FA Cup anyway.

Cheltenham Town's Steve Cotterill after first-round defeat against Lincoln City, 1998

It will be worse when we open the papers and realise we made history the wrong way round.

Coventry's John Sillett after FA Cup humiliation at Sutton United, 1989

I was seeing the headlines getting bigger by the minute.

Barnet's Ray Clemence as his team fought back from 3–0 down to force a Cup replay with Woking, 1994. The respite was short-lived since Woking won the replay

We are a young team, we've got a bright future and we will be back.

Defiant Arsenal boss Terry Neill after going down to Ipswich in the Cup final, 1978

When we got the two goals back, we were thinking of the breather before extra-time and lost concentration for a few vital seconds.

Manchester United's Dave Sexton after his team's last-gasp Cup final defeat against Arsenal, 1979

If I was the Kidderminster boss, I would really fancy my chances.

Birmingham City's Barry Fry before the third-round tie with GM Vauxhall Conference leaders Kidderminster Harriers, 1994

We've let the club down. A lot of Birmingham fans will be degraded and humiliated. They will go into work and take a lot of stick. It will take a long time for them to get over it. Never mind that we had so many chances. All they will see is that we are out of the Cup.

Barry Fry as his premonition came true with a 2–1 defeat, 1994

It was a Gross impertinence.

Howard Kendall, with a joke few bosses would be able to crack, after Everton lost to the Spurs-managed Christian Gross, 1997

Oh misery, misery. What's gonna become of me?

Graham Taylor as England surrender a two-goal lead against Holland, 1993

Together we made a pig's arse of the situation in Norway.

Graham Taylor, following a World Cup setback in Oslo, 1993

We played them on the wrong day.

Graham Taylor belatedly consulting his diary after England's humiliation at the hands of the United States, 1993

A bunch of schoolboys could probably have beaten my team today.

Watford's Graham Taylor in the aftermath of a 4–1 defeat at West Brom, 1998

It was hectic in midfield, like the Keystone Cops.

Tranmere's John King on a Coca-Cola Cup defeat against Birmingham, 1995

We didn't use any common sense and kept putting the ball in the air, even though the wind was a problem.

Steve McMahon, following Swindon's Cup defeat at the hands of Stevenage Borough, 1998

The ball was up in the air so much it was making me dizzy.

George Graham after Leeds' game at Highbury, 1998

We've got to stop believing in our own publicity.

Joe Kinnear after Wimbledon surrendered meekly 2–0 at Villa Park, 1995

There was a lot of space out there, but all the players abused it.

Sheffield Wednesday's David Pleat cracking down on any atmosphere of bad language following a goalless draw with Chelsea, 1995

You play this game with your hearts, but we didn't go to war. We didn't even get the bullets out – we fired blanks all day.

Tranmere Rovers' John King, still reeling from a 5–0 humbling at Derby, 1995

There were too many silver prizes being picked up by our players. We lost out in the individual contests, and when you do that, your chances are slim.

Maine Road caretaker boss Asa Hartford, the only person in years to mention 'silver' and 'Manchester City' in the same breath, following a League Cup humiliation at Lincoln, 1996

We went to see *Buddy* at the Victoria Palace last night. He's got more life in him now than we had out there today.

Dave Bassett after Sheffield United's 5–2 defeat at Arsenal, 1991

We were Billy Bigtime in the first half.

Dave Bassett moaning at Sheffield United's lack of effort at Barnsley, 1995

We had players who were self-indulgent, and that is detrimental to the team. We tried to play as individuals, and there were people not taking responsibility. All this fancy dan stuff doesn't get you anything.

Sheffield Wednesday's Danny Wilson in the wake of the club's Worthington Cup exit at the hands of Cambridge United, 1998

Whitley Bay had three or four men booked, but at least that showed they were competing.

Preston's John McGrath, upset at Cup surrender, 1989

You are disgraceful. You didn't show an ounce of character. I would stop your appearance money if I could.

Gordon Jago to his Millwall players following a tame FA Cup draw with Yeovil, 1975

It was a disgusting performance. Players were guilty of lack of concentration, lack of self-discipline, lack of everything. They are prima donnas.

Chelsea's Ken Shellito after a 3–1 defeat against West Brom, 1978

Their attitude was that they wanted to be winners. Ours was to be prima donnas.

Coventry's John Sillett, following FA Cup defeat at Northampton, 1990

We went out expecting things to happen. The Dutch went out and made things happen.

Jock Stein after Celtic's European Cup final defeat against Feyenoord, 1970

There, that's better.

Brian Clough spitting on Darren Wassall's injured hand and ordering him back on to the pitch after the Forest defender had wanted to leave the field during a reserve game, 1992. Wassall soon left Forest for Derby

If players want a non-contact game, they should stick to netball.

Queens Park's Eddie Hunter urging more fight from his men after a 2–2 draw with Stenhousemuir, 1992

We are too frail mentally. The goal killed the team and we seemed to have no legs after that.

Gerard Houllier suggesting physical as well as mental problems at Liverpool after a home defeat against Leeds, 1998

We have dropped more points against the non-Championship contenders. For some reason, against these teams, the same determination is not there.

Arsène Wenger as Arsenal fall to Wimbledon, 1998

How do I feel? Lower than a snake's belly.

Swindon Town's Steve McMahon summing up the pain of relegation, 1995

I have felt much lower than this. My wife and I counted eleven occasions as a player or manager when things have been a lot worse.

Gordon Strachan coping with Coventry's early-season struggles, 1998

Alex made a good substitution and I made a bad one. That's the way this game goes. Sometimes you get a pat on the head and others you get kicked up the backside. But we stopped doing the simple things. We suddenly thought we were better than we were.

Liverpool's Roy Evans reflecting on defeat at Old Trafford, 1994

I'm capable of showing anger at times, and half-time was one of those times.

Spurs' Peter Shreeves as his team slumped at home to bottom club Southampton, 1992

In one game we were 3–0 down at half-time. Jeff Astle came in and was looking for a cup of tea. I gave him one – all over his shirt! The rest of the team got the same treatment and went back out on to the pitch. We ended up winning 5–3 and Jeff got a hat-trick. The only difference these days is that I always make sure we use paper cups.

Barry Fry remembering a typical half-time pep talk during the 1970s at Dunstable, 1996

The lads will get slaughtered, I will get slaughtered – and we have to accept that.

Denis Smith prepares himself for the abattoir after West Brom's 3–1 home defeat at the hands of local rivals Birmingham, 1998

I am very pleased, delighted, ecstatic.

West Brom's Denis Smith dishes out the sarcasm following a 4–0 Cup defeat at Aston Villa, 1998

The perfect end to a perfect week.

A sarcastic Alex Ferguson after Manchester United's 5–2 FA Cup victory over Wrexham concludes the week of the Cantona incident at Selhurst Park, 1995

My players had sawdust in their heads today.

Bob Paisley after Liverpool's FA Cup third-round defeat against Chelsea, 1978

It was a bit of the old Chinese water torture.

Millwall's Mick McCarthy as his team missed a succession of chances and lost 1–0 to Barnsley, 1995

It will be Little and ten others against Blackburn in the Worthington Cup on Wednesday.

Crewe's Dario Gradi absolving only sub Colin Little from blame in a 4–1 home defeat against Tranmere, 1998

It's driving me to sobriety.

Luton's Jim Ryan declining an after-match drink following another defeat, at home to QPR, 1991

I couldn't believe seeing Martin Carruthers and Jason Beckford grabbing the ball out of the net and running back to the halfway line at a hundred miles an hour as if they were trying to win it with ten men. I'd have got the ball out of the net and kicked it over the Boothen End to waste a few minutes.

Lou Macari blaming a lack of professionalism as Luton were allowed to snatch a last-gasp winner seconds after his ten-man Stoke had equalised, 1994

I thought that I would have to throw another ball on the pitch for us to get a kick.

Sunderland's Bob Stokoe as his team were outplayed by Manchester City but still managed a draw in the FA Cup, 1973

The difference was that Tottenham stuck the ball in the net and we didn't.

Dave Russell, manager of non-League Marlow but in the Premier League for clichés, after a 5–1 FA Cup defeat at White Hart Lane, 1993

It was a nothing kind of cauldron.

Phil Neal with a nothing kind of comment after Coventry suffered a 2–1 home defeat against Wimbledon, 1994

It's going to be a long, hard winter. We must take it on the chin, that's all we can do. The odds get fearful, but we're not fearful of that.

Phil Neal, following Coventry's 4–0 home reverse at the hands of Spurs, 1995

Confidence is not something that players can get by taking a tablet.

Nottingham Forest's Dave Bassett, 1998

Bryan [Robson] will be opening a bottle of champagne while I'm having my cup of tea.

Blackburn's Roy Hodgson underlining the difference between victory and defeat after losing 2–1 at Middlesbrough, 1998

In our first four games we couldn't beat an egg.

Port Vale's John Rudge reading extracts from the Frank Carson joke book, 1998

We were a rag, tag and bobtail outfit in the first half.

Kettering Town player/manager Steve Berry after his team's second-half fightback against Farnborough Town, 1998

When their second goal went in, I knew our pig was dead.

Swindon Town's Danny Williams coming up with a new metaphor to describe FA Cup defeat at home to West Ham, 1975

It had been a finger-in-the-dyke job.

Crystal Palace's Steve Coppell summarising the defeat at Wimbledon, 1984

It was like the gun fight at the OK Corral – and they outshot us.

Coventry's John Sillett after losing 4–1 at Derby, 1990

I thought we could have been here to next Saturday and neither team would score.

Luton Town's Lennie Lawrence after a goalkeeping error saw them lose 1–0 at Gillingham, 1998

It was a festival of bad passing. In fact, United were more dangerous when we had the ball than when they had it.

Chelsea's Ruud Gullit on the Charity Shield fixture with Manchester United, 1997

We hardly got the ball up to the front pair. I think Peter Schmeichel got more passes from midfield than they did.

A dissatisfied Alex Ferguson despite Manchester United's win at Norwich, 1995

On Tuesday, I complained that they had passed the ball without purpose. The difference today was they didn't pass it, full stop.

Liverpool's Roy Evans, following disappointing performances against Burnley and QPR, 1995

We couldn't pass water.

Woking's Geoff Chapple, 1997

We committed football suicide.

Alvin Martin after his Southend team conceded two goals in the last four minutes to snatch defeat from the jaws of victory at Exeter, 1998

Graham must have seen some poor sides this season.

Mansfield Town's Steve Parkin after being told that his Rochdale counterpart Graham Barrow thought the Stags were the best team to visit Spotland all season, 1998

It looked as if we were worried about the reputations of some of their players, but if we are going to be intimidated by big names then we are in trouble, because there are an awful lot of them in this league.

Danny Wilson after Barnsley's 3–0 home defeat to Aston Villa, 1997

Our crisis will be someone else's crisis for the next few weeks, and then someone else's for the weeks after that. That's the way of the world we live in.

Blackburn's Roy Hodgson after victory over West Ham eased their precarious position, 1998

Any Premiership manager is one defeat away from a crisis.

Aston Villa's John Gregory, 1998

I think in life one has many disappointments.

Sir Alf Ramsey doing his Prince Charles impersonation after England's World Cup exit at the hands of Poland, 1973

We discuss everything before the game and then they go out and do the exact opposite.

Queen of the South's Rowan Alexander after defeat at Forfar, 1998

Nothing surprises me about what my side does any more.

West Bromwich Albion's Denis Smith, perplexed by a setback at Portsmouth, 1998

You hope you never get surprised by things that happen at this club, but you still do. It's a rollercoaster ride at times and we went off at the top.

Alex Ferguson as Manchester United crash at Sheffield Wednesday, 1998

When you concede one goal, then two more quickly, the game is over.

Tottenham's Gerry Francis presenting an irrefutable argument following a 3–0 defeat at Leicester, 1997

We can't consistently come back from a three-goal deficit.

Graham Taylor after Wolves' fightback at Charlton proved in vain, 1995

It was a carnival occasion and Barnet were the clowns. My defenders must have thought tackle is what they went fishing with.

Barry Fry as Barnet marked their Football League debut with a 7–4 defeat at home to Crewe, 1991

Every time the ball goes in our area, I shout 'Goal!'

Barry Fry on Birmingham's porous defence, 1994

It was kamikaze defending. Managers would be dead within six months if every game was like that.

Liverpool's Roy Evans after a breathless 4–3 win over Newcastle, 1996

I wish our defence had been as tight as that.

Tranmere's John Aldridge struggling to open a post-match bottle of beer following a 3–1 home defeat against Norwich, 1998

I was not surprised by the pace of the English game, but what did surprise me was the fact that my defenders did not play the way I told them.

Bristol City's Swedish boss Benny Lennartsson, whose first match in charge produced a 5–0 defeat at Bradford City, 1998

We had a weak defence when I arrived, and now they are even weaker.

Benny Lennartsson a week later after a 6–1 home drubbing by Wolves made it eleven goals conceded in his first two matches, 1998

We find it difficult to score goals, yet we concede them very, very easily.

Colin Todd putting his finger on the reasons for Bolton's lowly position in the Premiership following a 5–1 home defeat at the hands of Coventry, 1998

Our problem is that once we concede a goal, our unity goes out of the window.

Crystal Palace's Attilio Lombardo after a 3–1 home defeat against Spurs, 1998

We always forget to shut the back door.

Southampton's David Jones complaining about his leaky defence after conceding four to Aston Villa, 1998

Only he will ever know why he was in that position for the free-kick. Nobody told him to stand there. He'll take that to his grave.

Manchester City's John Bond on Tommy Hutchison, who deflected Glenn Hoddle's free-kick into the net for Spurs' equaliser in the FA Cup final, 1981. Spurs won the replay

He hasn't scored this season. It wasn't the best time to start, was it?

Slough Town's Dave Russell after Lee Harvey's own goal in the Cup against Plymouth, 1995

Lee's biggest asset is that he is not afraid to fail.

Arsenal's George Graham on Lee Dixon, 1992

The first game I saw was Bournemouth away at Reading. The doctor had told me not to go. So I got a friend to take me and I watched from the stands. We were winning 1–0, and then the goalkeeper made two terrible mistakes. It was sloppy. I went downstairs to the dressing-room and I coated the keeper. The players hadn't seen me for ages. They were probably thinking, 'Oh my God, Harry's back!'

Harry Redknapp recalling his first match back with Bournemouth following his horrific 1990 car crash, 1998

He made some good saves, but we can blame him for costing us the match because he made a mistake. If he doesn't hold his hand up, then I'll hold it up for him.

An unforgiving George Graham points the finger at Leeds' goalkeeper Nigel Martyn for gifting Newcastle an equaliser, 1998

I'd like to apologise to all the fans who paid good money to watch that. If people are subjected to that kind of garbage every Saturday, the crowds will be down to two hundred. If that game is the future of British football, I want no part of it.

Coventry's Terry Butcher after a dismal home defeat by Wimbledon, 1991. Six months later the club granted his wish

I genuinely do not look at League tables, but I know that if we play many more games like that one, we will not be top much longer.

Crystal Palace's Alan Smith after a 0–0 draw at Charlton, 1993

We were a nice present for him.

West Brom's Johnny Giles as Albion lost 4–0 at Highbury on Don Howe's first anniversary as Arsenal manager, 1984

I am a bit disappointed because I thought our stupid celebrations for the goal meant we lost our focus.

Bristol Rovers' Ian Holloway as Notts County equalised within two minutes of Rovers' over-elaborate goal celebration, 1998

I was truly elated – for fully fifteen seconds. We were still watching the action replay when they equalised.

Ron Atkinson after Sheffield Wednesday had conceded a quick Cup leveller at Watford, 1998

It was in the net in the time it takes for a snowflake to melt on a hot stove.

Leeds' Howard Wilkinson, 1995

Going behind that early made it like trying to run uphill in treacle.

Howard Wilkinson with more flowery prose, 1995

It was like trying to carry a ton weight up the down escalator.

Howard 'give us a simile' Wilkinson on the daunting task facing Leeds after conceding an early goal to Rangers in the European Cup, 1992

I feel like Korky the Kat when he gets run over by a steamroller, gets up and then somebody kicks him in the stomach.

Howard Wilkinson explaining that Leeds' weak title defence was far from dandy, 1993

We were kicked where it hurts.

Portsmouth's Jim Smith after missing out on promotion to the Premiership in the play-offs, 1993

Football can kick you in the teeth, and it has done that today.

Colin Todd after a 4–0 defeat at Derby increased the threat of relegation hanging over Bolton Wanderers, 1998

I only wish we could have won, because Bolton have not got a result here since 1908.

Colin Todd after Bolton conceded a late equaliser at Barnsley, 1998

Managers are being pressured from so many different angles now. They have got to expect that, if they lose, all sorts of things will be read into it. Everybody has to have their say in phone-ins and endless other things. Despite all the analysis, we might just have played badly and lost.

Honest Wolves boss Graham Taylor offering no excuses for defeat at Leicester, 1995

It was what they needed, because you can't play with your nerve ends showing like that. Football's just not worth it.

Graham Taylor telling his Wolves players at half-time in the game against Sheffield United that he wished he'd brought in his Tommy Cooper video to give them a laugh, 1995

Two things worried me at half-time. The way Villa were playing and the way we weren't.

Kevin Keegan after Newcastle had rallied for a 1–1 draw, 1995

Where did it go wrong for us? It was quite simple really: at the back, in midfield and up front.

Leeds' George Graham following a 2–0 defeat at Aston Villa, 1996

It was a case of the circus coming to town, but the lions and tigers didn't turn up.

Kevin Keegan watching Newcastle surrender meekly at Old Trafford, 1995

We don't consider we lost on football, but to a circus turn.

Jock Stein after Celtic lost their European Cup semi-final with Inter Milan on a penalty shoot-out, 1972

Penalty shoot-outs have nothing to do with football. It's like shooting poor wee ducks at a fairground.

Aberdeen's Alex Smith after winning the Scottish Cup at the expense of Celtic, 1990

Nobody beat us, did they? Sad, very sad.

Bobby Robson after England lost to Germany in the penalty shoot-out at the World Cup, 1990

I asked the players who wanted to take a penalty, and there was an awful smell coming from a few of them.

Mick McCarthy after Millwall's victorious penalty shoot-out against Chelsea in the FA Cup, 1995

You would not fight a war in those sort of conditions.

Leeds' Howard Wilkinson as the wind swept across Barnsley, 1991

I've never been so wet. Now I know how the cast of *Titanic* felt.

Bristol Rovers' Ian Holloway after a soggy 1–1 draw at Notts County, 1998

Hopefully, we can keep the rain going all season!

Leyton Orient manager Tommy Taylor after two wins in a week on saturated pitches, 1998

There's a certain jinx about programme writing. Feature a player and it's a fair bet he won't be in the team because of injury or being dropped.

Queens Park Rangers' Alan Mullery lamenting the absence of Simon Stainrod, profiled in the match-day programme but dropped, after an uninspiring encounter with Sheffield Wednesday, 1984

It was touch and go whether I kept him in the side, but we decided that if we played our best defenders we could win in normal time. That's football for you, the one you nearly dropped wins the FA Cup for you.

Alex Ferguson after Lee Martin had scored Manchester United's winner over Crystal Palace in the Cup final, 1990

No way would Francis have played if the others had been fully fit.

Nottingham Forest's Brian Clough after a goal from Trevor Francis (only in the team because of injuries to Archie Gemmill and Martin O'Neill) won the European Cup, 1979

If that was intentional, I'll drop me trousers and bare me bum in Burton's window.

Millwall's Mick McCarthy on Jan Fjortoft's 'fluke' Coca-Cola Cup goal for Swindon, 1995

We've seen off the Lions, we've beaten the Magpies and now we've got to do the same to the Cockerels.

Exeter City's Brian Godfrey on the club's Cup run in which they had beaten Millwall and Newcastle, among others, to earn a sixth-round tie with Tottenham, 1991. But Spurs won 2–0

We are going to slay the dragon in his lair.

John Beck of Cambridge United with bold words before his team's FA Cup visit to Highbury, 1991. United went down 2–1

People will probably start thinking we're favourites, and I don't like that.

I'm sure our name's on a cup somewhere, but it will have a saucer with it.

We're like Lady Di. She's not the Queen yet – she's not even married. But like us, she's nicely placed.

Everyone was talking about Eintracht. They said we were old, that Di Stefano and Puskas could no longer play together, but they said this before the semi-final too and we beat Barcelona 6–2.

If we were playing Barcelona in the Nou Camp tomorrow, I'd still believe we were in with a chance. Whatever I've done in my life, I've always thought I'd win.

This is the first time that the Cup final will be played at Hillsborough. The other semi-final is a bit of a joke, really.

Palace and Derby. That's my forecast for the FA Cup final.

West Ham will certainly know they've been in a match. We're going there to win.

Bury's Jim Iley before a 10–0 Milk Cup hammering at West Ham, 1983

Our recent record will have made them aware that no one can come to the Den with too much optimism.

Millwall's George Petchey before a 6–1 defeat at the hands of Ipswich in the quarter-finals of the FA Cup, 1978

The game in Romania was a game we should have won. We lost it because we thought we were going to win it. But then again, I thought there was no way we were going to get a result there.

A logical explanation from the Republic of Ireland's Jack Charlton, 1987

It's coming. Slowly, very, very slowly, but it's coming.

Alan Ball, heartened by Manchester City's 0–0 home draw with Leeds, 1995. The following week, City lost 6–0 at Anfield

Before City scored we could have been 3–0 up. We were playing so well I turned to our physio and said, 'I think I'll have a cigar. If we keep this up, we'll get double figures.'

Huddersfield Town's Malcolm Macdonald reflecting on losing 10–1 at Manchester City, 1987

Three of their goals were offside.

Malcolm Macdonald looking for sympathy after the same match, 1987

No. I've not got many teeth, and I wouldn't like to lose those I have.

Manchester City's Jimmy Frizzell when asked whether he'd had a word with Macdonald after the Huddersfield game, 1987

Our goalkeeper, Reg Davies, was never really tested – except of course for the five goals which passed him.

Millwall's Jimmy Seed after a 5–2 FA Cup defeat at Worcester City, 1958

We lost seven goals and yet I can't remember our keeper making a save.

Nottingham Forest's Frank Clark after a 7–0 drubbing at Blackburn, 1995

We couldn't lose and yet we lost. The whole thing was unreal, a freak of nature.

Sir Alf Ramsey on England's World Cup quarter-final collapse against West Germany, 1970

Our performance in the second half was a good one. I am not talking about the goals we lost.

Celtic's Dr Jozef Venglos as his team lost 4–2 in Zurich in the UEFA Cup, all six goals coming in the second half, 1998

Take away the stupid individual errors and it was as well as we've played all season.

Ian Branfoot after Southampton had conceded four at home to Sheffield United, 1992

The public's perception of this match is going to be clouded by the scoreline.

Scarborough's Billy Ayre after a 3–1 defeat at Barnet, 1994

I honestly believe we were desperately unlucky to lose those last four games.

Hull City's Terry Dolan, 1992

That's three games in a row now we've played really well. And we've drawn one and lost two.

Southampton's Alan Ball after being beaten at Blackburn, 1994

I'm very disappointed. We didn't play badly.

Tottenham's Keith Burkinshaw after losing at Bristol City, 1976

I'm very disappointed. We didn't play badly.

Keith Burkinshaw's reaction to defeat at Sunderland the following week, 1976

The heat was a great leveller.

Burnley's Chris Waddle after being held to a draw by Gillingham in tropical Lancashire, 1997

No excuses. The road to ruin is paved with excuses.

Coventry's Bobby Gould, following defeat at the hands of Leeds, 1993

It may sound daft, but until we let in those three goals just before half-time, I thought we were the better side.

Marine's Roly Howard searching for crumbs of comfort from an 11–2 FA Cup hammering at Shrewsbury, 1995

The score should have been 15–0 to Liverpool.

Bill Shankly overdosing on exaggeration after a 2–1 home defeat against Swansea in the quarter-finals of the FA Cup, 1964

We have been beaten before, but tonight we were defeated.

Inter Milan's Helenio Herrera, somewhat more gracious in defeat after losing 3–1 to Liverpool in the first leg of a European Cup semi-final, 1965. Maybe he knew he could afford to be generous, as Inter won the second leg to reach the final

The best team always wins. The rest is only gossip.

Notts County's Jimmy Sirrel, 1985

I have always been proud of what I've achieved in football, but I can't be proud of our Premiership results this season.

Newcastle's Kenny Dalglish bares his soul, 1998

Losing 3–1 to the potential champions is not necessarily a bad result.

Normal service has been resumed three months later as Kenny Dalglish tries to put a brave face on defeat at Arsenal, 1998

Performances are irrelevant in Cup games, as long as you get a result.

Kenny Dalglish as Newcastle scrape through against Tranmere, 1998

They played neatly, but didn't pose much of a threat. Sometimes you get games like that when you know you're best and get punished for it rather than a result.

Kenny Dalglish, magnanimous in defeat as Blackburn lose at home to West Ham, 1993

Superb . . . great football . . . we outclassed them at times.

West Ham's Billy Bonds with a somewhat different view of the same game, 1993

In terms of points we didn't come away with anything, but as the manager I got something out of the match.

Manchester City's Alan Ball after defeat at Stoke, a game in which both sets of supporters chanted 'Ball out' (the ginger one had been Stoke manager five years earlier), 1996. Exactly what Ball got out of the match remains a mystery since he resigned from Maine Road before the next game

You sometimes learn more from your defeats.

Mensa candidate Ray Harford following Queens Park Rangers' setback at Oxford, 1997

It is always interesting to see how young players react when they are three or four down.

Arsenal's Arsène Wenger after the 5–0 Worthington Cup humiliation at the hands of Chelsea, 1998

We gave them a grilling. We gave them a slap in the face.

Portsmouth's Terry Fenwick, seemingly forgetting that his team had just lost to First Division high-flyers Millwall, 1995

It might sound silly, but other than their three goals Bolton did not create any chances.

Terry Fenwick after Portsmouth's 3–0 home defeat, 1997

The positive side is that while other people are playing Cup games, we are going to be playing League games, and that will give us a chance to make ground.

Mark McGhee endeavours to convince himself that Wolves crashing out of the FA Cup at home to Portsmouth is a good thing, 1997

I am convinced the game was just a blip.

Mark McGhee after Wolves' 3–0 home defeat by Crystal Palace, 1997

Dave Beasant was so inactive in the first half I thought he had a cigar on at one point.

Dave Bassett after two second-half goals condemned Nottingham Forest to Worthington Cup defeat at Old Trafford, 1998

At certain stages, United were chasing us around, which is quite a nice thing to see.

Walsall's Jan Sorensen after a 5–1 Cup defeat at Old Trafford, 1998

How are things going? Well, we've tightened up defensively.

Everton's Walter Smith after letting in four at home to Manchester United, 1998

I think we are beginning to settle down.

Walter Smith after Everton's 3–0 drubbing at lowly Coventry, 1998

They'd have stopped it if it had been a boxing match.

Macclesfield's Sammy McIlroy after watching his team dominate Northampton but still lose 1–0, 1998

The defeat at Carshalton was not as bad as it sounds. But we gave away five bad goals.

Worthing boss Joe Boon reeling from his team conceding 23 goals in a week – losing 10–0 at Whyteleafe in the Vauxhall League and coming unstuck 13–0 at Carshalton in the Loctite Cup, 1991

Four very strange decisions by the referee totally changed the whole course of the game.

Graeme Souness after Liverpool's 5–1 defeat at Coventry, 1992

If we had won 5–1, it would have been called the greatest piece of man-management in the club's recent history.

Scarborough director of coaching Mitch Cook on his decision to take his players for a night on the town before their match at Plymouth, 1996. Instead, Scarborough lost 5–1

This was our poorest display of the season. But something as trivial as a change of month can sometimes make the difference. I hope it does the trick for us because I'm certainly glad to see the back of October.

Stoke's Brian Little after his team's dismal run continued with defeat at Notts County on the last Saturday in October, 1998. Sure enough, November sparked an instant improvement

We must begin to turn possession into goals. We can't score in the first half and are suffering. Short of black magic or getting a witch doctor in, we just have to keep going and keep believing it will change.

Dave Bassett after Nottingham Forest had failed to score in the first half for the twelfth time in thirteen games against Premiership opposition, 1998

If we continue to play this type of football, our turn will come.

Chelsea's Ted Drake after his team were crushed 5–2 at West Brom, 1953. But Drake was right: Chelsea won the First Division title the following season

Failed? Second in the Championship. Cup finalists. Ninety per cent of managers would pray for 'failures' like that.

Victorious Liverpool manager Bill Shankly on vanquished Leeds when asked whether Cup final defeat meant that Don Revie's season had been a failure, 1965

The Scottish Cup, the Dryborough Cup and now the League Cup – not bad for a side they say is falling apart.

Jock Stein after Celtic's 6–3 win against Hibs, 1974

I feel like jumping over the moon.

Alf Ramsey, possibly the first manager to use the cliché, as he celebrated Ipswich winning the First Division title, 1962

I am not one to jump over the moon or off a cliff.

Sir Alf Ramsey as the England going got tough, 1973

When it finally happens, you still keep waiting for somebody to come along and wake you up and tell you there's still a game to go.

Still determined to take each game as it comes even though the season has ended, Blackburn Rovers' Kenny Dalglish 'celebrates' the Championship win, 1995

God has helped us and our goalkeeper.

Iran coach Valdier Vierra after his team qualified for the World Cup finals at the expense of Terry Venables' Australia, 1997

We terrorised them for a lot of the time.

Terry Venables' view of the match with Iran, 1997

I don't want to have a team that wins things in one season and is then average again. It doesn't matter how well you do in the cups, the Championship is what matters. I want a generation that is at the top for four or five seasons.

Arsenal's Arsène Wenger, 1998

We don't just want to win this Cup. We want to win it playing good football, to make neutrals glad we've won it.

Celtic's Jock Stein before the European Cup final triumph over Inter Milan, 1967

What a performance. What a performance.

Celtic's Jock Stein, almost speechless after the match, 1967

Some people called me a visionary, others a reactionary, while a few called me awkward or stubborn.

Manchester United's Matt Busby on his quest for the European Cup, 1957

I had become increasingly obsessed about United winning the European Cup. It was almost as if this glittering trophy were the Holy Grail.

Matt Busby, 1973

We'll never win the European Cup now.

Matt Busby to Paddy Crerand after United's semi-final defeat against Partizan Belgrade, 1966

Like Satchmo says, it's a wonderful world.

Matt Busby, following Manchester United's European Cup semi-final triumph against Real Madrid, 1968

The moment when Bobby took the Cup it cleansed me. It eased the pain of the guilt of going into Europe. It was my justification.

Matt Busby reflecting on the European Cup success ten years on from the Munich air crash, 1980s

There is no way I would let the European Cup become an albatross. But that doesn't mean I am any less determined to win it.

Manchester United's Alex Ferguson, 1994

If we win, I'm taking the whole squad to Portugal for four days of sunshine and golf. If we lose, they'll be in for extra training and then off to a caravan site in Bangor.

Wimbledon's Joe Kinnear taking a leaf out of Judith Chalmers' book before the defeat against Everton, 1998

If we win, I'll climb the castle walls.

Colchester United's Dick Graham before the club's epic Cup tie against Leeds, 1971. Five days later, he was hunting out his crampons

If Clarke and Giles went to the toilet, I wanted my two men there as well.

Dick Graham explaining how he detailed John Kurila and John Gilchrist to do man-for-man marking jobs on the Leeds danger men before Colchester's famous 3–2 Cup triumph, 1971

If one of our forwards had gone off on a stretcher, Auxerre would probably have sent somebody with him.

Arsenal's Stewart Houston condemning the French team's man-marking policy, 1995

We are hoping to restore Nuneaton to their former greatness.

John Barton after Nuneaton drew at Swansea in the FA Cup, 1993

Who's got the Cup then?

Nottingham Forest assistant manager Peter Taylor brushing aside Liverpool protests that the penalty which won the League Cup should never have been given, 1978

I left the Cup on top of the TV for a couple of days so I could keep going back for a peek in case I thought I'd been dreaming.

Brian Clough after Nottingham Forest beat Luton in the Littlewoods Cup final, his first trophy for nine years, 1989

I lied to my grandson over the weekend and told him we had won the Cup. He's still in the stages of speaking Japanese, so he won't understand.

Brian Clough after Forest's Cup final defeat, 1991

Can't avoid the truth. Can't make it look any better than it is. Only one thing to be said: we're in the shit.

Brian Clough after Forest were crushed 3–0 by Norwich, 1993

The club became the victim of my personal stubbornness, my supreme but misplaced optimism. I was the one standing there, saying over and over again, 'This can't happen to me.'

Brian Clough on Nottingham Forest's relegation, 1993

It's totally my fault. We haven't played enough good football that's also successful. As Eric Morecambe used to say, 'There's no answer to that.'

Brian Clough on Forest's relegation season, 1993

I can't stress how important it is that when this game is over, you get in and out of the bath as quick as possible – we don't want to miss the 5.15 train back to Blackpool.

Blackpool's Joe Smith delivering his team talk before a vital relegation clash at Cardiff, 1955

I was delighted to get a point. Normally the only thing we get out of London is the train from Euston.

Oldham Athletic's Jimmy Frizzell after a hard-earned draw at Queens Park Rangers, 1981

I've seen Desert Orchid fall, I've seen Bestie refuse a drink, I've seen Emlyn Hughes buy one. So you never know.

Exeter City manager Alan Ball on his club's prospects for the FA Cup visit of Aston Villa, 1994. Villa won 1–0

A few fly bites cannot stop a spirited horse.

Cambridge United's John Beck quoting from Mark Twain before a 3–0 home defeat by Swindon, 1992

Just put your foot on the ball and pick your nose. Shock the defender and show him you are king.

David Pleat delivering a lesser-known line from literature when addressing his Sheffield Wednesday wingers before a match with Arsenal, 1996

See everything, adjust a little, be grateful for the burden.

Face triumph and disaster and treat those two impostors just the same.

Barrie Williams reciting Kipling to his players before the Cup tie at Norwich, 1989. Sutton lost 8–0

Sutton were a credit to the Vauxhall Conference, but we were a credit to the First Division.

Norwich City's Dave Stringer after the Sutton game, 1989

You've beaten them once. Now go out and beat them again.

Alf Ramsey to his England troops before extra-time in the World Cup final, 1966

My faith in the side was never shaken, even when the Germans scored the first goal. I still knew we would win.

Sir Alf Ramsey, from *They Think It's All Over* by Kenneth Wolstenholme (Robson Books, 1996)

Semi-finals are about winners – and we weren't the winners.

Chelsea's Glenn Hoddle assessing Cup defeat by Manchester United, 1996

I can't make that day, I'm going shopping with the missus.

Sheffield Wednesday's Trevor Francis after the FA bowed to pressure to stage the all-Sheffield FA Cup semi-final at Wembley, 1993

Right venue, right occasion. Fans get the tickets instead of the hangers-on. Nice day. Shame about the result.

Sheffield United's Dave Bassett on the same game, 1993

Great atmosphere. Great surface. Great players. Wrong result.

Kevin Keegan after Newcastle went down 2–0 at Old Trafford, 1994

We need twenty points from our last four games.

Oxford United's Mark Lawrenson confronting the reality of relegation from the First Division, 1988

The world is your lobster.

Mark Lawrenson quoting Arthur Daley as Oxford rise up the Second Division, 1989

I think having Wasps around here as well gives us that little buzz around the place.

Ray Wilkins on Queens Park Rangers' ground-sharing with Wasps rugby team, 1996

We are on the crest of a slump.

Jack Charlton, a few days before resigning from Middlesbrough, 1977

We can only go up. If we get any lower, we'll fall off the pools coupons!

Tommy Docherty as Manchester United struggle against relegation, 1973

Celtic were brilliant – when I had my eyes open.

Arbroath's Danny McGrain, unable to bring himself to watch his team's 9–1 Scottish League Cup hammering by Celtic, 1993

I knew it was all over when the seventh goal went in.

Danny McGrain after the Celtic game, 1993

I didn't see that incident: I had my head in my hands.

Charlton's Alan Curbishley as his team held on for a draw at Leeds, 1993

I didn't see anything of our goal because I was halfway to the dugout.

Manchester City's Joe Royle recovering from a hip operation at Wigan, 1998

It was a game of three halves.

**Grimsby Town's Kenny Swain on a draw with
Manchester City, 1997**

The better team drew!

**Mansfield Town's Andy King following a 2–2 draw at
Bury, 1995**

3 The Players

I said to one player, 'I'm Dodgin, the new manager.' He said, 'So am I mate, you haven't seen him anywhere, have you?'
Oldham Athletic's Norman Dodgin, 1958

I felt like the garrison commander at Rorke's Drift when the Zulus came pouring over the hill.
Alan Ball inheriting a squad of 42 players for his first training session at Manchester City, 1995

Players never know why they are taken off and substituted – until they become managers.
Bobby Robson at PSV Eindhoven, 1991

We have no reserves at this club, only good players.
Arsenal's Arsène Wenger, 1998

I don't drop players, I make changes.
Liverpool's Bill Shankly, 1973

How does he behave? What sort of life does he lead? Unless the answers are satisfactory, I do not pursue the matter further.
Arsenal's Herbert Chapman assessing a player, 1930s

I wouldn't check on a player I'm interested in under floodlights because he would look better than he really is.
Billy Walker of Nottingham Forest, 1960

I find out more about a player when he's injured. However much you try to involve him, he seems an outcast. You see the reaction, the character when a player is down.
Liverpool's Bob Paisley, 1982

How can I tell my players that this is the best club in the world when the bath is not clean and the tiles are dirty?

Kevin Keegan preparing to sign Carol Smillie for Newcastle, 1992

When I sign a player, I always arrange to meet him in a service station or a hotel, before he gets the chance to see our offices.

Luton Town boss David Pleat, 1981

There are no prima donnas, no heavy gamblers. We have a neat side, with no permed hair.

David Pleat on his well-groomed Luton outfit, 1981

I don't want my players having permed hair. I want them to look like footballers.

Mansfield's Mick Jones wields the scissors, 1979

Jason's got to learn to take some stick. If he doesn't like it, then there are two ways to cure it. Either he gets his hair cut or he scores more goals.

Nottingham Forest's Frank Clark as 'Pineapple Head' Jason Lee is ridiculed on *Fantasy Football League*, 1995

It was his lack of hair that did it!

Portsmouth 'Bald Eagle' Jim Smith on shaven-headed Chris Burns' failure to clear a cross against Middlesbrough, 1992

The only thing he's going to have to face at our club is one or two perverts – people who like dressing up in women's clothing!

John Gregory welcoming the troubled Paul Merson to Aston Villa, 1998

Generally, I like family men. The only single man I bought at Bolton was Alan Thompson and he was nineteen at the time. We put him into digs and worked on finding him a girlfriend.

Bruce Rioch taking over at Arsenal, 1995

A manager is sometimes forced to ask himself questions about a player's wife. What bearing does she have on his attitude to the game? Or on his physical condition? Does she feed him properly? Does she wind him up mentally, or help him to relax? Does she tuck him up on Friday nights whispering 'Good luck tomorrow', or does she say, 'I'm going to that party whether you go or not?'

Queens Park Rangers' Alec Stock, 1968

David Rocastle is a magnificent human being. If I had a daughter free . . .

Leeds' Howard Wilkinson getting carried away, 1993

Kenny is a wonderful asset to the club. I've talked about him so much this season, the players are beginning to wonder if I've got a thing for him!

Ross County boss Neale Cooper declaring his admiration for midfielder Kenny Gilbert, 1998

It hasn't affected his looks – he's still an ugly bugger!

Motherwell's Billy Davies after rugged defender Shaun Teale sustained a cut head against Kilmarnock, 1998

Billy is far more than a player to me. He is a friend, a very great friend. In the 21 years I have known him, we have never had a cross word.

Wolverhampton Wanderers' Stan Cullis on Billy Wright's retirement, 1959

He was as near perfection as man and player as it is possible to be.

Sir Matt Busby on Bobby Charlton, 1980s

I prefer players not to be too clever at other things. It means they concentrate on football.

Tottenham's Bill Nicholson, 1973

Son, you're too small to be a footballer.

Leicester City's William Orr to seventeen-year-old future England international Raich Carter after a trial against Watford Reserves, 1930

My biggest player was not as big as their smallest.

God knows what was wrong with him. When we get him home we'll put some scaffolding around him and have a look.

Oldham's Joe Royle, concerned about an injury to giant defender Brian 'Killer' Kilcline, 1991

If a jumbo jet was coming towards our area, he'd try to head it clear.

Birmingham City's Barry Fry on short-sighted centre-half Liam Daish, 1995

Just walk round him. He's a colossus.

Bill Shankly introducing journalists to Ron Yeats, Liverpool's new 6ft 2in, 14-stone centre-half from Dundee United, 1961

With him at centre-half, we could play Arthur Askey in goal.

Bill Shankly on Ron Yeats, 1962

Don't you recognise him? That man is the future captain of England.

Bill Shankly to a traffic policeman who had stopped him on his way back to Liverpool with his new £65,000 signing from Blackpool, Emlyn Hughes, 1967

Christ, son, I've just seen that Bobby Moore. What a wreck. He's got bags under his eyes, he's limping and he's got dandruff. He's been out to a nightclub again.

Bill Shankly to new signing Kevin Keegan before Liverpool's match with West Ham, 1971. A group of West Ham players including Moore had recently been caught in a Blackpool nightclub breaking the pre-match curfew

Jesus Christ, son. That Bobby Moore, he's some player. You'll never play against anyone better than him.

Bill Shankly to Keegan after the same match, which Liverpool had won easily despite an outstanding performance from Moore, 1971

This was Bobby Moore's greatest game. Technical perfection.

Ron Greenwood on West Ham's European Cup Winners' Cup triumph at the expense of TSV Munich, 1965

Bobby is not a bread-and-butter player. He is made for the big occasion. The more extreme the challenge, the more commanding he will be. He should play at Wembley every week.

Ron Greenwood, 1960s

The one thing that nobody ever found out was that he couldn't head a ball. He would always position himself so he'd catch it on his chest, or he'd let the ball run and turn on it, but you very rarely saw him head the ball. I don't think he wanted to spoil his hair.

Ron Greenwood paying tribute to Bobby Moore, 1993

He read the game twenty minutes before anybody else.

Celtic and Scotland's Jock Stein on Bobby Moore, 1960s

No footballer of talent should play in the back four.

Crystal Palace's Malcolm Allison, 1975

He is the greatest player of his age I have ever seen. Yet although he has soared up among the stars, his feet are still on the ground.

Manchester United's Matt Busby talking about Duncan Edwards, 1957

He played with tremendous joy and his spirit stimulated the whole England team. It was in the character and spirit of Duncan Edwards that I saw the true revival of British football.

England manager Walter Winterbottom pays tribute to Duncan Edwards on the day he died as a result of injuries sustained in the Munich air crash, 1958

I said, 'What happened?' She still said nothing. So I began to go through the names. She didn't speak at all. She didn't even

look at me. When they were gone she just shook her head. Dead
. . . dead . . . dead . . . dead . . . dead . . . dead . . . dead . . . dead.

**Matt Busby learning the worst from wife Jean as he
recovered in hospital after the Munich crash, 1958**

If ever there was a player who could justly be called a one-man
team, that man was Duncan Edwards. He was the most
valuable member of one team I ever saw anywhere.

Sir Matt Busby, 1980s

He is the most complete midfield player in the game. He can
defend, he can create and he can inspire all around him. He is
a great tackler, he's good in the air, he has superb range of
passing and he scores goals. He's like Duncan Edwards and
Dave Mackay – a scruff-of-the-neck player. He can take over
any game even when it is going against his own team.

**Ron Atkinson signing Bryan Robson for Manchester
United, 1981**

For the past ten years we've been trying to kick each other. He's
always been too quick for me and I've always been too smart
for him. I just hope he's slowing up and I am just as smart as I
was.

**Manchester City player/manager Peter Reid before a
derby game with Bryan Robson and Manchester United,
1991**

There's nobody fitter at his age, except maybe Raquel Welch.

**Ron Atkinson signing 39-year-old Gordon Strachan for
Coventry, 1996**

I want our best players in the team – old or young, big or small.
My first thought on taking the job was to reactivate Lothar. It
is ridiculous to see him playing so well week after week yet
having no role in the national team. The fact that he is 37 is no
obstacle. We need our most experienced players for the inferno
ahead.

**New German national coach Erich Ribbeck planning to
recall Lothar Matthaus, 1998**

We need young legs, quick legs. Some of our players will be playing charity games on a Sunday afternoon in a few years.

David Pleat on his ageing Sheffield Wednesday men, 1995

He can't run, can barely breathe, his legs have gone all soft and he can't kick a ball more than ten yards. Yet look what he does. He calms everyone down. It's just what we needed.

Notts County's Mick Walker signing veteran Peter Reid, 1994

He can't exactly run any more. But I don't know where we'd be without him.

Peterborough United's Barry Fry on his leading scorer, 38-year-old Jimmy Quinn, 1997

He can only make two to three sprints a match.

Derby County's Jim Smith on Paul McGrath's dodgy knees, 1997

What made me green with envy was his speed. It's not right for the over thirties to be skinning the youngsters. It's meant to be a young man's game! We used to hear these First Division coaches shouting from the bench: 'Take the old man on!' No chance! He was a great athlete.

Joe Mercer remembering Manchester City stalwart Tony Book, 1980s

He's a nice lad and he works hard. If the fence wasn't there, he'd run all the way down the A3.

Kingstonian's Micky Droy on Jamie Ndah, scorer of the FA Cup winner against Brighton, 1994

The work Carlo puts in, he defies science.

Plymouth Argyle boss Mick Jones on lighter-than-air striker Carlo Corazzin, 1998

Ten years ahead of his time.

Sir Alf Ramsey on Martin Peters, 1968

There was a moment when he took the ball off Hartson, dropped his shoulder, turned him and passed the ball to

Southgate, who launched it into the terraces – and someone around me asked: 'Which one of them played for England in mid-week?' It seems the only thing we can't teach him is to smash the ball into the stands.

Aston Villa's John Gregory drooling over teenage defender Gareth Barry's performance against West Ham, 1998

He proved he is amphibious! It doesn't matter to Denis which side he plays.

Oldham's Joe 'It's the way I tell 'em' Royle on his ex-player Denis Irwin, equally comfortable at right- or left-back, 1994

The first day Dave Mackay reported for training, everything at the club changed.

Former Tottenham manager Bill Nicholson remembering the presence of Dave Mackay, 1995

David was Derby County, the cornerstone. A competitor at every level who lost his temper with himself and his team-mates whenever we lost.

Brian Clough on the influence of Dave Mackay on the Derby team of the early 1970s, 1988

He needed five stitches – three in the first half and two at the interval when his brain started to seep through.

Alex Ferguson on Manchester United rock Steve Bruce, who sustained a head injury in a clash with Arsenal's Kevin Campbell, 1993

Nigel is a winner. He would want to win every game, even if he was playing for Wigan.

Arsenal's Arsène Wenger trying to engineer a transfer to Lancashire for Nigel Winterburn, 1998

What's the point of giving you the ball when there's a genius on the other wing?

Brian Clough to Martin O'Neill, who played on the right for Nottingham Forest, 1970s. John Robertson was on the left

Whenever I felt off-colour, I'd sit next to Robbo because then I looked like Errol Flynn. But if you gave him the ball and a yard of grass he became an artist. He was the Picasso of our game.

Brian Clough on the ample skills of Forest's John Robertson, 1980s

I remember calling off our first practice match because no one could get the ball off wee Jimmy Johnstone.

Scotland boss Tommy Docherty, 1970

We like the big, strong, powerful fellows here with a bit of strength and solidity in the tackle rather than the frivolous, quick-moving stylists like Jimmy Johnstone, small tiptoe-through-the-tulips type of players who excite the people.

Rangers' Willie Waddell, 1972

Most foreign opponents have never seen anything like him before, and they can lose concentration for twenty minutes trying to work him out. What will the fellas from Zaire think of him? They'll take him for a leprechaun or a hobgoblin.

Jock Stein considering the puzzle of Jimmy Johnstone on the run-up to the World Cup, 1974

You're at least a moving target. I'm stuck in the dugout.

Jock Stein to Jimmy Johnstone before Celtic's heated European Cup semi-final in Spain against Atlético Madrid, 1974

When he plays on snow, he doesn't leave any footprints.

Leeds' Don Revie on winger Eddie Gray, 1970

I didn't hold back when I met the players. I told Peter Lorimer he tried to con referees, I told Norman Hunter and Johnny Giles they were such good players they didn't need to go around kicking people. And I told Eddie Gray that, with his injury record, if he'd been a racehorse they'd have had him shot.

Brian Clough making friends at Leeds, from *Clough: The Autobiography* (Partridge Press, 1994)

He's like a bar of soap sometimes. When he's on song, it's difficult to nail him down.

Norwich City boss Dave Stringer on elusive winger Ruel Fox, 1991

It was like trying to tackle dust.

Oldham's Joe Royle on Ossie Ardiles, 1988

I wondered what on earth he was doing. Only Dean Saunders could have done that. He pulled a rabbit out of the hat.

Sheffield United caretaker boss Steve Thompson as Saunders aimed a throw-in at the body of Port Vale keeper Paul Musselwhite, collected the rebound and scored, 1998

I can't repeat what I said to him, but I had to call heavily on my Spanish.

Queens Park Rangers' Jim Smith after an Ardiles mistake had given away a late goal, 1988

I don't tell thoroughbreds how to play. It is the unexpected that excites people, and players, not coaches, provide that.

Stoke City's Tony Waddington, 1960s

The expectation was that Ray Wilson, who was the current England left-back, would dominate him, yet Ray just couldn't cope. It was mind over matter.

Stoke City's Tony Waddington remembering how 46-year-old Stanley Matthews, on his reappearance for Stoke against Huddersfield in 1961, ran rings around Ray Wilson, 1980s

Stanley was the matador, goading and provoking the opposition . . . He was the Maradona of his time.

Former England boss Walter Winterbottom on Stanley Matthews, from *Stanley Matthews* by David Miller (Pavilion, 1989)

Finney tended to have more 'assists' with goals than Matthews, a higher effectiveness, but Matthews gave the entertainment. Stanley tended to have either great games or ordinary ones.

Walter Winterbottom on the Finney/Matthews rivalry, 1989

Week in, week out, give me Tom. On his day, he was unplayable, even when the opposition threw two or three people at him.

Joe Mercer siding with Tom Finney, 1980s

I'd have played him in his overcoat.

Bill Shankly on his great hero, Tom Finney, 1970s

There would have been four men marking him when we were kicking in.

Shankly on Finney, 1970s

George Best probably is a better player than Tom Finney. But you have to remember Tom is 60 now . . .

Bill Shankly entering the debate as to whether Best was better than Finney, 1970s

George Best was the one who gave me the most enjoyment – as a footballer.

Sir Matt Busby on players under his wing, 1980s

A little elf, so brilliant that there was nothing to teach him.

Sir Matt Busby recalling George Best's 1963 arrival at Old Trafford, 1980s

He had more ways of beating a player than any other player I have seen.

Sir Matt Busby on Best, 1980s

Here at Old Trafford they reckon Bestie had double-jointed ankles. You remember how he could do those 180-degree turns without going through a half-circle, simply by swivelling on his ankles? As well as devastating defenders, that helped him to avoid injuries because he was never really stationary for opponents to hurt him.

Alex Ferguson, 1992

He was such a great player he could get away with almost anything, and that was the mistake. The club should have kept

110

him on a tighter rein for his own good and the good of United. As it was, he was allowed too much scope and began letting people down too often.

Former Manchester United manager Tommy Docherty on Best, 1990

Giggs was a problem for us all night, but the biggest problem is that he does not have a German passport.

Germany's Berti Vogts after his defenders were tormented by the Welsh wizard, 1995

He does things no other footballer would attempt. At 21 years old, he is a miracle.

Argentina's Cesar Menotti on Diego Maradona, 1982

With Maradona, Arsenal could have won the World Cup.

Bobby Robson, 1986

He takes all the knocks that are handed out. Yet he never retaliates, he just gets on with the game. He takes some whackings from defenders and yet he had that wonderful record for us of not missing a game in something like three seasons. That's a miracle, playing in the position he plays in. He is the target for all the hitmen in the game. He is the man they are after, yet few of them can kick him out of the game.

Liverpool's Bob Paisley on Kenny Dalglish, 1980s

When Kenny shines, the whole team shines.

Bob Paisley on Kenny Dalglish, 1981

Och, just let him on the park.

Celtic's Jock Stein ending the debate as to whether Kenny Dalglish was more effective up front or in midfield, 1978

We got him from Home Farm, the boys' club in Dublin, and I think the lads who come to you from that sort of background in the game are the best type. You get England schoolboys and

111

their heads are away before they arrive at the club. I think the failure rate is about 96 per cent.

Bob Paisley announcing the arrival of Ronnie Whelan at Anfield, 1982

We lose against England at youth level because we are more interested in talent than winning. We try to develop skills.

Former Holland manager Rinus Michels, 1994

They get them early at eight. In England, during my Ipswich days, we couldn't get players before they were fourteen.

Bobby Robson on the secret of the Dutch conveyor belt, 1995

By the time a club can sign up a promising youngster he is at an age when he must be pitched into a fiercely competitive world where the emphasis, almost from the start, is on winning.

Sheffield United's Ken Furphy, 1974

You have thirteen- and fourteen-year-olds who know everything there is to know about offside. Yet if you throw them the ball and say, 'Keep it up six times, five times, four times,' they can't do it.

West Bromwich Albion's Ossie Ardiles, 1992

At practice at Blackpool I saw one of our lads heading the ball about fifty times in succession. When I asked him what was the idea, he said, 'You couldn't do it.' 'I wouldn't want to,' I replied, 'this isn't a circus.'

Blackpool's Joe Smith, 1955

Kids are not allowed to develop naturally nowadays. They grow big hearts and lungs, but have no technique. You should allow a diamond to form, cut it out, polish it . . . and then maybe sell it for two million.

Stockport County's Danny Bergara, 1994

We have had to introduce a lot of young players into the team when ideally it should have just been one or two. But I knew the price when I bought the ticket.

Graeme Souness at Liverpool, 1994

He's used to crowds – he's the youngest of thirteen kids.

Leeds' Howard Wilkinson blooding young full-back Gary Kelly, 1994

They are a young side. It's like when you were eighteen with three girlfriends. The more you play, the more you learn.

Notts County's Mick Walker, 1994

The kids we had on the line against Middlesbrough last week were so young they were giving out jelly babies between them.

Spurs' Gerry Francis, 1997

If the team gets any younger, we'll have to play in the South East Counties.

Alan Smith as Crystal Palace search for their true level, 1994

With nine players injured, we are down to the kids. But we will not squeal.

Wimbledon's Joe Kinnear doing just that after losing to West Ham, 1993

If you let this lot play instinctively, they would need eleven footballs between them.

Terry Venables on his Barcelona players, 1985

I didn't have to teach our players how to play football, but I did have to teach them how to play as a unit, which is very difficult for Brazilian players because they are all such individuals.

Carlos Alberto Parreira, the Brazil manager, after winning the World Cup, 1994

No phone calls to me, not even from my mother. She'll only want to know why I don't pick Ronaldo.

Carlos Alberto Parreira explaining his 'no-call' policy at the World Cup, 1994

He is not just a footballer. I would call him a force of nature who takes the shortest route to the goal.

Brazil's Mario Zagallo on Ronaldo, 1997

Imagine if I hadn't picked Ronaldo and had left him on the bench and we had still lost 3–0. I'd have got the blame for losing Brazil the World Cup.

Mario Zagallo defending his action in playing an unfit Ronaldo in the World Cup final, 1998

The White Pelé? You're more like the White Nellie!

Liverpool's Bill Shankly as winger Peter Thompson struggled to repeat his international form in Brazil on the domestic stage, 1964

Tell him he's Pelé.

Partick Thistle manager John Lambie after being told that his striker, Colin McGlashan, had a head injury and didn't know who he was, 1993

The only problem with Sinclair is that we win a couple of games and he starts to think he's Franz Beckenbauer. I have to remind him a few years ago he was up a ladder for a living.

Raith Rovers' Jimmy Nicholl worrying that stocky defender Dave Sinclair was getting ideas above his station, 1995

He had a meander and decided he was Hidegkuti at centre-forward rather than playing midfield. When Glyn decides it's one of those days, he thinks he's the fairy on top of the cake.

Dave Bassett explaining why he substituted Sheffield United's Glyn Hodges against Southampton, 1991

Short of sending a couple of guys in balaclavas round with baseball bats, there's not a lot you can do to stop him.

Hibernian manager Jim Duffy pondering how to curb the threat of Rangers' Brian Laudrup, 1997

I told him he was playing and he smiled. I told him he was marking Juninho and he went white.

Leicester's Martin O'Neill issuing instructions to defender Pontus Kaamark before the game with Middlesbrough, 1997

If you whacked him, he didn't take umbrage, he just came back at you with the ball, pushed it between your legs or over you or under you or through you.

Former QPR maestro Alec Stock recalling the talents of Rodney Marsh, 1995

I bought him because he's got more skill than anybody else in English football, he can score goals and he's just got that thing. He affects people – like Bestie, Cassius Clay or Tom Jones. I don't know what it is, but he's got it.

Malcolm Allison on bringing Rodney Marsh to Manchester City, 1972

£200,000 is a lot of money to spend to throw away the Championship.

Manchester City general manager Joe Mercer, unimpressed by team manager Malcolm Allison's signing of Rodney Marsh, 1972. City finished fourth

He can play a bit – he's not just a big lump.

Joe Kinnear on Carl Cort, who scored on his Wimbledon debut at Newcastle, 1997

He is so enthusiastic he is like a two-year-old.

West Ham's Harry Redknapp on 34-year-old Ian Wright, 1998

Every single morning he is here an hour before everyone else – it's probably something to do with his wife kicking him out of the house.

Harry Redknapp on early-bird Ian Wright, 1998

Before the game, everyone was buzzing. Wrighty had his music going, but they wouldn't let me have my Max Bygraves on.

Harry Redknapp remembering Ian Wright's West Ham debut at Sheffield Wednesday, 1998

Spitting is part and parcel of the game now.

Arsenal's George Graham defending Ian Wright, who was accused of spitting at Oldham fans, 1991

In my experience, he just doesn't listen, or if he does, he chooses to ignore what you say.

Jack Charlton on Peter Beardsley, whom he managed at Newcastle, from *Jack Charlton: The Autobiography* (Partridge Press, 1996)

If young players do not learn from him, they have got to be thick.

Newcastle's Kevin Keegan on Peter Beardsley, 1993

People sometimes think I'm his agent, but he is a tremendous example for youngsters because of what he has achieved in his career and the way he carries himself. There is just no ego to the man.

Fulham boss Kevin Keegan on loan-signing Peter Beardsley, 1998

When I try to speak to him about his future, he tells me to talk to his agent. Well, it's not his agent he rings when the car won't start or the baby has earache. It is me or my wife at two in the morning.

Crystal Palace boss Alan Smith encountering communication problems with striker Chris Armstrong, 1995

God didn't shine on him the way he shone on Johan Cruyff, Kenny Dalglish or George Best. Keegan made himself into a player by work, work, work. In a way, it made him intolerant of some other players at Newcastle. He was intolerant of Chris Waddle at first. And for six months, Waddle fell by the wayside.

Arthur Cox, Kevin Keegan's former boss at Newcastle, greeting Keegan's arrival into the St James's Park hot-seat, 1992

I wouldn't play a man for England if he is with a foreign club. We have to fight against the trend of losing our best players.

Bob Paisley, irked by Kevin Keegan's move from Liverpool to SV Hamburg, 1977

One Kevin Keegan isn't enough.

**Denmark boss Sepp Piontek assessing England's
shortcomings, 1979**

I needed a midfield motivator, and there he was sitting across
the breakfast table from me.

**Gillingham's Keith Peacock on signing son Gavin from
Queens Park Rangers, 1986**

A team is like a nice clock; if just one piece is missing, the clock
is still beautiful but doesn't work the same.

Chelsea's Ruud Gullit, 1996

The only hooligans here are the players.

**Wimbledon's Dave Bassett after the club's fans
celebrated promotion to Division One by invading the
pitch, 1986**

They've mucked up my weekend, so I'm going to muck up
theirs.

**Dave Bassett ordering his Wimbledon players in on
Sunday following their FA Cup exit at Millwall, 1986**

The Borstal of football.

Dave Bassett on Wimbledon, 1987

Get your tin helmets out.

**Dave Bassett sounds the battle cry at Sheffield United
before the Yorkshire derby with Leeds, 1992**

This team is nothing like the one I had at Wimbledon – that
team would have been all right against Mike Tyson.

Dave Bassett on his Sheffield United charges, 1993

Some players collapse these days as soon as they get shoved.
You expect Sheffield United players to be more manly.

**Manchester United's Alex Ferguson claiming that
Sheffield's Tom Cowan was guilty of play-acting after a
clash with Roy Keane, 1993**

I don't like players behaving like poofters.

Straight-talking Dave Bassett's view of the Cowan incident, 1993

At the moment we couldn't hit a cow's arse with a banjo.

Dave Bassett bemoaning the struggles of Sheffield United, 1994

If you continually play Russian roulette, eventually you're going to get the bullet.

Dave Bassett as his Sheffield United team were finally relegated from the Premiership after a series of near misses, 1994

I know we are the team everyone loves to hate. They blame us for everything, from England's failure in the World Cup to the rising price of plums.

Wimbledon's Joe Kinnear, 1994

When I ask for one more charge they put the tin hats on and go over the top again.

General Joe Kinnear savouring the Wimbledon spirit as the Dons score twice in the last fifteen minutes to beat Sheffield Wednesday in an FA Cup quarter-final, 1997

The lads rolled up their sleeves and showed the bulldog spirit that years ago turned the defeat at Dunkirk into a victory.

Hereford United's John Sillett in Churchillian mood after a fightback at Gillingham, 1976

If good players don't battle against us, they are dead.

Watford's Graham Taylor, 1984

No more nicey-nicey stuff . . . I don't mind if we pick up a few yellow cards . . . I'm looking for a team which fights.

Swindon Town's new player/manager Steve McMahon, 1994. He was sent off in his first game in charge for receiving two yellow cards

Angels don't win you anything except a place in heaven. Football teams need one or two vagabonds.

Manchester City boss Billy McNeill, 1983

When the going gets tough, you have to hate.

Cambridge United's John Beck, 1991

We can all be mates and go on a beach in Spain at the end of the season, but for now we've got to be nastier with each other.

Shane Westley (a disciple of Beck's at Lincoln City) trying to instil some fighting spirit into his team, 1998

He'd run through brick walls if you asked him, and he never thinks about personal safety.

Manchester United's Dave Sexton on daredevil defender Kevin Moran, 1980

We've laid to rest the dogs-of-war bit. We're Cruft's now.

Joe Royle as Everton clean up their act, 1995

There will be no warpaint in the dressing-room.

Scotland's Craig Brown urging restraint before a European Championships qualifier against Finland at Hampden Park, 1995

We put bells on a football so he would know where it was. We had complaints from morris dancers saying he was kicking them all over the place.

Tommy Docherty on Jim Holton, the rugged centre-half he signed for Manchester United in the 1970s, 1988

I have heard Norman described as a one-sided player. It is true, and it is Don Revie's good fortune that his 'one side' happens to be Leeds United.

Aston Villa's Vic Crowe raids the Christmas crackers to pay tribute to Leeds hard-man Norman Hunter, 1974

Graham has kicked a few in England, now he can go and kick some in Scotland.

Spurs' David Pleat selling Graham Roberts to Rangers, 1987

I remember sitting in the stands watching him at Wealdstone, and after a few minutes he dumped the opposing winger in my lap. I thought, he'll do for me.

Bobby Gould recalling signing Stuart Pearce for Coventry, 1995

Before our European matches he used to stand in the tunnel and shout, 'Remember you're English!' It would confuse the likes of Alf Inge Haaland and Bryan Roy, but you knew what he meant.

Nottingham Forest's Frank Clark on the patriotism of Stuart Pearce, 1996

Football is like war. When the chips are down, you need fighters.

Southampton's Ian Branfoot after his team notched up thirteen yellow cards and one red in the space of three games, 1991

It's tough on the lad, but that is a sign of a good centre-half. All the best ones have broken noses and cut eyes.

Ian Branfoot consoling Saints defender Richard Hall, 1992

Sometimes you have to show the world what's between your legs.

Graeme Souness urging his Southampton team to get stuck in, 1997

He is more relaxed now. He will never lose that edge, and I am sure sometimes the red mist might still come down.

Republic of Ireland boss Mick McCarthy on Roy Keane, 1998

He's never hurt anyone. Mind you, he's frightened a few.

Matt Busby on Manchester United and England's Nobby Stiles, 1968

When it came to the more artistic side of the game, Norbert was not the kind of bloke to stand out in a crowd.

Jack Charlton on England team-mate Nobby Stiles, from *Jack Charlton's World Cup Diary* (Gill and Macmillan, 1990)

The last time I went to Anfield, I was playing for Manchester United Reserves, and Tommy Smith kicked me all over the pitch. I'll be looking for him in the corridor next week to get my own back.

Barry Fry after a goalless Cup draw with Liverpool at St Andrews had earned Birmingham a replay on Merseyside, 1995

Go in and shake his bones.

Bill Shankly's pre-match instruction to Liverpool hard-man Tommy Smith, 1970s

Tommy Smith would start a riot in a graveyard.

Liverpool's Bill Shankly, 1970s

Julian's in a different class altogether at the moment. I've just seen him in the shower and he looks in great nick.

West Ham's Harry Redknapp on Julian Dicks, a defender renowned for his tackle, 1996

He's a freak.

Harry Redknapp on Julian Dicks, 1998. Redknapp was referring to the lack of training Dicks needed to get match-fit

He could start a row in an empty house.

Manchester United's Alex Ferguson on Chelsea terrier Dennis Wise, 1990s

If Vinnie Jones had not come along, the *Sun* would have invented him.

Dave Bassett, from *Dave Bassett: Harry's Game* (Breedon Books, 1997)

He let everyone know that we weren't going to be a soft touch. I emphasised before the match that we had to be switched on from the start in all departments. Vinnie set the tempo of the game in that first minute.

Chelsea's Ian Porterfield defending Vinnie Jones, booked after just five seconds of the FA Cup tie with Sheffield United, 1992

Vinnie is a larger-than-life character who gets mistreated.

Wimbledon's Joe Kinnear after Jones is sent off again, 1992

I wouldn't only not sign him, I wouldn't let him in the ground.

Tommy Docherty on Vinnie Jones, 1993

Hartson's got more previous than Jack the Ripper.

Harry Redknapp after Welsh international John Hartson had been sent off again, for West Ham against Derby, 1998

It was the mis-match of the year: a fifteen-stone Welshman and a nine-stone Israeli.

Harry Redknapp a month later on X-rated video footage which showed Hartson kicking team-mate Eyal Berkovic in the head during a training-ground clash, 1998

It's just tough for Jimmy. What does he want me to do – go out and play instead of him and he can watch me from the dugout?

Airdrie's Alex MacDonald on the pleas of skipper Jimmy Sandison, tottering on the brink of suspension, to drop him in the run-up to the Scottish Cup final, 1995

If they don't want to be in the team, then they should carry on doing what they are doing.

Queen of the South's Rowan Alexander after his team collected six red cards in the opening eight weeks of the season, 1998

Gordon Banks deliberately left a gap to invite a shot and then, somehow, jack-knifed back and made a save.

Stoke City boss Tony Waddington revealing Banks's goalkeeping technique in one-on-one situations, 1971

He did pretty well in tricky conditions.

Charitable Barnet manager John Still on the debut of keeper Nicky Rust, during which he let in nine against Peterborough, 1998. Rust's reward was a two-year contract

Apparently the only time he's been to Ibrox was for a Rod Stewart concert. If he gives a performance like Rod does on stage, I'll be happy.

Alloa Athletic's Billy Lamont on keeper Jim Butters before a Scottish Cup tie at Rangers, 1994. Alloa lost 6–0

He's got the brains of a rocking-horse.

Dave Bassett contemplating the intelligence of his Sheffield United goalkeeper Simon Tracey, sent off at Spurs, 1992

I wouldn't go so far as to say he is a complete nutcase, but he comes very close to it.

Wales' manager Terry Yorath about keeper Neville Southall, 1993

Our goalkeeping coach Joe Corrigan has done a fantastic job on David's mental side. Though you'll never get that part completely right, because all keepers are mental anyway.

Liverpool's Roy Evans on the new, improved David James, 1997

I'm not worried about his knees or his back. The only danger is that his mouth will wear out.

Scarborough's Steve Wicks on 42-year-old keeper John 'Budgie' Burridge, 1993

I walked behind Schmeichel off the pitch at the end. Put it this way, there was not a lot of sunlight coming my way!

Crystal Palace terrier Steve Coppell follows the Great Dane, 1997

They might get through our midfield and, very occasionally, they might get beyond Larry Lloyd and Kenny Burns. But when they'd done all that, once they thought they were in the clear, they'd look up and see a bloody gorilla standing there with shoulders like Mr Universe, and they'd wonder where the goal had gone!

Brian Clough on Nottingham Forest and England's Peter Shilton, from *Clough: The Autobiography* (Partridge Press, 1994)

What can I say about Peter Shilton? Peter Shilton is Peter Shilton, and he has been Peter Shilton since the year dot.

Bobby Robson, 1986

Forest will go on and win it, because they have a goalkeeper, they have Shilton. European keepers are inept.

Bill Shankly correctly predicting European Cup success for Nottingham Forest, 1978

A clown.

Brian Clough's infamous pre-match verdict on Poland goalkeeper Jan Tomaszewski, whose unorthodox heroics knocked England out of the World Cup, 1973

He might be a bit vulnerable to a hard, low shot from the edge of the six-yard box.

Arsenal's Don Howe on Pat Jennings, 1983

I've always said there are roadsweepers and violinists who make up a football team. Bruce is a lead violinist.

Former Southampton chief Lawrie McMenemy in praise of Bruce Grobbelaar, 1994

After Kenny Dalglish scored our fourth goal there was a testimonial atmosphere about the whole thing, and I detest that. 'Brucie's going to Wembley', the crowd were singing. Brucie had gone to the bloody pictures at the end of the game!

Bob Paisley on Grobbelaar's more eccentric side as he let in two sloppy late goals to allow Ipswich to draw 2–2 in a League Cup semi-final second leg, 1982. Liverpool still won 4–2 on aggregate

Hoult was sitting in the stand finishing off a hot dog when he got the call to play. But it's no surprise – he's a big lad and doesn't seem to do anything but eat.

Leicester City's Brian Little on keeper Russell Hoult's last-minute call-up against Wolves, 1992

I'll have a chat with him in French this week. I'm taking a lesson on Tuesday and I'll probably speak to him on Thursday.

West Ham's Harry Redknapp, Gallic tongue in cheek, about the possibility of retaining on-loan French goalkeeper Bernard Lama, 1998

You have to remember, a goalkeeper is a goalkeeper because he can't play football.

Chelsea's Ruud Gullit, 1996

You rarely see goalkeepers booked or sent off for fouls. They must be the most protected species in the world – more protected than the golden eagle.

Manchester United's Alex Ferguson, 1991

I used to fine Jim Duffy, my assistant manager and sweeper, a fiver if he passed the ball back to him. He just could not deal with it. The change in the rule preventing him picking up the ball proved cataclysmic for James. We used to sit in the dugout and hold hands when he had to deal with a pass back.

Former Dundee manager Simon Stainrod remembering goalkeeper Jim Leighton's problems with the new back-pass law, 1998

I really could not see his style. I like to know what I am getting in a goalkeeper. I did not want to be surprised by the goals he prevented and I did not want to be surprised by the goals he conceded. He was, of course, the consummate professional. I just did not want him to play on Saturdays. I had to sleep at nights.

Simon Stainrod recalling why he gave Leighton a free transfer, 1998

Scotland might have found a goalkeeper.

Huddersfield Town's Brian Horton after 5ft 8in full-back Tom Cowan excelled as substitute goalkeeper against QPR, 1997

Reaction saves? That's not what goalkeeping's about.

Hard-to-please Everton boss Gordon Lee, 1977

That was just about the best goalkeeping display I've ever seen.

Fulham's Kevin Keegan, frustrated by Leigh RMI's 38-year-old David Felgate, 1998

Sooty played well.

Derby County boss Roy McFarland in praise of keeper Steve Sutton, 1994

We have to face the fact that there are some players utterly convinced they know more about the game than any coach.

Wolves' Stan Cullis, 1961

You can't give them the stick you used to give them now, or take the mickey. They're a bit precious nowadays.

Derby's Jim Smith on players' changing attitudes, 1997

The new freedom of contract for players is a warning to us all. It is going to make life more and more complex for managers. Give the game to the players, I say, and it will be a disaster.

Ipswich Town's Bobby Robson, 1979

The World Cup is on a disaster course. The players have become money mad.

Former Brazil manager João Saldanha, 1974

Players in the reserves are earning between £12,000 and £15,000 a week. As managers, we're dealing with a harder breed of player. They earn so much more than us. It is hard to get into their heads, to pass on the principles we know to be right.

Sheffield Wednesday's David Pleat, 1997

I remember talking to Marcello Lippi, the Juventus coach, at the World Cup. He was talking about the difficulty of getting through to the multi-millionaire players gathered around him in the dressing-room. His theory is that they will listen to the same voice for only a year. So the players must be changed every season, or the manager must go.

Tottenham caretaker boss David Pleat, 1998

I thought: What's the use? I'm talking to eleven millionaires.

Alan Ball struggling to get a half-time message across to his players, 1996

Players of today aren't facing up to their responsibilities in return for their salaries and adulation.

Manchester City's Alan Ball, 1996

Life today does not produce natural leaders. In football, there are no hungry players. Only as far back as my day, there were two or three in every team.

Arsenal's George Graham, 1989

I know what their approach is to their wages, cars, houses, agents and newspaper columns. I want to know what their attitude to football is.

Brian Clough lambasting his Forest players following a poor performance against Bolton, 1979

He is not going anywhere. He is under contract and he can't expect to change the rules just because he wants a few bob more.

Stoke City's Lou Macari laying down the law to restless striker Mark Stein, 1993. Stein was soon on his way to Chelsea

His wages were astronomical compared to what my boys get here. I had about as much chance of getting Alan Shearer.

Crewe Alexandra's Dario Gradi reflecting on his failure to sign striker Dean Windass from Aberdeen, 1998

You're not talking about £20,000 a week here – more like £20,000 a season.

Chester City's Kevin Ratcliffe on the wage gap between players in the Premiership and Division Three, 1998

There are players with swimming pools and tennis courts who haven't even won one Championship medal.

Bill Shankly, 1970s

There is a danger of the whole set-up going berserk and the game being ruined. People who sign contracts should honour them.

Liverpool's Bob Paisley, 1979

Loyalty went out of football a long time ago, and I'll never blame a player for wanting to move on at the end of his contract. That's the way life is now.

Terry Venables at Spurs, 1991

The trouble with this club is we have too many amateurs in the team.

Eddie Hunter, boss of amateur club Queen's Park, 1992

You just have to work intensely when you get them together. They won't move because their wives have jobs they can't afford to lose.

Carlisle United's Mick Wadsworth on his far-flung team, 1994

Are the players on big money? No – we'll buy them an extra drink in the bar.

Hednesford Town's John Baldwin after a 2–0 FA Cup triumph at Hull, 1997

There's two great teams in Liverpool: Liverpool and Liverpool Reserves.

Bill Shankly, 1972

Mind, I've been here during the bad times too. One year we came second.

Liverpool's Bob Paisley, 1979

I remember Jimmy Adamson crowing after Burnley had beaten us once that his players were in a different league. At the end of the season they were.

Bob Paisley, 1979

Sharing sums up Liverpool better than anything else. I don't think I could have survived at any other club, because here I can go from the top to the bottom, talk to people.

Bob Paisley, 1982

Too many of ours have no real interest or love of the football club – they are only interested in getting another move or another lump of money. People, even so-called stars, can say they are fully committed and passionate about this club. But talk is cheap, and we have a lot of talkers here. What matters is when you cross that white line on to the pitch.

Liverpool's Graeme Souness not mincing his words after the humiliating FA Cup defeat by Bolton, 1993

Anybody who plays for me should be a bad loser.

Graeme Souness, still smarting six months after Liverpool were pipped for the title by Arsenal, 1991

There were too many players who had come here for a pension and maybe thought, Let's join Leeds. Let's make a few quid and have a nice, soft time. There were players on enormous contracts with no will to deliver.

George Graham recalling what he had walked into at Elland Road, 1998

As a manager you have got to be a good judge of character and ask yourself, Is this guy coming to make a fast buck, and a year from now he will be off, or is he willing to stay and sweat? Under me, they have got to sweat. That's the least I require.

Leeds' George Graham, 1998

I think there have always been talented players at Spurs and they have underachieved in my opinion. I don't want to eliminate the nice football, but I want nice football that hurts the opposition.

George Graham on his move to Tottenham, 1998

The Drury Lane actors.

Bill Shankly mocking Spurs' perceived lack of determination, 1960s

I thought Paul Daniels was involved. It was amazing what he did.

Kevin Keegan on the wizardry of Newcastle's Andy Cole against Swindon, 1993

I don't want to talk about Andy Cole. I want to talk about players who want to play for the club in the right manner, week in, week out.

Kevin Keegan on the elusive Cole following Newcastle's 2–1 Coca-Cola Cup defeat at Wimbledon, 1993

I wouldn't swap them for anyone in the world.

Kevin Keegan praising Peter Beardsley and Andy Cole, 1995. Four days later he swapped Cole for Manchester United's Keith Gillespie, plus cash

If I've got it wrong, then there's a bullet with my name on it.

Newcastle's Kevin Keegan preparing to take the flak for the sale of Andy Cole, 1995

We used to say about George Cohen: 'He's hit more photographers than Frank Sinatra.' George was quick and broke up the flanks exceptionally well, but his final ball was rarely on target. Usually he would hit his cross into the crowd, or into the photographers.

Bobby Robson on former Fulham team-mate George Cohen, from *Time on the Grass* (Arthur Barker, 1982)

We are playing him further forward than he is accustomed to, because of his lack of defensive awareness in midfield.

Spurs' Keith Burkinshaw on Argentinian acquisition Ricky Villa, 1978

Sometimes I wonder if there is a poor Welsh player in the League. Every manager who has a Welshman in his team seems to give me a glowing report.

Wales manager Dave Bowen, 1972

They're wonderful things, videos. They never show you a bad player.

New Leeds boss David O'Leary, besieged by agents bearing videos of players, 1998

It's hard to believe that so many professionals in this country haven't been taught how to kick a football correctly.

Malcolm Allison back in management at Bristol Rovers, 1992

When I buy a player, I don't expect to have to teach him to play football.

Forest's Brian Clough on the technical limitations of million-pound signing Justin Fashanu, 1981

He couldn't trap a landmine.

Brian Clough on new signing Gary Megson, 1984

We reckon he covers every blade of grass on the pitch – mainly because his first touch is crap.

Southampton's David Jones on Carlton Palmer, 1997

He's as slow as a funeral, but has ball control and can stand on the ball while making up his mind.

Herbert Chapman on Arsenal schemer Andy Neil, 1920s

Now, boys, Crerand's deceptive – he's slower than you think.

Bill Shankly to his Liverpool players before meeting Pat Crerand and Manchester United, 1960s

I could not win a place in the present Arsenal team. I would be too slow.

George Graham, 1992

I call him 'The Crab' because he only plays sideways.

Manchester United's Ron Atkinson on midfielder Ray Wilkins, 1983

He can't run, can't tackle and can't head a ball. The only time he goes forward is to toss the coin.

Tommy Docherty on Manchester United's Ray Wilkins, 1987

Ray's got that horrible habit of passing to his own team. It's a disease we would like to catch.

Crystal Palace's Steve Coppell after defeat by a Wilkins-inspired QPR, 1989

We'll take his one or two little weaknesses. We know he isn't going to win headers against John Fashanu.

Kevin Keegan on Newcastle recruit Scott Sellars, 1994

John Barnes's problem is that he gets injured appearing on *A Question of Sport*.

Tommy Docherty, 1993

Wingers aren't luxuries as long as they produce. I'm not in favour of people just standing out there getting either a suntan or frostbite.

Everton's Joe Royle, 1996

He doesn't have days, that is the trouble. He has minutes. On his minute, he is one of the best wing men in the country.

Portsmouth's Jim Smith on the enigmatic Mark Chamberlain, 1992

He is a spasmodic player. He has so many spasms that he can win games.

Arsenal's George Graham on Swedish winger Anders Limpar, 1990

I'll bet yer man lives in a bungalow – he'd no want to be bothered wi' all that climbing stairs.

Bill Shankly to Watford manager Ken Furphy about midfielder Tony Currie, 1967

I'll let you off this time, but promise me you'll send me two complimentary tickets when you play for England.

Ken Furphy after Tony Currie had backed the Watford manager's car into a wall while in the process of cleaning it, 1967

Not every captain can be a Beckenbauer. It can cause problems, because there are those in the team who will not give as hard if the leader is a strolling type. The climate can be bad.

Former West German manager Helmut Schoen on the subject of Tony Currie's elevation to the captaincy at Leeds, 1978

We have bonding huddles, although we get injuries in it. I've done it all my career. With some of the players, it's the only time they get to win a tackle.

Bury's Neil Warnock, 1998

Trevor Brooking floats like a butterfly . . . and stings like one.

Forest's Brian Clough in his role as ITV pundit, 1981

You don't have to bare your false teeth to show you are a real he-man in football. Some people are morally brave, and Hoddle is one of them.

Brian Clough on Glenn Hoddle the player, 1980s

The players will receive only two-thirds of the bonus. Despite winning 6–1, there was some slackness and mistakes.

Dundee United taskmaster Jim McLean withholding the players' special entertainment bonus after trouncing Motherwell, 1981

Am I going to discipline them? No, I'm going to give the other six a rollicking for not trying hard enough.

Derby County boss Harry Storer after his Sheffield United counterpart Joe Mercer had complained that five Derby players had been 'clogging', 1957

Where did it go wrong? My lot wouldn't commit themselves. Their hearts weren't in it because they're a bunch of pansies like you and me.

Forest's Brian Clough before planting a kiss on the cheek of ITV's Gary Newbon following a 4–0 defeat, 1980s

He has a passionate side – he just doesn't show his emotions.

Arsenal's Arsène Wenger on Dennis Bergkamp, 1998

We have to analyse every case individually. If you have a decisive game where you can qualify for the quarter-final, say against Kiev, and on Saturday you play at home at Highbury against a normal team, you could say, 'OK, let's go for that game.' But of course if he has to go to Kiev with the bike, it is difficult to be back on Saturday.

Arsène Wenger on how Arsenal propose to handle Dennis Bergkamp's fear of flying in their European campaign, 1998

I think Bergkamp is one for the connoisseur.

QPR's Ray Wilkins, 1996

I started clapping myself until I realised I was Sunderland's manager.

Peter Reid applauding Dennis Bergkamp's solo goal for Arsenal in a 2–0 win at Roker Park, 1997

He could improve his heading. Dennis, as we know, does not like it in the air.

Arsène Wenger, asked to pinpoint Bergkamp's weaknesses, 1997

I considered that he was being disrespectful to a great player. I am trying to create better professionals.

Wales manager Bobby Gould after sending Robbie Savage home from the team hotel for tossing away Paolo Maldini's shirt during a TV interview prior to the European Championships qualifier with Italy, 1998

I'll invite him in, we'll sit down and talk about it for twenty minutes, and then we'll decide that I was right.

Brian Clough on his method of dealing with any dissent in the Derby dressing-room, 1972

A star? What is that? Only something in the sky.

Bayer Leverkusen coach Erich Ribbeck, 1994

Even if he was the world's best player, I wouldn't have a so-called star in my team. Stars may look good and flashy on the field, but they can play the very devil with team spirit in the dressing-room. Give me loyal club servants like Sam Bartram and we'll go places without the assistance of prima donnas.

Charlton Athletic boss Jimmy Seed, 1950

A wise old manager once told me that it's very difficult to change the mental attitude of footballers, sometimes you just have to change the footballers. That manager was Alex Ferguson.

Dundee United's Paul Sturrock, 1998

Players can easily become too confident and arrogant. I don't mind confidence, but it leads to lack of self-criticism . . . Good players shouldn't make mistakes, ever. That should be the aim, but if they do make one mistake, that should be it. They should be so furious with themselves that they vow never to do it again. But they won't admit mistakes so they don't try harder and do better.

Spurs' Bill Nicholson, 1972

Players have become impossible. They talk all the time about security but they are not prepared to work for it. I am abused by players. There is no longer respect.

Bill Nicholson quitting Tottenham, 1974

We're breeding a race of non-thinking players, players who go on making the same mistakes week after week, season after season. Today's thinking is done by people off the pitch, and it's turning players into stereotyped robots.

Hull City's Cliff Britton, 1969

There is no problem with the players' technique. But they must have strong minds and make no mistakes. For that, they need to concentrate, and this they do not do sometimes.

Sepp Piontek, coach of the Turkish national team, 1991

A mistake is only a mistake when it is done twice.

Derby County's Arthur Cox, 1990

The man who never made a mistake never made anything.

Glasgow Rangers' Bill Struth to young centre-half Willie Woodburn, 1938

I felt as if 'The Castle' which once perched so proudly on top of the Ibrox grandstand had come tumbling to the ground around my ears.

Rangers' Scot Symon recalling the 1954 suspension *sine die* of tough defender Willie Woodburn, 1964

I listen to players. But that doesn't necessarily mean that I take any notice of them.

Middlesbrough's Bryan Robson, 1996

Venables had always set himself up as something of dressing-room spokesman. He started to challenge my authority in training. He would make sarcastic comments about what I was trying to put across. He wanted to be Mr Big in front of the lads, but what they didn't know was that he would often come to my office after training and apologise, saying he didn't mean any disrespect.

Tommy Docherty on life with Terry Venables at Chelsea in the 1960s, from *Docherty* by Brian Clarke (Kingswood Press, 1991)

He's a big-time Charlie.

Manchester United's Alex Ferguson on Paul Ince, the self-styled 'Guv'nor', 1998

This is not a theatre after all. It is a place where passions run high, and sometimes players let their feelings get the better of them.

Liverpool joint manager Gerard Houllier after Paul Ince and Chelsea's Graeme Le Saux were allegedly involved in a post-match fracas, 1998

He is our captain, and he simply wants to look after our players in any troubled situations. I felt really sorry for him.

Gerard Houllier defending Paul Ince's sending-off in a UEFA Cup tie in Valencia, 1998

Incey should have had nothing to do with it. He should have been the cool captain who keeps everybody else away. Instead, he got involved and got another red card.

England's Glenn Hoddle taking a less blinkered view of the Valencia incident, 1998

If I was Glenn Hoddle, I would never pick him again. In an important match, where he is playing or captaining his country, there is no guarantee that he is going to last the ninety minutes.

Tommy Docherty stating his position on Paul Ince, 1998

I cannot defend David's actions, but it was a foul on him in the first place.

Portsmouth's Terry Fenwick contradicting himself in sixteen words over the sending-off of débutante David Hillier at Oldham, 1996

We're quite a good team when we have eleven men.

Peter Reid bemoaning Sunderland's poor disciplinary record, 1996

I call Brace my vision in Versace.

Sunderland's Peter Reid admiring Paul Bracewell's collection of designer suits, 1994

I just wanted to give them technical advice. I told them the game had started.

Aston Villa's Ron Atkinson revealing why he abandoned his seat in the stand in favour of the dugout fifteen minutes into the game with Sheffield United, 1993

I always make sure I write Atkinson D. on the team sheet. Sometimes I wonder if I'm making a mistake.

Ron Atkinson on his Villa namesake Dalian, 1993

I don't go much for this hugging and kissing in soccer – that's one Continental idea we'll never bring to Upton Park.

West Ham's Ted Fenton, from *At Home with the Hammers* (Nicholas Kaye, 1960)

He never smiled. I couldn't have that. He might have made the other players miserable.

Joe Mercer, pledged to putting the fun back into English football, on why he dropped grim-looking Stoke City full-back Mike Pejic from the national side, 1974

I admire the way he plays with a smile on his face.

Kevin Keegan on Jurgen Klinsmann, 1994

He does more in celebrations than he does in a week's training.

Newcastle's Kenny Dalglish on flamboyant Georgian Temuri Ketsbaia, who ripped off his shirt and kicked advertising boards after scoring a last-minute winner against Bolton, 1998

He gets goals like that every day for us in training and leaves us all knock-kneed.

Coventry City's Bobby Gould hailing a Peter Ndlovu strike against Norwich, 1992

In training on Friday, he was sensational. I thought he had peaked a day early, but he proved me wrong.

Birmingham City's Trevor Francis after Peter Ndlovu's two-goal salvo against West Brom, 1998

There would be a poll among the players to find the one they felt had given the worst performance. The player who got the highest number of votes would have to buy a Mars bar for each member of the winning team . . . and then run across Putney

Bridge in a yellow goalkeeper's jersey with the words TOSSER OF THE WEEK emblazoned across the chest!

Fulham boss Malcolm Macdonald on the club's six-a-side training matches, from *Malcolm Macdonald: An Autobiography* (Arthur Barker, 1983)

I am sceptical when people say that training should be fun. I don't see how it can be if you are at the bottom of the table and facing relegation.

George Graham inheriting a precarious position at Tottenham, 1998

We probably do less training at Derby than any other team in the League.

Brian Clough, 1973

I don't care how you train just so long as you perform for me on a Saturday. I'm just trying to extend your career.

Southampton's Lawrie McMenemy to flamboyant striker Frank Worthington, 1984

In my opinion, he's as fit as a butcher's dog.

Portsmouth's Jim Smith after defender John Beresford failed a Liverpool medical, 1992

They can get fitter. I have six levels. When I was boss here previously, the players were at level six. When I came back, I did level one and most didn't make it.

Gerry Francis on his return to Queens Park Rangers, 1998

Not many of them want the ball when it's over. Mainly they want a basin.

Gerry Francis on the fitness runs he introduced at Tottenham, 1994

All he does is lie on the treatment table twice a day.

Rangers' Dick Advocaat on reluctant Italian striker Marco Negri, 1998

He either improves or he doesn't.

Leeds United's Howard Wilkinson on dropping his £4.5 million Swedish signing Tomas Brolin, 1996

I thought he was very quiet. He looked better when he had a bandage on his head. Perhaps one of his eyelashes had fallen out.

Leeds' George Graham seeing Brolin turn out for Crystal Palace following his cut-price transfer from Elland Road, 1998

Is he match fit? I don't know. I never saw him fit. I got on all right with him, I honestly did . . . when I saw him.

George Graham on Brolin, 1998

The days when you shouted down a pit and came up with a young inside-forward are over. Now you'll probably get a long-haired guitarist.

Portsmouth's sergeant-major George Smith, 1968

After one game Barnsley wanted to sign him. After two they decided to send him back.

Derby's Jim Smith on Dean Burton's loan spell, 1998

I was stopped for speeding as we hurtled through Perth in the middle of the night. Fortunately the policeman was a football supporter.

Leeds United's Don Revie racing to head off rivals for the signing of Scottish schoolboy sensation Peter Lorimer, 1962

Apparently his dinner would have been thrown in the bin if he didn't make it home by 1 p.m.

Aston Villa's John Gregory on the David Unsworth transfer saga, 1998. Unsworth's wife allegedly didn't want to move to Birmingham, so less than a week after signing for Villa from West Ham, the defender left to join his original club, Everton

You couldn't buy a decent pie lady for that.

Swindon's Steve McMahon rejecting Stoke's £150,000 bid for striker Peter Thorne, 1996

He nearly went to Middlesbrough, but I told him that Newcastle was nearer London. Luckily, footballers believe things like that.

Kevin Keegan persuading the geographically challenged Robert Lee to sign for Newcastle from Charlton, 1992

If you asked leading players which club they would join if they had the chance, ninety per cent would say Newcastle. There's no doubt that, at the moment, we are the place to be.

Kevin Keegan, 1992

As soon as players know I'm from Workington, they immediately go off the idea of signing for me. The town is so isolated I feel if I offered a player £100,000 to sign, he still wouldn't. You can imagine the problems I have trying to persuade free-transfer men to come here!

Workington manager George Aitken, 1972

I didn't want Tommy to be burdened with a £30,000 price tag.

Matt Busby signing Tommy Taylor from Barnsley for £29,999, 1952

In nine matches out of ten, Blanchflower has the ball more than any other two players on the field. It's an expression of his tremendous ego, which is just what a great captain needs.

Spurs' Arthur Rowe justifying the £30,000 transfer fee – a record then for a half-back – to bring Danny Blanchflower to White Hart Lane from Villa Park, 1954

In a poor side Danny was a luxury. That's why I dropped him. But in a good side his creativity, his unorthodox approach, was priceless – a wonderful asset.

Former Tottenham boss Bill Nicholson on Danny Blanchflower, 1982

A £100,000 transfer is nothing these days. It's like bananas – they used to be two-a-penny, but they're not any more.

Crystal Palace's Bert Head complaining about the price of fruit, 1972

McSherry refused to come to Shawfield, considering that our ground was not a football stadium but a dog track.

Clyde's Craig Brown on being turned down by Jim McSherry of Ayr United, 1977

There are still good players in the lower divisions; you just have to be prepared to work hard with them.

Sunderland's Peter Reid, 1998

Look at Liverpool – they have a goalkeeper from the Fourth Division [Ray Clemence], a centre-half from Division Three [Larry Lloyd], an outstanding forward from Division Four [Kevin Keegan]. That's the value of clubs like Crewe. We can find and develop youngsters and introduce them to the League game earlier than the top First Division clubs.

Crewe boss Jimmy Melia, 1973

I predict he will be the first ten-million-pound signing in British football.

Manchester City boss Alan Ball on paying Exeter City £750,000 for winger Martin Phillips, 1996. Two years later, Ball signed Phillips for his new club, Portsmouth, for under £50,000

Despite the fact that he is my son, I would always want him in my side whichever club I was with. His character and ability will stand the test of time.

Manchester City's John Bond defending the signing of son Kevin to club shareholders, 1981. Three months later, Kevin asked for a transfer

All managers make mistakes. There's no guarantee, no matter how much you pay, that a player will be a success.

Everton's Howard Kendall giving a free transfer to Mo Johnston, his £1.5 million signing from Rangers, 1993

I haven't seen the lad, but my coaches have, and he also comes highly recommended by my greengrocer.

Brian Clough signing Nigel Jemson for Forest from Preston, 1988

If he's a success, he'll be one of my signings. If he blows it, he'll be one of Ronnie Fenton's.

Brian Clough prepares to lay the blame for the signing of Forest's latest misfit striker Robert Rosario at the feet of assistant Ronnie Fenton, 1993

He leaves over my dead body.

West Brom's Ronnie Allen before the sale of Bryan Robson to Manchester United, 1981

John's given his word he'll sign for West Ham . . . He's one of the most honest professional footballers around.

West Ham's Harry Redknapp, the day before John Barnes signed for Newcastle, 1997

Burnley could become the team of the 1970s.

Jimmy Adamson, 1972. They finished the decade being relegated to the Third Division

Palace are a club of the future. I know that everything here is right. The only thing that is out of step at the moment is the way the first team have performed.

Malcolm Allison, with Crystal Palace bottom of the Second Division, 1973

We're the best team there's ever been in the Third Division.

Malcolm Allison on his Crystal Palace side, 1975. They didn't even get promoted

I'd like to think Palace are becoming the Liverpool of the Third Division.

Terry Venables, 1977

You could write the retained list on a postage stamp.

Darlington's Alan Murray, 1994

I'm always telling Craig Russell to run at players with the ball. And he does it. Do you know why? I tell him I'll break his legs if he doesn't.

Sunderland's Mick Buxton improving team spirit, 1994

If I sense that any player of mine is not psyched up and giving absolutely everything, I'll put a bullet in the back of his neck.

Barcelona's Johan Cruyff introducing a novel method of team discipline before a UEFA Cup tie with PSV Eindhoven, 1996

If I'd had a gun at the time, I think I would have shot him.

Aston Villa's John Gregory reacting calmly to Dwight Yorke's decision to join Manchester United, 1998

He's a nervous footballer . . . he sort of runs on nervous energy, and sometimes I don't think he knows where he's going. Like a chicken with its head off.

Aberdeen's Alex Ferguson on St Mirren striker Frank McGarvey, whom Fergie had developed at Love Street, 1978

He was so nervous that we had to push him out on to the pitch, and he would have a cigarette lit up within seconds of coming off.

Blackburn's Jim Smith on flying 1970s winger Dave Wagstaffe, from *Bald Eagle: The Jim Smith Story* (Mainstream, 1990)

I was on a drip in a hospital bed and this player came in to see me. I thought he was enquiring about my health. He never even asked how I was. All he was interested in was how he stood regarding his contract. He'd even brought his agent in.

St Johnstone's John McClelland, 1994

If I had five centre-forwards on the books, Iván Zamorano would be fifth in line.

Real Madrid's Jorge Valdano, 1994. But the Chilean striker stayed and scored thirty goals to help Real to the Spanish title

He'll score you twenty-odd goals a season, but he can't play!

Burnley's John Bond assessing Irish international striker Billy Hamilton, 1983

No experience, no finesse, mediocre technique.

Argentina boss Daniel Passarella leaving little room for misinterpretation as to why he decided to leave young striker Martin Palermo out of the World Cup squad, 1998

Play him for ninety minutes and he's useless.

Birmingham City's Barry Fry on professional substitute Ken Charlery, 1995

One of the lads just tried to jump in the bath and fell out of the window.

Tommy Docherty bemoaning his Manchester United team's lack of accuracy at Villa Park, 1975

Having seen him finish on a day-to-day basis, I would think his last hat-trick was at primary school.

Crystal Palace's Steve Coppell on Bruce Dyer, three-goal hero of an FA Cup victory over Leicester, 1998

Devon Loch was a better finisher.

Ron Atkinson on Aston Villa's goal famine, 1992

Our strikers couldn't score in a brothel.

Tommy Docherty on his goal-shy Wolves, 1985

We don't use a stop-watch to judge our golden goal competition now, we use a calendar.

Tommy Docherty on Wolves, 1985

Relegation was the outcome of fifteen years of neglect.

Tommy Docherty giving his reasons for the decline of Wolves, 1985. The club didn't neglect to sack him that summer

People say his first touch isn't good, but he usually scores with his second.

Wolves' Graham Turner on the prolific Steve Bull, 1988

Yes, he misses a few. But he gets in the right place to miss them.

Bill Shankly on the merits of Liverpool and England forward Roger Hunt, 1966

All I'm prepared to say about him is that we have had two one-to-ones – and I'm not talking about mobile phones.

Leeds United's David O'Leary addressing the lack of goals from striker Jimmy-Floyd Hasselbaink, 1998

I'll tell you what we have obtained for our money – a player who has shown the ability to hit the target nine times out of ten when striking at goal, though I point out this is merely an indication of accuracy and not goals scored.

Manchester City's Malcolm Allison adding a timely disclaimer regarding the worth of £1.25 million man Kevin Reeves, 1980

It will probably be another fifty or sixty matches before we see his best.

Wolves' Mark McGhee pleading for extreme patience to be shown towards striker David Connolly, 1998. Five days later the board had lost patience with the manager supporters christened 'Mr Magoo'

Jimmy Greaves was the greatest finisher of all time.

Former Wolves boss Stan Cullis, 1970s

He's a fantastic centre-forward. I've had 54 centre-forwards since I've been here and he's the only one to have kept his place.

Birmingham's Barry Fry waxing lyrical about Steve Claridge, 1995

The boy's a mean machine. A real gunfighter. It doesn't matter who you are, he'll shoot you down when he's in the box.

Tranmere's John King on the evergreen John Aldridge, 1992

He is like a lethal weapon.

He was like a fox in that area, the way he hunted for his goals.

Liverpool's Gerard Houllier praising Robbie Fowler for a hat-trick against Aston Villa, 1998

Playing at number nine for the reserves was this youngster who looked like a clothes-line prop. He was just eighteen and can't have weighed more than nine stone. When I sold him to Fulham, I told their manager, Vic Buckingham, that he was getting one of the top six strikers in the country. I think Vic thought I was exaggerating.

Former Walsall boss Ray Shaw recalling the discovery of Allan Clarke, 1973

He's playing better than ever, even if he's going grey and looks like a pigeon.

Chelsea's Ruud Gullit on Mark Hughes, 1997

He has the best two feet in the game; the best I can remember. He doesn't know one from the other either.

Alf Ramsey attempts a rare joke at the expense of Ipswich forward Ted Phillips, 1961

Denis Law could dance on egg-shells.

Bill Shankly, 1960s

If you give him ten decent crosses in a game, he'll get a minimum of two goals.

Ray Harford on his former Blackburn protégé Alan Shearer, 1998

He's got a baby face when he plays football, but when he tackles he knows what he's doing.

Aston Villa's John Gregory on Liverpool's Michael Owen after the latter had been involved in a clash with Stan Collymore, 1998

You would rarely see him hit a shot over the bar. He will usually hit it low and make the goalkeeper work. You get so many strikers who want to give it a blast, but he concentrates on hitting the target.

Terry Venables signing Gary Lineker for Barcelona, 1987

He wants to burst the ball, but there are times when you have to stroke it in.

Bolton's Colin Todd on left-sided midfielder Alan Thompson ,1997

From now on, we'll make him take any penalties from 25 yards and ask the opposition if they want to stick a wall up!

Aston Villa's John Gregory after new signing Alan Thompson had missed a penalty against Middlesbrough before making amends with a 25-yard free-kick a few minutes later, 1998

Trevor said he had a system when he scored a penalty earlier in the season, but that's obviously rubbish.

Queens Park Rangers' Jim Smith relieving Trevor Francis of penalty-taking duties after two misses in a month, 1988

The player who kicks the last penalty either has the key to the hotel or the plane tickets home.

Argentina's Carlos Bilardo on the lottery of the penalty shoot-out, 1990s

Strikers win matches, defenders win championships.

John Gregory, 1998

It only takes a second to score a goal.

Brian Clough, 1984

If Stan Bowles could pass a betting shop as well as he could pass that ball, he wouldn't have had a problem.

Crewe Alexandra's Ernie Tagg, who tried to save Bowles' career, 1974

There was no question of them gambling – they did not have Argentinian money.

They can't gamble here because they don't get any money!

We have a TV in the dressing-room, but it's only switched on at five o'clock for the football results. I honestly don't think we have many players who follow the horses. I've never seen a *Racing Post* left lying around.

Wherever you are, there will be the lazy bastard you've got to get after, there will be the diamond you'd love to take with you wherever you go, there will be the good player whose personality doesn't quite dovetail with your own, and however much you try, you can't fall in love with him. There will be the player who gets by, but doesn't really have the talent, and there will be the one who has all the talent in the world but isn't prepared to do the work to maximise it.

Very often these days a player will get his place in the side because he can run for ninety minutes rather than because he has skill and flair. The 1966 World Cup was won with workhorses like Hunt and Hurst while the magical Jimmy Greaves was left out, and a large proportion of the managers in England followed Sir Alf's lead.

Supporters want to be excited. They go to see the skilful players, not the workmanlike so-called one hundred per cent players.

I don't go along with those who say that a player is born with character. Character is a lot of hard work and experience.

Brighton's Pat Saward, 1972

Players from the north are harder and more competitive. To be honest, I rarely bother looking at players born in London. They lack some of the qualities I believe are so important in a player.

Bury's Allan Brown, 1973

Tiredness is mostly in the head. We had seven players involved in the last four matches at France 98, but it's not about tired legs, it's about getting your head around a friendly against a Second Division team after playing in a World Cup final.

Barcelona coach Louis Van Gaal, 1998

I wouldn't pay money to go and watch Stan Collymore. I'd pay to watch Shirley Bassey. She's got real, undisputed talent. But not Stan. I think he is a guy who cannot find himself, he's lost in a mist of his own mind. I don't think we know who the real Stan Collymore is, and I don't think he knows.

Wycombe Wanderers' Alan Smith, who once sold Collymore on the cheap from Crystal Palace to Southend, from *I Think I'll Manage* (Headline, 1996)

I'd be delighted, because our agreement with Southend is that we only pay them more money if he plays for England!

Nottingham Forest's Frank Clark responding to stories that Stan Collymore might be eligible to play for the Republic of Ireland, 1994

I got hold of him a couple of minutes before the kick-off and told him not to get into trouble. After thirty seconds of the game he got himself booked.

Aston Villa's John Gregory finding that his words to Stan Collymore fell on deaf ears during the goalless draw at West Ham, 1998

I spoke to four people – Glenn Hoddle, a lad I know who's a coach in France, Michel Platini and his assistant – and they all said there's no problem with the boy.

Howard Wilkinson signing Eric Cantona for Leeds, 1992

Eric likes to do what he likes when he likes it –
and then fucks off. We'd all want a bit of that.

**Howard Wilkinson, two months after selling Eric
Cantona to Manchester United, 1993**

In the big games, against Inter Milan or whoever, I think
Cantona will go missing. He's a cry-baby when the going gets
tough.

Arsenal's George Graham, 1994

When he feels he has been done an injustice, he's got to prove
to the world that he's going to correct it. But he can't control
his temper. Love him or hate him, we have to live with it.

**Manchester United's Alex Ferguson on Eric Cantona,
sent off against Rangers in a meaningless wooden
spoon match as part of a pre-season tournament, 1994**

He is so mild-mannered when the volcano inside him isn't
erupting.

Alex Ferguson on Cantona, 1994

It doesn't matter whether Eric Cantona or Mickey Mouse
kicked him, he should not have reacted.

**Sheffield United's Dave Bassett after Charlie Hartfield
was sent off in an FA Cup tie against Manchester
United, 1995**

I don't think any player in the history of the game will get the
sentence he got unless they had killed Bert Millichip's dog . . .
When someone is doing well we have to knock him down. We
don't do it with horses. Red Rum is more loved than anyone I
know, but he must have lost one race.

**Alex Ferguson reflecting on Eric Cantona's
seven-month ban following the fracas at Selhurst Park,
1995**

Part of the problem is, Eric can't tackle. He couldn't tackle a
fish supper.

Alex Ferguson, from *A Year in the Life: The Manager's Diary*
(Virgin, 1995)

It's one of his first goodbyes. I'm sure there will be encores.

Auxerre coach Guy Roux on the retirement of his former pupil Cantona, 1997

Technically, he is a very good player – but he's a bit of a loony and can be hot-tempered.

West Brom boss Alan Buckley on winger Lee Ashcroft, 1995

Don't tell me Sherwood did not make a crucial mistake. Don't tell me he didn't cost us three points today, and possibly three points in the future. If he does not know that, it's a sad day.

Roy Hodgson refusing to defend his Blackburn captain Tim Sherwood, sent off against Manchester United, 1998

Fine him? £5,000, £50,000, £150,000 – ban him *sine die*? It doesn't matter, it's too bloody late.

Roy Hodgson, still on the warpath over Sherwood, 1998

There's a silly wee boy inside him who comes out now and again, but hopefully that Peter Pan will disappear.

Coventry's Gordon Strachan on Noel Whelan, 1998

It was an insult – like asking Cruyff to go on trial for Lincoln City.

Derby County's Tommy Docherty after Charlie George had only been selected for the England B team, 1977

The phone's been off the hook and the faxes have been switched off!

Bradford City's Paul Jewell, anxious to avoid a Republic of Ireland plea for midfielder Gareth Whalley not to play against Swindon, 1998

I told Charlie that if I caught him without socks it would cost him.

Billy McNeill of Celtic on Charlie Nicholas's habit of not wearing socks, 1981

Tommy had to realise he is part of a team and not a pin-up boy.

Notts County's Neil Warnock on why he dropped star striker Tommy Johnson, 1991

If you don't start treating the senior pros around here with a little respect, you're out the frigging door, and I'll see that you never get another club.

Newcastle boss Jack Charlton trying to keep a straight face while laying down the law to a young Paul Gascoigne after complaints from senior players about his pranks, 1985

Daft as a brush.

Bobby Robson on Paul Gascoigne, 1990

I thought he would have lasted ninety minutes, but he used up so much energy in the dressing-room he knocked himself out.

Terry Venables on Gascoigne's display in the FA Cup semi-final with Arsenal, 1991

He is the type of guy who needs to know you are concerned about him. You have to find the root of his problems. He may have come to me with a sore thumb and asked why he was feeling bad. The real reason wouldn't be the sore thumb.

Spurs' Terry Venables trying to get inside Gazza's head, 1991

It's like watching your mother-in-law drive over a cliff in your new car.

Terry Venables seeing his former protégé Gazza sign for Italian club Lazio, 1992

I only hope it's someone else's body with his face painted on.

Lazio's Dino Zoff seeing topless pictures of an overweight Paul Gascoigne at a nightclub, 1992

Paul tends to react abruptly and often uses the wrong word. It is because he doesn't have a big vocabulary.

England assistant manager Lawrie McMenemy on Gascoigne's four-letter response to a Norwegian TV reporter, 1993

I think it's the lightest he has been since he was four.

It's a talent wasted. He has dissipated his talent, and I don't think the image he gives the game is good.

His actions have tarnished the club's and my own image a great deal . . . The tragedy is that he has so much talent and yet may only be remembered for his off-field exploits.

There are certain things he needs to change in his life.

I will make sure he does not go on a bender this year, by going with him.

A player like him always tries the difficult things because most of the time they come off. But when you have that little rustiness, they might not, and he can look a bit of an idiot.

Gazza has got to help himself. He can't be going out to pubs and bars and places like that – he understands that.

We quickly realised that he liked a drink – certainly a lot more than the other players.

I know he lives for his football. It seems that out on the pitch is the only place where he can really be happy. It's his opportunity to escape the pressures. If he can't get football back into his life, then you have to fear what might happen to him.

Zdenek Zeman fearing for Gascoigne's future, 1998

I think he's cut down from nine pints a night to six!

Forest's Dave Bassett on a revitalised Steve Stone, 1998

If any of my players had a drink problem I'd nip it in the bud, but a lot of them don't drink. John Fashanu never touched a drop. Now we've got Kenny Cunningham and Michael Hughes. They're both Irish, but we have to force them to have a beer.

Wimbledon's Irish boss Joe Kinnear, 1998

You can't be a boozer and get away with it in the Premiership. You get found out in training within five minutes. People say Vinnie Jones liked a drink, but he's one of the most dedicated footballers I've known. He used to train for fun here.

Joe Kinnear, 1998

If they lose and play badly, they don't get a beer on the bus home.

Ford United's Dennis Elliott before his Ryman League team's Cup tie at Preston, 1998

David has not been focused for this tournament. Half the problem is what he has to cope with. Maybe his club need to look at that further.

England coach Glenn Hoddle expressing concern about David Beckham's showbiz lifestyle, at the World Cup, 1998

I have too much respect for football to be involved with players who do nothing but tarnish it and the image of Falkirk.

Falkirk's Jim Duffy announcing his resignation after a succession of nightclub incidents involving Falkirk players, 1989

Our problem is not keeping the players out of nightclubs, it is keeping them out of the bank.

Luxembourg coach Paul Phillipp on his country's well-paid part-timers, 1998

It's not chasing women and having sex that tires out young footballers. It's staying up all night looking for it.

Nigeria coach Clemens Westerhof, 1994

When I went to the South American Championship in 1977, from a squad of thirty players there were twenty on drugs.

Seville coach Carlos Bilardo, 1993

Players are under ever greater pressure, and it gets harder for them to resist the temptation of the magic little pill. I'm sure that many players in Serie A, probably even in my own Roma side, have difficulty giving up on certain substances.

Roma coach Zdenek Zeman, 1998

In my day, once I'd finished playing on a Saturday afternoon, I came in, had a cup of tea, got in the bath, had a cigarette – or the manager gave me a cigarette if I'd had a good game – then I got dressed and went to the bar for a drink. After that, I remember I was so light-headed I used to have to get my wife to drive me home. But nobody knew any different then.

Notts County manager Sam Allardyce, 1998

When I was playing, we were nothing more than glorified labourers. An hour's training in the morning, then off to play billiards or golf. Today's player is paid the same as an executive in industry. So he's got to think, behave and be treated like one.

Brighton's Pat Saward, 1972

I've had no complaints from the players. I've had to take mine home before. That's what I pay the missus for.

Swindon Town's new boss Jimmy Quinn introducing his own form of 'Ariel bombardment' whereby players have to wash their own kit, 1998

Trailing round the shops with your missus for three hours can wear you out. I don't want my players lugging heavy bags of shopping around days before a game. If it upsets the missus and

156

means sleeping in the spare room for a couple of nights, then so be it if it will improve performances on the pitch.

Jimmy Quinn introducing a ban on supermarket shopping for his Swindon players in the three days before a match, 1998

His knee played up in the supermarket. He's not used to pushing the trolley.

Ipswich caretaker boss Mick McGiven on the latest injury to striker Ian Marshall, 1994

Make love before matches? My lads can do as they like, but it's not advisable at half-time.

German coach Berti Vogts advocating a flat back four, 1998

German footballers don't get a good education. I would love to let them play a more modern game, but it wouldn't work.

Germany's Berti Vogts at the World Cup, 1998

I want time to stand still. You only get a generation of players like this once in a lifetime.

Yugoslavia coach Slobodan Santrac, 1997

I never thought I'd see the day when I'd say we needed a few more Englishmen in our squad!

Manchester United's Alex Ferguson getting to grips with UEFA restrictions regarding the number of foreigners able to play in European matches, 1991

Foreign managers don't have the knowledge of the lower leagues that we possess, so it's easier for them to bring in foreign players. Chairmen may get seduced by that, but we can pluck a player from the lower leagues of equal ability or potential without the problems of settling into a new culture.

Wimbledon's Joe Kinnear discussing the influx of overseas players, 1998

How does he feel? How do you think? And the lad doesn't even celebrate Christmas!

Crystal Palace's Steve Coppell after a missed penalty by Itzak Zohar cost Palace a first home win of the season, against Southampton on Boxing Day, 1997

He'll have no problems settling in. Our game is all about craft and technique, and it's much the same in Africa.

Rob Kelly, boss of Sevenoaks Benevolent League pub team Robin Hood, whose midfielder Mohammed Sasso was called up for the Sierra Leone national squad, 1996

At the beginning it was difficult understanding the Cockneys and Scots. I ask them, 'Do you speak English?' Now we understand each other.

Ruud Gullit on the United Nations that is Chelsea, 1997

When he came to the club, all he could say in English was 'Yes', 'No' and 'Morning'. A week later he'd added 'Thank you' and 'Budweiser'.

Hibernian boss Jim Duffy on Czech defender Dusan Vrto, 1998

The interpreter couldn't understand me.

Millwall's Irish manager Jimmy Nicholl explaining why a five-minute meeting with Russian imports Sergei Yuran and Vasili Kulkov took 45 minutes, 1996

He is definitely the worst professional I have ever seen. The only thing the other players could have possibly learnt from him was how to steal a living.

Jimmy Nicholl on Sergei Yuran (one goal in fifteen games and a drink-driving charge), 1996

I would never advise Italian players between twenty and twenty-five to come to play in England. Instead, I would tell them to achieve their peak in Italy and only go abroad once they have had their fill.

Chelsea boss Gianluca Vialli, 1998

I enjoy watching the foreigners and I am picking up Italian quite well – but struggling with Croatian.

Jim Smith on the foreign influx at Derby, 1997

Foreign players are a gamble. They're not a long-term prospect.

Jim Smith, 1998

I like to gamble. I don't play the casinos, so I have to do my gambling on the football field.

Arsenal's Arsène Wenger contemplating signing Inter Milan's Nigerian World Cup forward Nwankwo Kanu, despite doubts about the player's fitness, 1998

The game is in danger of being flooded with foreigners, and it is affecting all levels. What worries me is that some youngsters with the potential to develop will find their path to the first team barred by imports.

Sheffield Wednesday's Danny Wilson, 1998

You can't say all the foreigners are mercenaries, here just for the money, but a lot of them are.

Leeds' George Graham, 1998

The administrators are called Ernst and Young. My lot probably think I've signed a couple of German strikers.

Terry Cooper, boss of cash-strapped Exeter City, 1994

It's not my scene to have eleven foreign players because I don't speak any foreign languages and they wouldn't understand me.

Nottingham Forest's down-to-earth Dave Bassett, 1998

I'm not interested in what he's said, and I can't be bothered with him. He's made his bed – he's got to lie on it. The sooner he finds another club, the better for everybody.

Dave Bassett on stay-away Dutch star Pierre Van Hooijdonk's belated attempt to apologise, 1998

Suggesting that he will call is like saying I'm going to marry a pop star.

Dave Bassett on the Van Hooijdonk affair, 1998

Who does he think he is? He is on strike and he is history as far as I am concerned. Does he seriously expect us to go to Holland and offer him an olive branch? No way! Maybe he'd like Tony Blair to go over as well! We could all go together. He can pick up the phone and ask to come back here – cap in hand,

159

tail between his legs – any time he wants. He can then do a pre-season, play for the reserves and try to get a place in the first team. That's his only way back.

Dave Bassett with his (almost) last word on Van Hooijdonk, 1998

If I had been the multi-millionaire of the club, I would have left him to rot in Holland. I don't know whether I'll shake his hand. That's something I've not even considered, but if you see him running awkwardly you'll know where I've stuck his olive branch.

Dave Bassett reluctantly welcoming Van Hooijdonk back to the City Ground, 1998

I'm irritated by it. It was embarrassing and made the club look a bit of a laughing stock.

Dave Bassett on striker Jean-Claude Darcheville's failure to remove his earrings before coming on as substitute during Forest's Coca-Cola Cup tie with Cambridge United, 1998. The referee promptly sent the Frenchman off for hasty repairs

If he doesn't want to play in our first team, perhaps he can play in our reserves.

Sheffield Wednesday's David Pleat over a dispute with Romanian defender Dan Petrescu, 1995

If I have to go to Grimsby next season, then Ravanelli will be coming with me.

Middlesbrough's Bryan Robson considering the ultimate punishment for want-away Italian striker Fabrizio Ravanelli, 1997

There's no way I am going to see him walk out of here, stick two fingers up at us, after all the work we've done in helping him become a top-class player.

Southampton's Lawrie McMenemy cracking down on want-away defender Mark Wright, 1984

He's handed in a written transfer request. The handwriting was beautiful.

Newcastle's Kenny Dalglish admiring the 'ealthy-looking 'and of David Ginola, 1997

If I've learnt anything, I've learnt not to sign any more Romanians.

West Ham's Harry Redknapp after striker Florin Raducioiu went shopping at Harvey Nichols instead of turning out in a Coca-Cola Cup tie against Stockport, 1996. The Hammers lost 2–1

I have a good relationship with Stoichkov, more than good. But if you play 28 games as a striker you have to score more than eight times. That's it. Don't talk about relationships, those are facts. If it's my best friend or my biggest enemy, if you don't score enough in his position, then you're out.

Barcelona's Johan Cruyff addressing rumours of a rift with Bulgarian forward Hristo Stoichkov, 1992

When you've lost 5–0 to Real Madrid the Sunday before, you don't go to a party. You should be modest. I'm the one who decides whether or not he should train, not him.

Johan Cruyff after refusing Stoichkov permission to skip training in order to attend an awards ceremony, 1995, from *Ajax Barcelona Cruyff: The ABC of an Obstinate Maestro* by Frits Barend and Henk Van Dorp (Bloomsbury, 1998). **Soon afterwards, Cruyff sold him**

The players have tried to say who should run the national team. Gullit was like a spoiled child before the last World Cup. He said he didn't like the coach so he would not play. Unfortunately, this side of Dutch football has been there for everyone to see. The players become too powerful.

Bobby Robson, from *Football, Fussball, Voetbal* by Colin Cameron (BBC Books, 1995)

We Dutchmen are pig-headed.

Barcelona's Johan Cruyff, 1995

He's only 21 and still learning, but he is giving the best defenders terrible trouble. He doesn't know what he's going to do, we don't know what he's going to do – so how can they?

Derby County's Jim Smith on unorthodox Costa Rican forward Paulo Wanchope, 1997

Paulo was way out of order, but I deny any suggestion I ever said he was a poof.

Jim Smith dismissing rumours of a dressing-room row with Paulo Wanchope, 1997

I'd like everyone to stop calling him 'O Animal', which isn't a nice nickname to have. He's just a sensitive lad who, because of his own timidity, sometimes reacts in a particular way.

Fiorentina boss Giovanni Trapattoni on Brazilian striker Edmundo, 1998

Anyone who knows him will tell you he's a very pleasant young man and isn't a bad lad at all.

Everton's Joe Royle acting as character witness for his striker Duncan Ferguson, jailed for head-butting an opponent while playing for Rangers, 1995

Duncan could be the biggest thing here since Dixie Dean. The fans love him. He's massive. He's the Prime Minister of Merseyside.

Joe Royle goes OTT after Ferguson scores the winner against Manchester United, 1995

When people like him do have a bad game, it will be a real stinker, because they never stop trying to turn it into a good one.

Celtic's Tommy Burns on striker Paolo Di Canio, 1997

I've had a chat with Paolo and he understands me, and I think I understand him.

Sheffield Wednesday's Danny Wilson trying to overcome communication problems with Italian star Paolo Di Canio, 1998

We have suspended the player with immediate effect. He will be kept away from the ground indefinitely, for as long as it takes. The severity of the incident is beyond question. I just don't know what went through the boy's mind.

Danny Wilson later that same day after Di Canio had pushed referee Paul Alcock to the ground having been sent off against Arsenal, 1998

Paolo doesn't have a bad bone in his body.

Juventus coach Marcello Lippi speaking up for the troubled Paolo Di Canio after his transgression at Hillsborough, 1998

He's from Latin America. That's the way they are.

Newcastle's Kevin Keegan seeking to explain the behaviour of Colombian Faustino Asprilla at Maine Road in an incident which brought a misconduct charge from the FA, 1996

By the end he was knackered-o. I think that's the Spanish for it.

Kevin Keegan after Asprilla's Newcastle debut, 1996

He does put his foot in, but fairly. That does not always happen to him.

Arsenal boss Arsène Wenger on French midfielder Patrick Vieira, 1998

It is standard practice here for players to fall over far too quickly.

Rainer Zobel, coach of Kaiserslautern, on play-acting in German football, 1992

It was a very honest and human reaction, especially in the light of all the negative human reaction we've seen this season. Now whether that is the right thing professionally, whether Roy Evans would be happy with that, whether I would be happy with that if he did it playing for me, that's a different kettle of fish.

England coach Glenn Hoddle after Liverpool's Robbie Fowler had appealed to the referee *not* to award a penalty against Arsenal's David Seaman, 1997

From that moment on, I was the villain.

Graham Taylor, never forgiven by some for substituting Gary Lineker in his final international, against Sweden, when he was one goal short of Bobby Charlton's England record of 49, 1992

He's not completely squeaky clean by any stretch of the imagination – I would imagine he has the odd half of lager.

Aston Villa's John Gregory on his England defender Gareth Southgate, 1998

I don't care whether you are Alan Shearer or the Pope – you don't do that.

Leicester City's Martin O'Neill after Shearer appeared to kick Neil Lennon, 1998

The football season is a marathon. Now they want us to follow the marathon with a sprint!

Tranmere's John King, none too happy about the introduction of end-of-season play-offs, 1987

We are treating top-quality athletes like shire horses.

Crystal Palace's Steve Coppell addressing the argument that footballers in England have to play too many matches, 1991

They don't ask racehorses to run four times in a week, but we had to play four games in eight days, and the 'system' says that we have to play again on Saturday. It wouldn't happen in any other country in the world.

Sunderland's Bob Stokoe, 1973

Even I'm knackered. When I wake up, it takes me five minutes to work out where I am. Instead of coaching and managing, I'm acting as a travel agent and a courier.

Leeds' Howard Wilkinson on the problems caused by two games a week, 1991

The problem is keeping the kettle simmering rather than boiling, and sometimes keeping it from boiling over.

Howard Wilkinson on Leeds' punishing schedule, 1992

It's hard to be passionate twice a week.

George Graham on Arsenal's demanding programme, 1991

4 The Opposition

No one. I fear nobody in the world, except my wife.

Zambia's German coach Burkhard Ziese when asked who he feared in his country's World Cup group, 1998

England are great opponents, but they can be defeated.

Hungarian coach Gusztav Sebes before his country's historic 6–3 victory over England at Wembley, 1953

Some time, some day we have got to win in Belfast.

Northern Ireland's Danny Blanchflower before meeting England, who hadn't lost in Belfast for 52 years, 1979. England won 5–1

I know their spirit, their pride and their luck. Their luck is important. We keep dismissing it, but they have got four decades of it.

Manchester United's Alex Ferguson putting the boot into German teams (Bayern Munich were in United's European Cup group), 1998

I admire the English mentality because you are so strong, so hard-working. But we have talent.

Benfica coach Sven Goran Eriksson after eliminating Arsenal from Europe, 1991

I tried to watch the Spurs match on television in my hotel yesterday, but I fell asleep.

Arsenal manager-elect Arsène Wenger dozing through Tottenham's home defeat by Leicester, 1996

Everton do not have a great record here at Highbury, but then the same can be said for a fair number of teams.

Everton's Walter Smith, 1998

I think the core of the Arsenal team has that winning mentality. They've got a lot of players who would be finished at other clubs because of their age, but their inner strength drives them on.

Tottenham's George Graham on his old club, 1998

At one stage I thought they had fifteen on the park.

Ron Atkinson, following Sheffield Wednesday's defeat against Arsenal, 1998

Thank goodness Milan cannot play in the World Cup. No one else would stand a chance!

Brazil manager Sebastião Lazaroni, 1990

They are all so good that they are willing to let you take control of the ball and then set out to kid you into passing it where they want it to go.

Jock Stein marvelling at Brazil, 1982

They all seemed to have longer legs than my players. When they came forward, it was like the Charge of the Light Brigade.

Brian Hall after Yeovil Town went out of the FA Cup 3–0 to Queens Park Rangers, 1988

The good thing is that we now have a replay at our place; the bad thing is, it's against them.

Brighton's Barry Lloyd after a 2–2 FA Cup draw at Anfield, 1991

I remember the days when you used to come to Anfield and do well to get a corner.

Sheffield Wednesday's Trevor Francis, 1994

Fred sent me to see if I could spot a weakness, and I found one. The half-time tea's too milky.

Shrewsbury Town coach Kevin Summerfield, sent by manager Fred Davies to spy on the club's FA Cup fourth-round opponents Liverpool, 1996

Every time their coach, Robert Herbin, saw us play we won. He came over to watch, we won and played well. He came over again, we won again and played even better . . . He might well have worried his players. In the end we beat them 4–1 away and 3–1 at home.

Bobby Robson on Ipswich's 1981 UEFA Cup success against St Etienne, from *Football, Fussball, Voetbal* (BBC Books, 1995)

Two days ago, the Bavarians were dead. Today they played like gods.

Atlético Madrid's Juan Carlos Lorenzo as Bayern Munich recovered from a lacklustre 1–1 European Cup final draw to win the replay 4–0, 1974

You have to be careful in this division because anything below the top three is the relegation zone.

Steve Wignall, boss of Second Division Colchester United, 1998

There really is only a very narrowing gap between the top and bottom of the Football League these days.

Newcastle's Joe Harvey, 1968

We may be in the same division as Liverpool, but we are trying to do different things. There are two leagues in one division.

Charlton Athletic's Lennie Lawrence, 1988

There are three trophies in the Premiership: winning it, getting a top-six place and staying up.

Spurs' George Graham, 1998

Whatever you think of the morality of the Premier League, the reality is you've got to be in it. There's a big black hole beneath it.

Lennie Lawrence, by then in charge of Middlesbrough, 1992

Without Rangers and Celtic, we, along with the rest, are basically playing in a sort of B Division within the Premier

League. It isn't a nice thing to admit, but at some point myself and the other seven bosses have got to be honest.

Dundee boss Jocky Scott suddenly realising what everyone south of the border has known for years, 1998

I am worried. The corner shop is going out of business. The breeding grounds could disappear if we don't act soon.

Luton Town's David Pleat on the widening gulf between the Premiership and the Football League, 1993

The chairmen of the big clubs want to be on that ship to go to the moon and leave the rest behind.

Southampton's Alan Ball, 1995

It will be dog eat dog, and the best players will end up at three or four clubs who can afford the wages. Manchester United will eat up Wimbledon, we will eat up teams in Division One. One day, you might find the entire England side at one club.

Joe Kinnear, 1997

We have just seen the champions of England . . . the rest of us are merely fighting for the scraps. United have the title sewn up. They are a nightmare to play against. There is only one other place in Europe on offer – everybody else will have to catch the ferry next season.

Newcastle's Kevin Keegan admitting defeat in the race to catch Manchester United, 1993

Unless the authorities give everybody six points for a win and United none, I don't think they will be caught.

Aston Villa's Ron Atkinson, 1993

It looks as though we are going to be happy just to stay on the same page of Ceefax as Manchester United.

Ron Atkinson, 1994

I don't suppose anyone has given them a harder time over two League games than us this season. But we don't have a point to show for it.

QPR's Gerry Francis after a 3–2 home defeat at the hands of Manchester United, 1994

How do I view United? Preferably on television, but unfortunately we have to go down the East Lancs Road and get a bit closer.

Howard Kendall, boss of struggling Everton, before the visit to Old Trafford, 1997

It can be an intimidating place with no way out. So we've got to look on it as a nice wee challenge.

Coventry's Gordon Strachan preparing for the trip to Manchester United, 1998

They have that feeling that they are head and shoulders above the rest. We had that at Liverpool. It gives you the strength to get scratchy results when not playing well.

Coventry's Phil Neal expressing his admiration for Manchester United, 1993

We refused to go as lambs to the slaughter.

Kevin Keegan after Newcastle's honourable draw at Old Trafford, 1993

You get the feeling you are supposed to go to Old Trafford and let them walk all over you.

Nottingham Forest's Frank Clark after Alex Ferguson accused them of time-wasting and incessant fouling during Forest's surprise 2–1 win, 1994

It's hard when you've got that useless player Bryan Robson and that not bad centre-half Pallister as subs.

Sheffield United's Dave Bassett envies Manchester United's embarrassment of riches, 1991

It's frightening when you see someone like Ryan Giggs sitting on the bench. All you feel is envy.

Everton's Howard Kendall echoing the theme, 1993

I wouldn't even have minded some of the players who couldn't get on United's substitutes bench.

Derby County's Jim Smith, 1998

Alex has fielded his second team, but most of them would walk into an average Premiership team.

Nottingham Forest's Dave Bassett after being knocked out of the Worthington Cup by what amounted to Manchester United Reserves, 1998

Matt has got a bad back. I tell you it's two bad backs! And not much of a midfield either.

A Bill Shankly jibe about Manchester United, 1960s

Nothing any good ever came out of Belgium. You name me one famous Belgian footballer. You'll take them apart.

Bill Shankly preparing his Liverpool team to play Anderlecht in the European Cup, 1964. His talk worked: Liverpool won the first leg 3–0 en route to a 4–0 aggregate victory

If Everton were playing down at the bottom of my garden, I'd draw the curtains.

Bill Shankly, 1960s

Aye, Everton.

Bill Shankly to a barber who asked him if he wanted anything off the top, 1960s

I know their side better than I know my own.

Harry Catterick, boss of injury-ravaged Everton, handing in his team-sheet before a game, 1971

If you are successful with Newcastle, son, there's not a block of granite at Aberdeen big enough to build you a throne.

Bill Shankly to Arthur Cox on taking over at Newcastle, 1980. He never quite made it to King Arthur

Frankly, I wish they'd get relegated.

Gerry Francis in the wake of Tottenham's third defeat by Nottingham Forest in the season, 1996

I'm just pleased we only play Blackburn twice in a season.

Forest's Frank Clark after a 12–1 aggregate defeat at the hands of Rovers, 1996

If they have got a weakness anywhere, they just go out and buy the best player and plug it.

Norwich's Mike Walker reeling from a 7–1 thrashing at Blackburn, 1992

I suppose having spent thirty-odd million pounds, they are entitled to be top of the League.

Wimbledon's Joe Kinnear following a 3–0 defeat by Kenny Dalglish's big-spending Blackburn, 1994

We lost to the better side, even if it did cost about six million.

Ian Atkins, boss of hard-up Northampton Town, after going down to moneybags Reading, 1998

Their team might have cost more, but ours is probably worth more.

Crewe's Dario Gradi after victory over Birmingham, 1995

Blackburn can only throw the League away now. We can only hope they do a Devon Loch. It's going to take a real major boob by them.

Alex Ferguson apparently conceding the title to Blackburn after dropping two points at home to Leeds, 1995

Is Devon Loch an expanse of water in Scotland?

Quick-witted Kenny Dalglish refusing to take the bait, 1995

We wish them well in the FA Trophy – I hope they get beat in the next round.

Newcastle's Kenny Dalglish in the wake of an acrimonious FA Cup encounter with Stevenage Borough, 1998

It didn't fall down. I was quite pleased about that.

Stevenage's Paul Fairclough on the club's temporary stand which Cup opponents Newcastle had deemed unsafe, 1998

I hope I never have to take a team there again!

Leeds United's Don Revie after a stormy Fairs Cup clash in Napoli, 1968. Although Leeds lost 2–0 on the night, they won through to the next round on the toss of a coin

The Italians were spitting at my players all through the game, but they were doing that against the Leeds team I played for twenty years ago.

Birmingham City's Terry Cooper after a bad-tempered encounter with Bari, 1992

Leeds should have been instantly relegated after being branded one of the dirtiest clubs in Britain . . . It's like breathalysing a drunken driver, getting a positive reading, giving him his keys back and telling him to watch it on the way home.

Brian Clough, angry at Leeds' lenient treatment from the FA, 1973. A year later, he was appointed manager at Elland Road

The thing with Leeds was that they were cynical. It wasn't just being stronger and stopping the other team, it was cynical. There was no need for it. They were the best team in England, a great side, but greedy.

Malcolm Allison, from *The Mavericks* by Rob Steen (Mainstream, 1994)

It was like the old Leeds team. The first foul comes in the first minute and they apologise.

Luton manager Jim Ryan, 1990

I'm not even thinking about what changes Leeds may make. Imagine a side that can bring in three internationals . . .

Bristol City's Alan Dicks on Leeds' supposed injury problems for an FA Cup replay, 1974. City created a major shock by going to Elland Road and winning 1–0

They're wolves in sheep's clothing.

Southampton's Alan Ball sums up Leeds United, 1994

Leeds are a big, powerful outfit. Most of my back four are downstairs with aspirators.

Wimbledon's Joe Kinnear, 1995

Wimbledon are killing the dreams that have made football the world's greatest game.

Tottenham's Terry Venables, 1989

Poor old Margs has probably never seen anything like that in his life. It's certainly not how they play in Chile.

West Ham's Harry Redknapp on the problems faced by his Chilean World Cup defender Javier Margas in coping with Wimbledon's aerial bombardment, 1998

They are kicking the ball fifty yards instead of sixty.

Norwich City's Mike Walker when asked whether Wimbledon had changed their style, 1993

They came at us playing direct football. They were more English than the English.

Graham Taylor as England were beaten by Sweden in the European Championships, 1992

Your father has got a twenty-year start, but I'll pass him in three.

Malcolm Allison stokes up the City/United rivalry to Matt Busby's son, 1965

I bet they're right cheesed off now!

Rochdale's Terry Dolan after a Cup win over Whitley Bay, who had described Rochdale as a Mickey Mouse club, 1990

I think they've got more problems than we've got.

Marlow manager Dave Russell's pessimistic view of Spurs' future after the teams' FA Cup clash, 1993

They may have to go down to the Second Division to sort themselves out.

Lincoln City's John Beck after knocking Manchester City out of the League Cup, 1996

They just lump it.

Lincoln City's Keith Alexander on John Beck's Preston, 1993

When you arrived at Cambridge, there used to be no hot water, cold tea, and for your warm-up, the balls used to be the worst kicking balls you've ever seen in your life. It was definitely a psychological ploy to try and undermine our morale.

Mark McGhee recalling trips to John Beck's Cambridge United with Reading, from *I Think I'll Manage* (Headline, 1996)

It's the sort of place you get into as late as possible, bring your own grub, go to bed, get up, play the game and get out.

Republic of Ireland boss Jack Charlton's postcard from Tirana, Albania, 1993

They took me to this terrible place, and told me this is where we would be staying. I told them they would stay at the best hotel in England when they came to us, so I wanted Spurs to stay at the best hotel in Katowice. They said this *was* the best hotel in Katowice.

Spurs' Bill Nicholson after the trip to Poland to play Gornik Zabrze in the European Cup, 1961

Eastern Europe is bad. Romania the worst of the lot. Dirty hotels, bad food, bad water. Hungary? I went there as a player with Preston in 1938 and it was the bright city of Europe. Now? I don't think it's had a coat of paint since.

Bill Shankly's Rough Guide to Europe, 1972

Rapid were the dirtiest side I've come across in thirty years of football. If this is European football, I'd rather have a Combination match.

Bill Nicholson on Spurs' UEFA Cup opponents Rapid Bucharest, 1971

How on earth are you expected to play good, attractive football when the opposition's sole intentions are to spoil by shirt-pulling, time-wasting etc. I could get eleven fellas out of a pub and line them up to make it difficult for everybody. Is this

what we must do to achieve results? If so, I'll pack up
tomorrow.

**Walsall's Doug Fraser attacking Chester's negative
approach, 1975**

All Palace did in the second half was to hit high balls up the
middle. They had two men chasing them against four defenders,
and they did it well. Two men beat us.

**Spurs' Bill Nicholson after FA Cup defeat by Crystal
Palace, 1970**

You don't want a date with your wife or girlfriend after playing
Crystal Palace. It would be difficult to kiss them without
smooth lips.

**Everton's Howard Kendall after a fiery clash with
Palace, 1991**

Uruguay are a disgrace. They have no respect for other people's
dignity.

**Alex Ferguson after Scotland's elimination from the
World Cup, 1986**

Other countries have their history. Uruguay has its football.

Uruguay manager Ondino Viera, 1966

We have still to produce our best football. It will come against
a team who come to play football and not act as animals.

**Alf Ramsey after the infamous battle with Argentina in
the World Cup, 1966**

I am not a man who is easily scared. But I am ashamed to admit
I was terrified. I have never been so angry as I sat on the bench
and watched my players being spat at, slapped on the face and
kicked by the opposition.

**Jock Stein after Celtic's World Club Championship
decider against Racing Club of Argentina, 1967**

The two teams reflected the different kind of people that Glenn
and I are. We'll probably kick, shout and bite a bit more than
what they will.

**Southend United's Dave Webb after a 3–2 win over
Glenn Hoddle's Swindon, 1991**

Next time we'll play Mexico in winter and see what happens.

Jack Charlton after his Republic of Ireland team had gone down 2–1 to Mexico in the extreme heat of Orlando at the World Cup, 1994

You could grow tomatoes on it. It's like a League ground on the last day of the season – bone hard and full of bare patches.

Bill Shankly casting a critical eye over the AEK Athens pitch prior to a UEFA Cup tie, 1972

Why is it that a nation with the technology to put a television in my wristwatch can't grow some bloody grass in its Olympic stadium?

Brian Clough casting a disapproving eye over the state of the Tokyo pitch before Forest's World Club Championship final, 1981

It'll never replace plastic.

Luton's Ray Harford inspecting the grass at Coventry, 1988

You could smell the pressure.

Bury's Neil Warnock on a trip to under-fire Wolves, 1998

The beach is all right.

Canvey Island's Jeff King when asked what he thought of Brighton after a 2–2 FA Cup draw, 1995

People expected us to win today, and that's very unusual for Queen's Park.

Spiders' boss John McCormack after a 3–0 win over bottom club Montrose, 1998

The only thing I can see going south this year is rain.

Manchester City's Malcolm Allison, 1969

We are doing reasonably well in the First Division, so I do not think we shall worry unduly about meeting Newport.

Sheffield Wednesday's Vic Buckingham before FA Cup defeat at Fourth Division Newport, 1964

Obviously for Scunthorpe, it would be a nice scalp to put Wimbledon on their bottoms.

Wimbledon's Dave Bassett before a League Cup tie, 1984

It's all too easy for the big boys of the First Division to look down on us and offer solutions to our problems. Unfortunately, they have no knowledge of football at this lower level. It's an entirely different game down here to the one they play.

Ken Furphy, manager of Third Division Blackburn Rovers, 1972

Some of these clubs play in graveyards.

Newcastle's Joe Harvey discovering how bad things had become for lower-division teams, 1968

I didn't understand just how physical the football would be in this league.

Reading's former Celtic boss Tommy Burns adjusting to life in Division Two, 1998

It's yoicks and tally-ho football.

Malcolm Allison on Second Division soccer, 1973

They're the First Division's banana-skin club.

Norwich's Bruce Rioch on party-poopers Port Vale, 1998

You don't know what you're going to come across – you don't know whether they've had a fight with the missus the day before or been doing extra time at work. We don't know how they're going to approach this game. They could be tired, they could be lethargic or they could be up for it.

Scunthorpe's Brian Laws, apprehensive before a Cup tie at Woking, 1998

Are they Italian?

Tommy Docherty learning that his Derby team may face AP Leamington in the next round of the Cup, 1977

Where's Torquay? I've never been there in my life and have no idea how to get there.

Enfield's George Borg facing a possible Cup trip to the West Country, 1994

I don't even know where these bloody places are on the map.

Jack Charlton as the Republic of Ireland draw Latvia and Lithuania in their World Cup qualifying group, 1992

If the opposition score four goals, we'll score five.

Adventurous Barcelona coach Johan Cruyff, 1992

If they were a well-coached team, they'd win the League by streets. Cruyff should start taking notes and go back to school to take his coaching badge.

Embittered Deportivo la Coruña coach Arsenio Iglesias after his team were unluckily pipped for the Spanish League title by Cruyff's Barcelona, 1994

I don't care what you say, as long as it's loud!

Altrincham's John King encouraging his players to make a row outside the opposing dressing-room before going on to the pitch, 1995

There's method in my madness. When we met last, it was like two boxers who were not compatible. So I'm having a little go at them, because I'm looking forward as far as April, hoping they'll be so narked, they'll bypass midfield and open up the game a little bit.

Liverpool's Bob Paisley practising sports psychology on Arsenal, 1982

Let's hope they play the same next week as they did against us.

Rangers' Dick Advocaat noting that Aberdeen always seemed to raise their game against the men from Ibrox, 1998

On that performance, they should be a top-six team. They're not. They're struggling, so they've been cheating their manager.

Leeds play Newcastle next and I would like to see a video of that one.

When you do that with footballers like he said about Leeds . . . I've kept quiet, but I'll tell you something, he went down in my estimation when he said that. We have not resorted to that. But I'll tell you, we're still fighting for this title and he's got to go to Middlesbrough and get something. And I'll tell you, honestly, I will love it if we beat them. Love it!

I feel for them. I feel for the whole club. Newcastle have had a fantastic season. Their supporters were brilliant to us when we played up there. There was no bitterness, no spite. We are not gloating, but we are quietly satisfied.

When did I know the game was won? When I saw their team-sheet.

What we don't want is for Chelsea to go out in their flip-flops like they have been doing in recent games.

The nearest we get to a Latin influence is when the lads go down to the local restaurant on a Friday lunchtime before a home game.

There are three types of Oxo cubes: light brown for chicken stock, dark brown for beef stock, and light blue for laughing stock.

Tommy Docherty enjoying Manchester City's struggles, 1988

They smoke and drink a lot – especially whisky.

Tunisian manager Abdelmajid Chetali on the Scotland team who were sharing a training camp with Tunisia in Argentina for the World Cup, 1978

This is an unusual Scotland side because they have good players.

Spain's Javier Clemente taken aback by Scotland's Under-21s, 1996

Yesterday I thought Mr Ramsey's team would win the World Cup. Today it is another picture.

Austria coach Rudi Fruwirth following his team's shock 3–2 win at Wembley, 1965

Poland are a young team on the way up. England are an old team on the way down.

Luxembourg coach Paul Phillipp comparing his country's recent opponents, 1998

We'll start worrying about the Italians when we sober up tomorrow.

Republic of Ireland boss Jack Charlton at the World Cup, 1990

I've seen them on television most Sunday mornings.

Jack Charlton on World Cup opponents Italy, 1994

We have nothing to learn from Brazil.

Sir Alf Ramsey after the World Cup, 1970

5 The Tactics

Everyone tries to complicate the game. Getting round the back? That's what burglars say, isn't it?

Liverpool's Bob Paisley, 1980

Football is a simple game and should be kept simple.

Bill Shankly of Liverpool, 1960s

Football matches are played on football pitches and not in exercise books.

Bill Shankly decrying the trend for dossiers, popular with Don Revie at Leeds, 1970

Simplicity is genius.

West Ham's Ron Greenwood, 1960s

I tried to keep our football as simple as possible. We had good players, but I didn't want them to indulge themselves too much as individuals. I used to tell them they had to be effective, not exhibition players.

Former Spurs boss Bill Nicholson, 1982

When we get the ball, we attack. When they get it, we defend. It's as simple as that.

Norwich City's Dave Stringer explaining his team's rise to the top of the First Division, 1988

Tactics are irrelevant when you have great players.

Milan's Fabio Capello, 1995

Cut out what eats up energy and wastes time, such as laboured and needless moves, and you get on with the purpose of football, which is to score goals.

Manchester City's Joe Mercer, 1968

We are taking far too many passes to go nowhere.

Forest's Dave Bassett thinking there must be a quicker way to go nowhere, 1997

The words and phraseology are new, but the game isn't. It never changes and it never will. In the year 2000 it will still all be about scoring goals and stopping them.

Sheffield Wednesday's Derek Dooley, 1972

I'm looking forward to seeing some sexy football.

Chelsea's Ruud Gullit, 1996

Unfortunately, we aren't allowed to study style. So severe is the competition that we are compelled to sacrifice whatever ambitions we may have for effect. With us, it is a case of goals and points. At times one is persuaded that nothing else matters.

Herbert Chapman answering criticisms of Arsenal's lack of style, 1930s

You ought to get a bunch of clowns if you want entertainment.

Stoke City's Alan Durban responding to criticism of his team's negative tactics at Arsenal, 1980

All managers want to see their sides play attractive football, but they also want to stay in a job.

Arsenal's George Graham, 1992

I would rather play ugly football and win than play attractive football and lose.

Brazil coach Mario Zagallo, 1997

When I came to this country twenty years ago, my dream was to combine English organisation, spirit and guts with South American skill. If you want to be successful, you can't have one without the other. You have to have players who can kick a bit, especially at the back.

Stockport's Danny Bergara, 1994

We were returning home from a match at Bradford Park Avenue and were all dead pleased at our two-pound win bonus, talking over the game and the last-minute goal which had done the trick for us. I spread the sugar around, trying to map out the moves leading up to our goal. It was one to savour because there were about seven passes starting out from our own penalty area. I argued that if we could plan moves like that instead of just hoping for it to happen, we would score more often.

Spurs' Arthur Rowe on how the push-and-run style originated in season 1949–50, from *And The Spurs Go Marching On* by Phil Soar (Hamlyn, 1982)

I took our style back to the streets, the way we played it as kids – off the kerb, off the wall, taking the ball at different angles, enlisting the kerb as a team-mate who'd let you have the ball back immediately after you had played it quickly . . . the quicker the better.

Arthur Rowe on push-and-run, from *And The Spurs Go Marching On* (Hamlyn, 1982)

Supple and imaginative, that's how the game has always been played at Spurs . . . It's the man *without* the ball who is the most important.

Former Tottenham manager Bill Nicholson, 1982

I believe that even in the days when England had great players like Stanley Matthews, Tom Finney and Raich Carter, the team would have been even better with a rigid plan. Any plan must be adapted to the strengths and weaknesses of the players and must be acceptable to them. That is the secret of football planning . . . It is exciting. I want to do it. You see, I believe in England, and Englishmen, as well as English football.

Alf Ramsey setting out his stall on his appointment to the England job, 1962

We've all followed Ramsey. The winger was dead once you played four defenders. Alf saw that in 1966, and it took the rest of us a little longer to understand.

Wales boss Dave Bowen, 1973

It's better to have a bad system than no system at all.
Liverpool's Bill Shankly, 1960s

I wouldn't give you tuppence for our players individually, but collectively, in a 4–4–2 formation, they are the best team in Europe – reputedly.
Liverpool's Bob Paisley, 1979

It's not enough to say that you are going to play 3–5–2 or 4–4–2. What's important is having a group that can vary the play.
Brazil coach Vanderley Luxemburgo, 1998

Rigid 4–4–2 systems can be boring. Our style is a bit like Newcastle's.
Carlisle United's Mick Wadsworth, 1994

My team take their style from Manchester United.
St Mirren's Tony Fitzpatrick, 1998

I was making notes about switching around my team formation to 4–4–2. When I looked up, Dion was jogging off the pitch and I thought it would have to be 4–4–1.
Coventry's Gordon Strachan forced to re-jig things after the sending-off of Dion Dublin, 1997

I've done it before unsuccessfully and I probably won't ever do it again.
Crewe's Dario Gradi after a switch to 4–4–2 resulted in a 3–0 home defeat against Charlton, 1998

It might be true that 75 per cent of sides in the World Cup played with three at the back, but 75 per cent of the semi-finalists used four defenders. I would always have four at the back – I think this gives players elsewhere on the pitch the maximum opportunity.
Howard Wilkinson arguing against the use of wing-backs, 1998

There were no words, no diagrams, no tactics, just a group of players playing for each other.

David Pleat as Sheffield Wednesday kept their first clean sheet in twenty games, beating Aston Villa 2–0, 1996

Good teams are built on clean sheets.

Bolton's Colin Todd, 1995

The best place to defend is in the other side's penalty box.

Celtic's Jock Stein, 1970s

The whole idea of compensatory play is absolute bollocks.

Claude Le Roy, French coach of Cameroon, defending his tactic of throwing men forward in the World Cup, 1998

It is possible to win the title by playing the way that we play. Of course there comes a time when we have to scrap for a draw because teams impose themselves on us, but what's the point of going out to defend when we have so many creative players here?

Kevin Keegan at Newcastle, 1994

Defensively, our record isn't the best. We can give away goals without the other team having to do anything. It makes you wonder if you wouldn't be better playing eight defenders back, but I don't believe in that. No matter what, you have to try and entertain people, and, one way or another, we certainly do that.

Len Walker of Aldershot (53 goals for, 72 against, in 30 matches), 1991

Some people consider my idea somewhat naïve, but I would like to see an end to the points system which decides the honours and base the whole of the League set-up on the number of goals scored. The team that scored the most goals during the season would finish on top of the table, the side scoring the fewest would finish bottom.

Cambridge United's Bill Leivers, 1973

We always try to attack attractively.

Rochdale's Mick Docherty contemplating kitting out his forwards in something by Vivienne Westwood, 1995

How can you ever attack unless you have a solid base?

Newcastle's Ruud Gullit realising the need for sensible shoes, 1998

Maybe I dream too much . . . I would play with a goalkeeper and ten front players.

Ossie Ardiles revealing the philosophy which has got him the sack on such a regular basis, 1993

We believe in striking quickly from defence. A team is most vulnerable when it has just failed in attack. If I had to suggest an ideal number of passes, I would say three. It is difficult to generalise on such a fluid game as football, but generally the second pass out of defence I would regard as the most vital.

Alf Ramsey explaining his success with unfashionable Ipswich, 1961

It can't be fast, fast, fast. I think there has to be a slow, slow, quick, quick, slow.

Bruce Rioch watching too much *Come Dancing,* 1996

It's all about playing to your strengths and making the best use of what's available. After all, if you go into a pub and there's no Guinness, you just have to drink something else.

Airdrie's Alex MacDonald justifying his team's reputation for uncompromising play, 1995

There was no point in us trying to follow them and beat them at their own game for they had a ten-year start. So instead of attempting to play the ball through them, I decided we would go over them.

Jack Charlton on how his Republic of Ireland team set out to counter the great passing nations of the world, from *Jack Charlton's World Cup Diary* (Gill and Macmillan, 1990)

Northampton had devised a plan by which their outfield players had five seconds to get to the halfway line for a long kick out by their goalkeeper. When the ball dropped, they had invariably more players in the other half of the pitch than the opposition and, by heading it on, they were then in the position to trade on percentages. They won the Championship by a mile.

Jack Charlton on using Fourth Division Northampton as his inspiration, 1990

We beat England by playing the English way, and my bible is the English coaching book, *Tactics and Teamwork* by Charles Hughes. We have great respect for English coaching courses.

Norway's Egil Olsen, 1993

I bought Kevin Francis, not Pelé.

Stockport County's Danny Bergara defending his team's aerial route to the 6ft 7in striker, 1994

My lads think you survive in the Premiership by going out and playing football all the time. Their first goal was a boot down the middle, we let it bounce, and it was in the back of our net. If that's what keeps you in the division for 28 years, I'll have some of it, please.

Crystal Palace's Alan Smith on a tactical lesson learned from defeat against Coventry, 1995

We concentrate on doing the simple things well.

Graham Taylor steering Lincoln City to the Fourth Division title, 1976

Possession and patience are myths ... Goals come from mistakes, not possession.

Watford's Graham Taylor, arch exponent of the so-called long-ball game, 1982

Part of a nation's culture, its heritage, is the way it plays its sport. And the English way is with passion and commitment.

Graham Taylor, 1982

Bloody hell, I'll have to stop that!

Graham Taylor, informed that his England team had strung together thirteen passes in the build-up to a goal, 1991

Nobody here gives a damn about technique any more. It's all up-and-unders.

Keith Burkinshaw deciding to go abroad after resigning as manager of Gillingham, 1989

I couldn't manage a club playing the long ball. I'd prefer to be out of the game than have to do that.

West Bromwich Albion's Keith Burkinshaw, 1994

In some teams, the playmaker is the goalkeeper. It's embarrassing to see.

West Brom's Ossie Ardiles, 1992

One day they'll try to stick the sinking of the *Titanic* on me!

Dave Bassett, haunted by accusations that he is an advocate of the long-ball game, 1989

If we do play a long ball occasionally, it's a long ball. If anyone else does it, it's a wonderful pass.

Wimbledon's Joe Kinnear, 1995

We might have to become a long-ball team.

Joe Kinnear, tongue firmly in cheek, after defeat at Queens Park Rangers, 1994

I can't watch Wimbledon, Watford or Sheffield Wednesday. Football wasn't meant to be run by two linesmen and air traffic control.

Tommy Docherty, 1988

If God wanted the game played in the air, why did he put grass on the floor?

Nottingham Forest's Brian Clough, 1980s

That's the ball. Keep it. Play with it. Treasure it. Look after it, and if you do, it will come back to you. The most you ever do is lend it to somebody else.

Brian Clough's team talks, 1992

If you have the ball, you command the game. If you kick and rush, it depends on luck.

Chelsea's Ruud Gullit, 1996

In Holland it's different. Every player is a footballer whether he has a number five on his back or a number nine. Everybody has a touch of the ball, has a little cuddle. Pass it, pass it, pass it, don't lose it. In Britain, there is still a tendency to look for the early ball up behind defenders.

Bobby Robson at PSV Eindhoven, 1998

My time at Hamburg had taught me that players can work in a variety of ways if they are comfortable on the ball. British teams usually have five or so players who are comfortable when the opposition have the ball.

Reading's Mark McGhee, 1994

I don't think there's a better footballing side in the division, but perhaps good footballing sides don't always get their just rewards.

Glenn Hoddle singing the praises of his Swindon team, 1992

It's difficult to try and tell our players to play the disciplined way they have to play in Europe, because they have to play all out every week.

Rangers' John Greig on the difficulty of British players adapting to Europe, 1978

People ask me if we practise them. Yes. That is why we are so good at them.

Swansea City's John Toshack praising his team's stream of back-passes during a goalless draw at Chelsea, 1980

The biggest disappointment is to find the game so defence-orientated here. All these teams rushing up to the halfway line, at every chance they get, simply crucifies the game that was invented for Stanley Matthews, Tom Finney, Jimmy Johnstone, Danny Blanchflower, Denis Law, Rodney Marsh, Pelé, Garrincha and Maradona.

Dave Mackay returning to England with Doncaster Rovers after nine years abroad, 1988

I described soccer in England as being the working man's ballet. It's more like a clog dance now.

Former Stoke manager Tony Waddington, 1991

I've even seen youth coaches running about with clipboards. They're marking channels where the goalkeeper is required to kick the ball and pen in the opposition. How can a boy improve in a team where the goalkeeper is an attacker?

Bristol City's Joe Jordan, 1989

I do not like Spanish football. Often it is more concerned with crippling opponents than with technique.

Argentina coach Cesar Menotti, 1982

Football is a game of skill, not combat.

Crewe Alexandra's ex-Wimbledon boss Dario Gradi, 1995

The modern team isn't like the modern car. You can't just put in a spare part and expect the machine to run the same as before.

Everton's Harry Catterick on the need for positional changes when making a substitution, 1967

They all laughed when I said we could beat Manchester United, but I knew our men to be capable of winning. I planned two lines of defence. Right-half Roy McCrohan stayed back with the centre-half and full-back, while Matt Crowe operated in front. As soon as a Norwich move broke down, inside-right Terry Allcock doubled back with Crowe. That way we were able to break up most of their moves before they started. I reckoned Billy Foulkes could be beaten, so I told inside-left Jimmy Hill to stay on the wing with Bobby Brennan, and that was where our goals came from. It worked to perfection. Terry Bly had all the room he needed in the middle and could have had half a dozen goals.

Norwich City's Archie Macaulay plotting the FA Cup downfall of Manchester United, 1959

I still can't believe it. Our plan was to attack whenever we could and then defend like dervishes. And that is what we did.

Alvechurch manager Wyn Bowen after the Cup win at Exeter, 1973

I don't think they realised we could play so well. Club coach Brian Hall and I were up until two o'clock this morning scrapping, then reconsidering ideas as to how we could beat them. We produced a fifteen-page dossier. It might have been different if Bob Stockley had been skinned three times by Leighton James in the first ten minutes, but he wasn't. We worked out that they got their attacks to a certain point, usually on either flank, and then used the cross. We had to stop them reaching this stage or deal with the crosses. It went as planned. They were too predictable.

Wimbledon's Allen Batsford after his Southern Leaguers won at First Division Burnley in the Cup, 1975

Fortunately our chaps are proper chaps and they do have some intelligence. Therefore they are able to countenance a multiplicity of set plays suited to the occasion.

Sutton United's Barrie Williams on the tactics which outsmarted Coventry in the FA Cup, 1989

We have had them watched several times and, as Baldrick would say, 'I have a cunning plan.'

Hayes' Terry Brown before the first-round FA Cup tie with Mansfield, 1998

I don't work off my nervous pre-match energy on giving the boys useless dressing-room tactical talks. I go into my office and get out my crossword. I find the challenge of it drives out my own anxieties and pre-match nerves.

Carlisle United's Tim Ward, 1968

What do I say to them in the dressing-room? Nothing really. Most of the time I don't even know what they are going to do myself.

Kenny Dalglish on his Liverpool team, 1988

Nothing. I went in prepared to give them hell, but not a word came out. I kicked over the tea urn and left. They must have guessed I was angry.

Joe Mercer recalling the occasion when he revitalised his Aston Villa team from a 4–0 half-time deficit, 1960s

There was a lot of shouting and slamming of doors during the interval.

Cambridge United's John Beck getting his ideas across to his players and inspiring them to FA Cup victory over Middlesbrough, 1991

It was all down to a wonderful team talk by me at half-time. To be honest, what I said was just the usual cobblers. Sometimes it works, sometimes it doesn't.

Straight-talking Mick McCarthy inspiring a second-half revival for Millwall, 1994

I thought the World Cup was played in a negative sense, and England won with negative football.

Liverpool's Bill Shankly offering the unbiased view of a Scot on England's World Cup triumph, 1966

Football is about football.

Coventry City's plain-talking Bobby Gould, 1992

6 The Ref

That, that's unbelievable. That's actually unbelievable. Unbelievable. The referee's five yards away and gives a penalty. That is unbelievable. It is unbelievable. In a couple of weeks, that decision won't really matter because at the end of the day we are beaten in this competition, but that is shocking.

A disbelieving Martin O'Neill watching a TV replay of the controversial last-minute penalty which sent his Leicester team crashing out of the FA Cup at Chelsea, 1997

Tell your friend out there that he's just got me the sack.

England's Graham Taylor telling the linesman what he thinks of German referee Karl Josef Assenmacher for allowing Holland's Ronald Koeman to stay on the pitch following a professional foul on David Platt and score the decisive goal in a crucial World Cup qualifier against Holland, 1993

There is a vast gulf between what referees from different countries are prepared to allow. English referees generally are the best in the world, but others need rigorous briefings to stop cynical and brutal play.

Leeds' Don Revie, an expert on cynical and brutal play, 1973

Tinkler ruined nine months of hard work.

Don Revie on referee Ray Tinkler's decision to allow an 'offside' West Brom goal in a 2–0 win at Leeds, a result which cost them the Championship, 1971

It's just too much. We should have had at least three penalties. When you get decisions like that going against you, what can you do?

Don Revie after defeat at Wolves in the final game of the season saw Leeds pipped for the First Division Championship by a single point for the second successive year, 1972

We are practising for the one we expect around 1995.

Dave Bassett pointing out that Sheffield United hadn't had a penalty for 47 games, 1992

The last time I got anything away from home, I was playing for Tottenham.

Wimbledon's Joe Kinnear, 1996

The last time we got a penalty away from home, Christ was a carpenter.

Charlton's Lennie Lawrence, 1989

Sure, we get our share of penalties. But then we get in the penalty area more often than most teams.

Liverpool's Kenny Dalglish, 1988

After the match an official asked for two of my players to take a dope test. I offered him the referee.

Tommy Docherty after a 5–1 defeat by Brighton condemned his Wolves team to relegation, 1985

I know where he should have put his flag – and he'd have got plenty of help!

Coventry's Ron Atkinson, unimpressed by a linesman's decision at Stamford Bridge, 1996

If that was a penalty, I'll plait sawdust.

Ron Atkinson after his Sheffield Wednesday team lost 1–0 to Chelsea, 1998

It's a physical game, and to get beaten like that is sickening. It's sad that week in, week out, managers are talking about referees' decisions, not how good a game it was.

Bradford City's Paul Jewell after a controversial last-minute penalty had denied his team a win at Norwich, 1998

One of Cadette's strengths is holding off people with his back to goal. If that wasn't legal, nor were many of Kenny Dalglish's during his career.

Falkirk's Jim Jefferies after Richard Cadette had been penalised for holding off his marker in the build-up to a disallowed goal against Rangers, 1992

He must have been a very little player, because I didn't see him.

Brighton's Liam Brady after a Brentford winner had been disallowed because the linesman had seen 'a little player' in an offside position, 1995

The nearest player offside was at White Hart Lane.

Millwall's John Docherty after a Les Briley effort at Arsenal was ruled out for offside against Teddy Sheringham, 1989

If he's not interfering with play, what's he doing on the field?

Brian Clough, 1970s

It's a crap rule. You're either offside or you're not offside. It's getting beyond a joke.

Stranraer's Campbell Money, angry at the award of a last-minute goal to Ayr, 1998

It would have been a travesty if we had lost. We dominated 75 per cent of the game, our passing and movement were really good, and I thought we played really well against the fourteen men of Wycombe.

Grimsby's Alan Buckley with a thinly veiled reference to the referee and his assistants after a draw at Wycombe, 1998

We were playing against twelve men.

Shrewsbury Town manager Jake King, unhappy at the performance of referee Andy D'Urso at Exeter, 1998

All I said was his decision to send off Aspinall for handball was garbage. I didn't swear.

Swansea boss Frank Burrows, sent off along with captain John Cornforth by referee Kevin Lynch for allegedly making abusive remarks over the dismissal of Warren Aspinall, 1993

It was handbag stuff. If you start sending players off for scratching at each other, then you might as well send a team out wearing skirts.

Walsall's Kenny Hibbitt playing down the sending-off of Chris Marsh against Cardiff City, 1992

The lads say it was an incident that would not have hurt a baby.

Portsmouth's Alan Ball after midfielder Russell Perrett was sent off at Grimsby, 1998

I didn't see any blood.

Blackburn's Roy Hodgson after Kevin Gallacher was sent off for supposedly elbowing West Ham's Eyal Berkovic, 1998

What happened to the man's game of football I used to know? I don't want to go back to the days when players kicked lumps out of each other, but this kind of stuff is morris dancing. No one seems to be able to tackle any more.

Nottingham Forest's Dave Bassett after Steve Stone was sent off for making minimal contact with Spurs' David Ginola, 1998

It was an incredible decision, the worst I've seen in nearly thirty years of football. Even a few of the Huddersfield players were laughing at it.

Birmingham City boss Trevor Francis seeing red after referee Rob Styles sent off Peter Ndlovu for diving in the top-of-the-table clash with Huddersfield, 1998

These days you get a yellow card for kicking the ball away, you get a yellow card for breaking somebody's leg. It doesn't look sensible to me.

Liverpool's Roy Evans after Steve Harkness was injured against Coventry, 1996

If my players played as he reffed, I couldn't defend them publicly.

Blackburn's Kenny Dalglish criticising the performance of referee Martin Bodenham in the 1–1 draw with Wimbledon, 1992

It was an abysmal performance. The referee totally lost control. We managers get done for disrepute and referees get away with murder.

Wimbledon's Joe Kinnear weighing in with his verdict on Martin Bodenham after the same match, 1992

He's past his sell-by date.

Arsenal's Bruce Rioch on referee Martin Bodenham following defeat at Chelsea, 1995

A referee who is not in the 'established' category will worry about what the assessor is thinking, and he'll stick rigidly to the code rather than use his own personality to control the game. Too many referees have this season stuck too severely to the letter of the law and not the spirit of the game. I believe the assessor sitting anonymously in the stand has a lot to do with this.

Southampton's Ted Bates, 1973

I'll give the referee what we got from him – a big fat zero. I won't even give him one for turning up, because I wish he hadn't.

Stockport's Gary Megson on referee Gary Willard, who sent off two County players in a Cup defeat at Birmingham, 1998

There was thuggery going on in the first few minutes, but the referee did nothing about it. Then he booked five of my players in the defensive wall while Burnley were moving the ball forward behind his back. I know I'll get into trouble for saying it, but the referee was a joke.

Cambridge United's John Docherty after referee Peter Reeves sent off two of his players and booked a handful more at Burnley, 1979

The referee booked ten players when there wasn't a bad tackle in the match. We've worked hard to improve our disciplinary record, but now we feel butchered.

Gateshead's Colin Richardson, following a draw with Kettering, 1995

He was handing those cards out like tram tickets.

Ipswich's Bobby Robson on the refereeing in a 3–3 draw with Everton, 1977

Six bookings? What do you expect from a referee from Great Bookham?

Sheffield United's Dave Bassett on referee Ray Lewis after the derby with Leeds, 1992

I'm very disappointed with Keith Hackett, who is one of the top referees in England. If he failed to see certain things, what chance do we have in this game?

Spurs' Ossie Ardiles after Gary Mabbutt sustained serious injuries in a clash with Wimbledon's John Fashanu, 1993

I thought I was the only Irishman around here.

Leicester's Martin O'Neill, puzzled by some of the decisions of referee Mike Riley in the game against West Ham, 1996

The referee did his best to even the game up.

Myopic Middlesbrough boss Bryan Robson moaning because he had a man sent off during the Cup semi-final draw with Chesterfield, this despite the fact that referee David Elleray admitted disallowing a perfectly good Chesterfield goal, 1997

As a manager, you're like a prostitute. You depend on other people for your living.

Steve Coppell considering giving up the game after Crystal Palace lost to a disputed penalty in an FA Cup tie at Hartlepool, 1993

You certainly know what city you are in when this sort of thing happens.

Partick Thistle boss Murdo MacLeod on referee Jim McGilvray's decision to book Partick's Rod McDonald for crossing himself as he left the pitch at the end of the first half against Rangers, 1996

I went naked because I'm tired of working honestly only to be scandalously robbed. Football in Rio de Janeiro is a disgrace.

Paulo Mata, coach with Brazilian club Itaperuna, who did a streak at the end of a match in protest at having three players sent off and a late goal disallowed, 1997. Denied access to the referee by the police, Mata made his point by mooning at a TV camera

The linesman said at half-time that if he had made a mistake, he was sorry. That's a comfort for the lads when they look at the papers in the morning and see they've only got five points!

Gordon Strachan after Coventry lost to a suspiciously offside goal against Aston Villa, 1998

The referee told us that he had lost a contact lens when he was hit in the face. He thought the ball was still in play, but admitted that he couldn't see properly and that his decision may have been wrong.

Alloa Athletic boss Tom Hendrie after conceding a controversial goal at Livingston minutes after an injury to referee Jim Herald, 1998

The referee looked at it, moved to one side, looked again, then maybe he thought, 'I'm at Chelsea. It's a bit dicey.' Five of our six away games this year have been against teams who are in Europe. It is fair to say we haven't been given many decisions when it has counted.

Charlton's Alan Curbishley, denied a penalty by referee Steve Dunn after Chelsea's Michael Duberry appeared to handle, 1998. Chelsea won 2–1

No one needs to tell me how hard a referee's job is. I wouldn't take their place for a million pounds.

Alex Ferguson, manager of Aberdeen, 1985

I can now understand why clubs come away from here having to bite their tongues and choking on their own vomit, knowing they have been done by referees. It would be a miracle to win here. It is the whole intimidating atmosphere and the monopoly

Liverpool have enjoyed here for years that gets to them eventually.

Manchester United's Alex Ferguson on winning a hard-earned point at Anfield, 1988

The referee? I thought he had a good game.

Liverpool's Kenny Dalglish after the same match, 1988

There's no rapport with referees these days. If you say anything, you get booked, and if you don't, they send you off for dumb insolence.

Sheffield Wednesday boss Jack Charlton, 1983

You can't even talk to referees now. If you get into the dressing-room and try to speak to them, they ask you to leave. And if you start talking to them, you don't get an answer. Football is about players, not officials.

Kenny Dalglish at Blackburn, 1992

We prefer to lose because of the ability of the opposition rather than the inability of the referee.

Blackburn's Kenny Dalglish, 1994

It's a difficult enough job for the referee without us being over-critical, but I think he was the worst person on the pitch.

Newcastle's Kenny Dalglish on referee Peter Jones, who booked seven players during the home defeat by Manchester United, 1997

Referees are following rules made by men who don't pay to watch football. Those rules are ruining the game for those who do.

St Mirren boss David Hay, 1991

We work all hours God sends to try and achieve our own standards of perfection. We make sure that every eventuality in the modern game is planned for. But all this can be upset by referees making wrong decisions.

Preston's Alan Ball senior, 1972

I saw in the programme that the referee's interests included the theatre – and he wanted to be centre stage.

QPR assistant manager Iain Dowie acting up after defeat at Swindon, 1998

Our players asked the referee how long to go, and he said, 'Thirty seconds.' We kept the ball down in the corner for more than thirty seconds, then they broke upfield and scored.

Tamworth's Paul Hendrie feeling cheated by Exeter's FA Cup equaliser five and a half minutes into injury time, 1998

The referee made it very difficult for us. He had too much influence on the game. We've not been beaten by the opposition, we've been beaten because of decisions.

Newcastle's Ruud Gullit blaming the 3–0 home defeat by West Ham on referee Graham Poll, 1998

They've got a fanatical crowd here and they scream for everything. They screamed for penalties that weren't penalties. The referee was strong enough not to give them when a weaker ref might have buckled and gone with the crowd.

West Ham's Harry Redknapp taking a somewhat different view of the same game, 1998

In the end I was pleased for the referee that Bellamy missed it. He would have been very embarrassed about his decision when he saw the incident again on television.

Bury's Neil Warnock after Craig Bellamy of Norwich missed a dubious injury-time penalty awarded by referee Barry Knight, 1998

The ref was so excited about giving the penalty that he forgot.

Neil Warnock on why Bury defender Chris Lucketti was not sent off after giving away a spot-kick against Bristol City, 1998

Almost all foreign referees ask for my autograph. It's always been like that. For their friends, their sons, themselves, I don't know.

Barcelona coach Johan Cruyff, 1994

The referee was determined to see the game through, but if you don't have goalposts, a ball and a pitch, it's a bit of a struggle.

Jimmy Case, boss of crisis club Brighton, after the game with visiting York was called off, 1996

I've served more time than Ronnie Biggs did for the Great Train Robbery.

Plymouth Argyle's Malcolm Allison appealing against his touchline ban, 1978

He ordered me off the pitch in his normal Hitler fashion. He was a dreadful referee, and I know I've got myself into trouble again. He was up for it all night, and also threatened to send off Sam Hammam . . . With these refs it depends on what shirt you're wearing.

Wimbledon's Joe Kinnear on referee Robbie Hart after the game with Manchester United, 1995

The referee lost the plot towards the end, but I do not want to give him the satisfaction of getting myself into trouble.

Barnsley's Danny Wilson restraining himself from commenting on Gary Willard's handling of the game with Liverpool, 1998

I've already been fined by the FA this season for speaking out, and I'd like to build up my bank balance before I say anything.

Newcastle's Kevin Keegan refraining from criticising the referee after a game against Swindon, 1993

I'm not going to say too much. I've been fined enough times, and the FA could probably go on holiday with the amount of money I've given them over the years.

Leicester's Martin O'Neill biting his tongue, 1996

I'm not saying anything because I'm still paying the fine from the last time I said anything about a referee.

Bryan Robson after referee Paul Alcock sent off two Middlesbrough players in the 3–3 draw at Southampton, 1998

7 The Fans

If the crowds start chanting, 'Turnip, Turnip, give us a wave', then you give them a wave.

Graham Taylor starting afresh at Wolves, 1994

It's not the first time this has happened. The fans are too close to the tunnel and we are very easy targets. It's not a very nice feeling, someone else's phlegm on your face.

Wolves boss Graham Taylor after a spectator spat at him at Sheffield United, 1995

I suppose I'll only know how they feel when I return on Thursday and if I have to pay for my own Guinness.

Jack Charlton, following the Republic of Ireland's exit from the World Cup, 1994

I don't know if the people are still behind me or not. I'll soon find out when we kick off.

Glenn Hoddle before England's European Championships qualifier with Bulgaria, 1998

It's not nice to see a manager get booed like that, and it saddens me that we still crucify the manager. But that's the public response. It's a vicious game, vitriolic at times. In other countries they don't do it so viciously.

Former England boss Bobby Robson on the abuse meted out to Glenn Hoddle after the Bulgaria game, 1998

There are two possible ways I can end this tournament. Either I shall be kissed all over my bald head or I will have tomatoes thrown at it.

Italy's Arrigo Sacchi before the European Championship finals, 1996

The problem is that the public treats footballers and football managers as public property, and almost as if they don't have feelings or families, don't have a wife and children, but are simply tools there to run a team. They feel we can cope and are impervious to hurt, and therefore at times they treat us very badly.

Wolves' Mark McGhee, 1996

When some fans tried to run John and his wife off the road after a match, it made him think twice about football.

Falkirk caretaker boss Gerry Collins revealing the reasons behind John Lambie's exit, 1996

There was even a threat to kidnap me and take me to the zoo, but it didn't materialise.

Ian Branfoot, a victim of the Southampton boo-boys, 1994

Look at that, Southampton only drew. What a shame!

Ian Branfoot, after his escape from The Dell, celebrating a rare win as manager of Fulham, 1995

It's a yob culture, the only thing they know. Supporters are less tolerant and more hostile than they used to be.

Ian Branfoot reflecting on his miserable stay at Southampton, 1995

There were parents bringing their kids to matches and encouraging them to shout abuse at me. It's pathetic. I just hope the fans are happy now.

Steve McMahon resigning from Swindon, 1998

Stickers saying things like SACK DOLAN which are issued to kids in the same class as my daughter at school is taking things a bit far.

Hull City's Terry Dolan, 1997

Part of the problem is that the modern soccer spectator has become too sophisticated and well educated.

Middlesbrough's Stan Anderson yearning for the days when fans were happy with a cup of Bovril and a 5–0 defeat instead of putting pressure on managers to do their job, 1972

I went to a supporters' night and half of them were cheering and half were booing. The problem was that the half that were cheering were cheering the half that were booing.

Scotland boss Craig Brown recalling his management days at Clyde, 1996

The last thing the players need is criticism. This has been the biggest change I have noticed at the club since my return. There was never the kind of booing aimed at certain individuals during my playing days.

Dundee United's Paul Sturrock, shocked by the atmosphere at Tannadice, 1998

It was a losing battle with the supporters. There I was, window smashed, driving along the M25 with the rain soaking me and feeling miserable as sin after such a bad defeat. I thought, Someone is trying to tell me something here.

Queens Park Rangers' Ray Harford resigning after a 4–1 defeat at Oxford and having his car broken into for the third time in a year, 1998

I had tough times with relegation seasons at Sheffield United and Aston Villa. On the day Villa were relegated, I received a telegram from a Sheffield United supporter that read: Congratulations. You have done it again.

Joe Mercer, 1988

I get a hundred letters a week blaming me, saying I'm a traitor to the Welsh cause.

Alex Ferguson on repeatedly having to withdraw Ryan Giggs from the Welsh squad, 1995

Neither the club nor the fans were prepared to take one step back to ensure that they could move forward. For that blindness alone they deserve exactly what they have since got – football in the lower divisions.

Dave Bassett on his unhappy spell at Watford, from *Harry's Game* (Breedon Books, 1997)

I don't write a column in the programme because the fans wouldn't buy it if I did.

Doncaster Rovers' Mark Weaver on his stormy relationship with the club's supporters, 1998

I'll fight you all if it'll get us a result. I'll wear a tin hat to cope with the abuse.

Southampton's Dave Jones addressing the club's supporters, 1998

I've got about as many friends as Al Capone.

Leeds' Howard Wilkinson struggling to keep the support of the fans, 1994

All I can remember is shouting instructions to the right-back. He wears the number two shirt, doesn't he?

Brian Clough rejecting complaints that he had directed a V-sign to some Forest fans, 1993

We are top of the League, but with people like that there is no point in carrying on. If that is the fans' attitude after our first defeat in fifteen games, I will resign.

Brentford's David Webb, barracked by some travelling fans after a 1–0 defeat at Preston, 1997

You can't become a bad coach overnight.

Ronnie Whelan finding that the honeymoon is over as he comes under fire from the Greek media and fans of Panionios of Athens, 1998

I can live with the pressure, but it gets to the young players when the crowd start chanting 'Adamson must go' when the team bus arrives at the ground.

Leeds' Jimmy Adamson, 1979

It's not so long ago they were throwing things at me.

The fans are fickle. A few weeks ago, they were shouting for my head.

Those same supporters who were begging me to stay were baying for my blood when I first joined.

I'm thinking of sending him to Blackheath Hospital to get five thousand fans off his back.

Do the crowd always referee the game here? If we'd scored a winner, I don't think we'd have got out of here alive.

The most violent offenders should be flogged in front of the main stand before the start of home games. I'd volunteer to do the whipping myself.

The first thing I would advocate for these people is the birch. You don't stroke a wild dog – you blow its brains out.

I have to ask myself: Do you really want to be a manager of a club like this?

Football is the great god of exhibitionism. The big stadia are the only places frustrated youngsters can vent their emotions.

Everton's Harry Catterick on the upsurge of hooliganism, 1972

Their support can be an embarrassment sometimes, but I'd rather have them as an embarrassment than not at all.

Manchester United's Tommy Docherty on the club's notorious Red Army, 1974

It's 2,000 of us against 70,000 drunkards.

Spain's Javier Clemente before the England game in Euro 96

I know how much it means to everyone but, at the end of the day, it is football, not war. I just hope the fans understand that.

England coach Terry Venables before the semi-final with Germany at Euro 96

When we picked up the money, we were very rich, but there were no francs.

Standard Liege coach Arie Haan after his team were pelted with coins during a European Cup Winners' Cup tie in Cardiff, 1993

They've obviously never been to a Glasgow wedding.

Alex Ferguson making light of warnings about the hostile atmosphere Manchester United would face for a European Cup tie with Galatasaray in Istanbul, 1993

I've been frightened that I wouldn't be let into the ground with all these skinheads about.

Colchester United's close-cropped Dick Graham, 1970

There will not be any trouble. The average age of our supporters is eighty.

Worthing's John Robson before the FA Cup tie at Bournemouth, dubbed 'the pensioners' Cup final', 1994

The supporters didn't want anyone to take the job. I didn't expect to be received with open arms, but the depth of their feelings towards the board took me by surprise.

Brighton's Steve Gritt in the Goldstone Ground cauldron, 1997

The fans were writing GRIT OUT graffiti before my first game. If they'd spelt my name right, I might have gone.

Steve Gritt at Brighton, 1997

They made it clear they didn't want me from the outset. My every word and action was scrutinised for its level of devotion towards Tottenham Hotspur.

Former Arsenal stalwart Terry Neill on his unhappy two years in charge of North London rivals Spurs, 1976

I thought I'd have to get the armour plating.

Leeds' George Graham, fearing verbal attacks from both sets of supporters at the Spurs v. Leeds game, 1998. Leeds fans didn't want him to take the White Hart Lane job, while some Spurs fans didn't want him as their new manager because of his Arsenal connections

It's the first time I've had two sets of supporters shouting for me to get out.

Chelsea's John Hollins after a Simod Cup exit at the hands of Swindon, 1988

I didn't know I was so popular.

Birmingham City's Barry Fry after receiving a welcome that was heated rather than warm from fans at his old club, Southend, 1994

I don't often wish a day of my life away.

Aston Villa's Brian Little making an exception for the return to his old club Leicester, where he was greeted with cries of 'Judas', 1994

What you wish to do if and when Mark McGhee visits us with Wolves is at your own discretion.

Leicester boss Martin O'Neill asking the fans to go easy on Brian Little this time, but suggesting that a visit from McGhee, who also walked out on the club, might be another matter, 1997

Now the players applaud the crowd at the end of a match. When I was playing, it was the other way round.

Alan Ball at Manchester City, 1996

If I can just get them to a respectable position in the League, then I will leave it to the supporters to worry about my European record.

Everton boss Walter Smith dismissing concerns about his European misfortunes with Rangers, 1998

At Manchester United you become one of them, you think like a supporter, suffer like a supporter. They have been waiting 22 years for a League Championship. I've been waiting less than three years, but in terms of frustration it seems like 22 already.

Alex Ferguson, 1989

The Kop's exclusive, an institution, and if you're a member of the Kop, you feel you're a member of a society, you've got thousands of friends around you and they're united and loyal.

Liverpool's Bill Shankly, 1960s

When the ball's down the Kop end, they frighten the ball. Sometimes they suck it into the back of the net.

Bill Shankly, 1960s

I'm a people's man – only the people matter.

Bill Shankly, 1965

I know I can never have the same rapport with the fans that Bill had. I just hope I can let the team do the talking for me.

Bob Paisley taking over from Bill Shankly, 1974

The whole of my life, what they wanted was honesty. They were not so concerned with cultured football, but with triers who gave one hundred per cent.

Bob Paisley on the Kop, 1982

The highlight of the game was not our two goals or the three points we won. It was when our fans made the Kop sing 'You'll Never Walk Alone'. It was as if they couldn't come here and go home without hearing it sung in all its glory. It was very emotional, and something I'll remember for ever.

Kevin Keegan on Newcastle's 2–0 win at Anfield, 1994

I will always remain convinced that those Liverpool fans who died were killed by Liverpool people ... If all the Liverpool supporters had turned up at the stadium in good time, in orderly manner and each with a ticket, there would have been no Hillsborough disaster.

Brian Clough's controversial comments on the 1989 Hillsborough disaster, from *Clough: The Autobiography* (Partridge Press, 1994)

The FA Cup isn't worth it. There is nothing worth one death, let alone one hundred.

Liverpool's Kenny Dalglish on the futility of that season's competition following the semi-final tragedy at Hillsborough, 1989

Half of them can't read and the other half are pinching hubcaps.

Brian Clough winning more friends on Merseyside, 1994

When they see the quality of the football we are playing now, it's like a drug to them – they can't get enough of it. You've got to remember these fans have driven down motorways and watched some really abysmal sides in Newcastle shirts.

Kevin Keegan with Newcastle on the way up, 1992

Support means getting behind the team through thick and thin. Newcastle supporters have, in the last few years, been through thin and thin.

Kevin Keegan, 1993

I've told the players that if they keep playing the way they are then there won't be five thousand fans watching them train. They will be able to get straight in their cars and drive home.

Kevin Keegan with Newcastle on the slide, 1996

The fans want it [style of football] in a certain way and I think that's where Kenny, if you like, lost the plot.

Kevin Keegan on Kenny Dalglish's departure from Newcastle, 1998

All the time I am seeking ways and means to exploit my attacking potential. The public here demand it. They wouldn't stand for the stuff the Italians and Spaniards have had to put up with.

Walsall's Ray Shaw, 1968

The crowd want the ball forward, but you can't do that all the time. Sometimes they can't understand why the ball was going backward, but we all have to learn to be patient.

Ruud Gullit finding his feet at Newcastle, 1998

Attacking football and goals are the bait that is going to catch the fish.

Luton Town's Harry Haslam, 1973

They have been brought up on it here. The tradition was a hard week's work down the pit followed by going to the match on a Saturday, and they wanted to come and watch the skill. If you see people flogging their guts out all week, you don't want to pay to watch 22 lads huffing and puffing on the pitch. They want to come to see a bit of class, a bit of guile; they want to see people get the ball down and play.

Danny Wilson considering the demand for good football at Barnsley, 1995

I like to play football from the back, and there has been a certain amount of re-education both of players and the fans. The crowd get very restless and want to see it banged up the field, but gradually I think we are winning them round.

Sheffield United's Nigel Spackman, 1997

You can feel the buzz beforehand – the electricity right throughout the crowd.

Leeds' Don Revie on the highly charged atmosphere at Elland Road, 1972

I can still hear Denis Smith saying they were the best supporters in the world. Denis had tried to play good football without money and they gave him a standing ovation. He was crying in the tunnel.

Peter Reid, once of Manchester City, recalling how Sunderland under Denis Smith had visited Maine Road three years earlier and been relegated from the top flight, 1994

The best-selling T-shirt in town at the moment says CLARKIE'S A MACKEM.

Peter Reid on how Sunderland fans have accepted Geordie and ex-Newcastle player Lee Clark (a Mackem is a native of Sunderland), 1998

When Frank McLintock and I went into the Royal Archer with the Championship trophy, I think most of our fans thought I was a cardboard cut-out. They couldn't believe that we wanted to have a drink with them and let them hold the Championship trophy, but for me that sort of moment is what the game's all about.

Millwall's John Docherty celebrating winning the Second Division title, 1988

I hope they go away feeling that I'm not such an idiot as they thought.

Pat Saward organising meetings with Brighton fans, 1972

The players learn to appreciate just how hard people, like the dockers for example, have to work for their money and just what they expect when they pay their forty pence to stand on the terraces on a Saturday afternoon.

Southampton's Lawrie McMenemy arranging factory trips for his players to meet real people, 1974

The adulation is really embarrassing. You can't walk down the street without them coming up to you, putting their arms around you, offering you lifts on their rickshaw things.

Colin Murphy, a hero in Vietnam, 1997

I had to smile when they chanted, 'It's just like watching Brazil.' Maybe they were taking the mickey, but we had little spells where they might actually have meant it.

Lawrie McMenemy as Northern Ireland fans got behind his team in the European Championships victory over Finland, 1998

Many times it's the fans who get you the sack, but our crowd at Port Vale is the reason I've stayed.

John Rudge on his fifteen years at the Vale Park helm, 1998

The task was enormous, but if things went wrong the board could turn around to the fans and say they had acted on demand.

Rotherham United's Ronnie Moore, appointed by fan power, 1997

The working man now has too many choices to take his fancy on a Saturday. From my own experience, I know that he is looking towards the more unusual sports and participating freely in them.

Ken Furphy as Blackburn staged the Sex Olympics, 1972

More time is taken up around the home and the high street than in the days when most men worked on Saturday mornings and then went straight to the match. I believe Sunday soccer has far more appeal to potential women spectators than Saturday football, played at a time when the shops are at their busiest.

Bristol City's Alan Dicks advocating Sunday football, 1974

You won't find a trophy room, or even a cabinet, tucked away under our homely stands. Any success, however minor, is a godsend to our loyal band of fans. That's why we enter the Welsh Cup every season.

Chester's Ken Roberts, 1973

We're a farming community and traditionally farmers don't go to football matches.

Lincoln City's Shane Westley explaining the reason behind the low gates at Sincil Bank, 1998

One of Ipswich's main problems has always been a geographical one. Support-wise, we'll never be able to compete with the big-city clubs. We don't have chimney pots surrounding Portman Road as far as the eye can see. Travel eleven miles east of the ground and you reach the sea. I've always said we can't expect the fish to come and watch.

Bobby Robson abandoning plans for an aquarium on one side of Portman Road, 1973

Cumberland people love their rugby, but they are ripe to join the expanding soccer crusade if we can only give them something. We have started a Golden Girl [*sic*] competition and we have other attention-boosting plans on the stocks.

Workington's Frank Upton, 1968

Bradford has a lot of Pakistani immigrants, so it stands to reason that if we got a couple of Pakistani players good enough for the Third Division, at least a few of their nationality would come along to watch.

Bradford City's Bryan Edwards, 1972. Acting on this initiative, it was rumoured that Torquay had signed up two holidaymakers and Bournemouth were about to field a team containing three pensioners

People may not realise it, but King's Lynn is a real football town.

King's Lynn manager Peter Morris, 1997

I just wish there were ten thousand more in the ground chanting for my blood.

Aldershot's Len Walker after fifty fans gathered to call for his head following a home defeat by Hartlepool, 1983

It's difficult to play when the ground is that quiet you could hear a coin drop.

Notts County's Neil Warnock on the lack of atmosphere at Meadow Lane, 1992

It was like a morgue out there. The sooner we move to Dublin the better. We would only upset four thousand people.

Joe Kinnear failing to take into account the number of Dubliners who might be upset by Wimbledon's proposed move to their city, 1996

I thought the mural was noisier than the crowd.

Arsenal's George Graham after a 1–1 draw with Sheffield United in front of the demolished North Bank, 1993

Before this, the biggest crowd we've had was for a firework display.

Bedlington Terriers' co-manager Keith Perry before the FA Cup tie with Colchester, 1998

The glory days of regular big crowds have gone for ever. Fans see clubs spending millions while they are expected to pay one pound for a programme. They see executive boxes installed while they are peeing down one another's legs in scruffy, inadequate toilets. They read about huge sponsorship deals while they are drinking stewed tea and paying more for a piece of stale cake than they paid last year.

Graham Taylor endearing himself to the Villa Park catering corps, 1988

It gets depressing when you see supporters from this area going to Ibrox or Parkhead.

Kilmarnock's Bobby Williamson lamenting the drift to Glasgow despite the fact that Killie were second in the Premier League at the time, 1998

It's frustrating when I see soccer fans living in Bury going eight miles or so on a Saturday afternoon to City or United, but I think we've re-directed a few of them towards Gigg Lane this season.

I expect to win. Let me do the worrying – that's what I'm paid for. You get your feet up in front of the telly, get a few beers in and have a good time.

People kept saying, 'Get the champagne out, George.' I'd reply, 'Not until it's mathematically certain. The fat lady is just clearing her throat.'

Perhaps I gave them too much caviar last season. When you've had caviar and you have to change, it's difficult to come back to sausage.

8 The Media

Can I go storming out now, please?

Jack Charlton, irritated by recent sensationalist media coverage, concluding a press conference after his Republic of Ireland team had been surprisingly held by Northern Ireland, 1995

I've never had much success in the Cup as a player or manager, so you can make up your own superlatives as to what it means to the club and the town.

Chesterfield's John Duncan to reporters after his team reached the quarter-finals of the FA Cup, 1997

They make from a little mosquito a big elephant.

Chelsea's Ruud Gullit on the magical powers of the British press, 1997

Some aspects of the story are absolutely ludicrous. For a start, I've never been to Sainsbury's – which the report said I frequented – in my life.

Howard Kendall refuting newspaper allegations that a drink problem cost him his job at Notts County, 1995

They had us down as 'Villa' instead of 'Aston Villa', and this meant we were eight places lower than we should have been on alphabetical order. That could cost us a place in Europe!

John Gregory ringing the Wolverhampton-based *Express and Star* after they published the first League table of the season, 1998

They examined us, analysed us and lived with us. They pulled us apart and put us together again. I had one call from Jack Milligan, a reporter on the old *Daily Graphic*. He was after a new angle, and while we were talking the subject of our slope cropped up. Nothing much had ever been written about it, but I thought, Why not? and gave him the facts – the way the slope dipped, its ten-foot drop and so on. Next morning the *Graphic* announced to the world that the pitch sloped fourteen feet from one side to the other, and in the next few days every other reporter seemed to add a couple of feet to its steepness. By the time match day came round, everyone must have had the idea we played on the north face of the Eiger.

Yeovil's Alec Stock turning press interest to his advantage before the famous 1949 Cup win over Sunderland, from *The Giant Killers* by Bryon Butler (Pelham Books, 1982)

Every time we lose a match it seems I have to get the psychological armour out to counter all the despondency and negativity that engulfs the club from the outside.

Wolves' Mark McGhee, 1998

There are a lot of people around who would love to see Blackburn Rovers fail because of jealousy. The national press put the club on a pedestal and then can't wait to boot it away.

Kenny Dalglish after big spenders Blackburn slipped up to First Division basement boys Port Vale, 1992

Envy is the worst fault in human nature. This club has been the most successful in history. People have waited a long time to have a go at Liverpool, and now they've got the chance.

Graeme Souness, 1992

I have never come across the situation we had in the closing weeks of that season. Our failure seemed to make a lot of people very happy. I find it difficult to understand. It is bitter and twisted.

Alex Ferguson reflecting on the previous year's near miss for Manchester United, 1993

Without newspapers and television, the game would lose much of its public appeal. Yet most of us feel we must always play politics. If there are some misinterpretations, the fault is usually ours. We speak, I'm afraid, with forked tongue.

Manchester City's Joe Mercer, 1969

By and large I get on well with the press, but I think the pressure on them to get a story has made them much less professional.

Jim Smith, from *Bald Eagle* (Mainstream, 1990)

I can work quite happily alongside most sports writers, but I no longer include any of them among my closest friends.

Dave Bassett, from *Harry's Game* (Breedon Books, 1997)

Of course, there are some black sheep among press men.

Leicester City's Matt Gillies complaining about the club's coverage, from *Farmers' Weekly* (1969)

You're welcome to my home phone number, but don't ring me during *The Sweeney*.

Ron Atkinson to journalists on taking over at Manchester United, 1981

I'm not here to help people fly kites. I will be the first to speak if there is something to speak about, but it is not my job just to fill the pages of newspapers.

Atkinson's taciturn predecessor at Old Trafford, Dave Sexton, under the headline COLD TRAFFORD, 1979

I appreciate that everyone feels he is a football expert and that everyone feels he has a right to make known his own opinions, but I also feel I have a right to keep my own opinions to myself when I feel it is important to do so.

England manager Sir Alf Ramsey, 1970

Too many managers say too much publicly these days. The only thing that matters in the long run is that table at the end of the season. And you can't talk your way to the top in this business.

Notts County boss Jimmy Sirrel, 1971

I tolerate the press as a necessary evil, but there is too much evil at the moment.

Port Vale's Gordon Lee, 1973

I stopped talking to the press when I found I was spending more time with the press than I was with my players. I work hard at my job and I don't see why I have to stand in draughty corridors after a game giving time to the Sunday papers, then the Monday ones. Hell fire, if they can't do their job without me, then they're poor journalists.

Brian Clough at Nottingham Forest, 1980s

Young man, you couldn't ask me a hard question to save your life.

Brian Clough to a BSkyB reporter, 1992

Talking to the press is dangerous. You must have super concentration or you make mistakes. And if you make one little slip here, a minute later it's telexed to Holland and every other country.

Barcelona's Dutch coach Johan Cruyff after deciding to cut down on the number of press conferences he gave, 1989

If a journalist likes to get things out of you, you just got to dribble around it.

Chelsea's Ruud Gullit, 1997

Dealing with some of the characters who are in the media now is a real strain. They come with something in their minds and that is what they want you to say. I usually see things in black and white, but being clear and telling the truth is unacceptable. If you give a direct answer, you're accused of whingeing or being cynical. Integrity and veracity count for nothing.

Manchester United's Alex Ferguson, 1997

We don't have reporters any more, we have QCs. Nowadays they aren't interested in how many goals a player scores, but where he's scoring at night.

Everton's Joe Royle, 1994

With Luton the pressure is probably greater than it was at Queens Park Rangers. In London, the press have more clubs to cover and don't build up such a tense atmosphere as a local paper does when there is only one club to follow.

Former QPR boss Alec Stock sampling life at Luton, 1971

I read the papers and saw that one or two obituaries had been written beforehand.

Under-fire Roy McFarland clinging to power at Derby, 1994

If I'm in Ireland, I'll buy a few of the Irish papers. I do a column for one of them, but I can't remember its name.

Jack Charlton, 1994

One advantage of being manager of Northern Ireland is, because I live in England, I don't see the papers. They offered to send me cuttings, but I said no thanks.

Lawrie McMenemy, 1998

We are described as the team of mercenary multi-millionaires – a club where nobody even speaks English.

Gianluca Vialli bridling at newspaper stories about his Chelsea players, 1998

I don't know whether to seek political asylum or settle for an ordinary old-fashioned asylum.

Scotland boss Willie Ormond as the press homed in on stories about Jimmy Johnstone's late-night revelry near the team hotel, 1974

Reporters have a job to do. They have to ferret out information, and I acknowledge that if they find out anything then it is their duty to print it. My job as a club manager is to ensure there is nothing to ferret out within our club.

Queens Park Rangers' Gordon Jago, 1972

Events conspired to push me out of things at Tottenham. They tried to take my life; they didn't. They tried to take my brains; they couldn't. It was trial by press. I don't wish that on any person.

David Pleat on the allegations about his private life which had brought about his 1987 resignation from Spurs, 1994

I have told my players never to believe what I say about them in the papers.

Graham Taylor at Aston Villa, 1988

You people, you never check your facts. Only three of my teams have gone down out of seven.

Alan Ball defending his management record as he took over struggling Portsmouth, 1998. Against all the odds, he kept them up

A Bengal tiger could not do that.

Graeme Souness rejecting claims in a libel case against a newspaper that he tried to dominate his ex-wife Danielle, 1994

Former players have always had a pop. When that happens I am always disappointed. Most of them have tried the job of managing and failed. Now they know all the answers to the questions. Maybe they are in need of a few bob to say these things.

Roy Evans reacting to criticism from ex-Liverpool players Mark Lawrenson and Jan Molby, 1998

We are like Unicef at the moment – everyone is feeding off us. The ones who really get to me are the ex-players who are out of work and jump into the media to have a go at us.

Leeds' Howard Wilkinson responding to criticism, 1994

Some of today's writers who were once professional players seem to have grown sour with old age.

Fulham's Alec Stock, 1972

The game needs stimulating, not slating.

Middlesbrough's Stan Anderson, 1972

If I walked on water, my accusers would say it is because I can't swim.

Berti Vogts, coach of Germany, 1996

I might see out my contract just to kick the press in the balls.

Javier Clemente holding firm after Spain's shock 3–2 defeat at the hands of Cyprus, 1998. He quit shortly afterwards

Now that the bad guy in this film is going, I hope the press begins to get behind the players. I've still got the knife wounds from all the people I trusted but who stabbed me in the back. This has been a persecution with long knives. Some of you didn't deserve to be born.

Javier Clemente announcing his departure from the Spain job, 1998

They can't take your house away from you. They can't take your family away from you. They cannot come along with big sticks and batter you. All they can say is 'You're not a very good manager', and, one day, you might have to accept that.

Coventry's Gordon Strachan on press coverage, 1998

I've asked all the players in the squad to read the book, and I hope they find it a good read.

England coach Glenn Hoddle trying to boost sales of his controversial World Cup diary, 1998

At the end of the day, none of these people at this moment in time have read the book, so I think when you read the book in the context of everything, I think you'll understand where the situation falls.

Glenn Hoddle launches a dual attack on the English language and the press as the fuss intensifies over the *Sun*'s serialisation of his book, 1998

I've been accused of a lack of passion. I can't win. If I go the other way, I'm called too passionate and I've lost my head.

Glenn Hoddle finding himself, like England, in a no-win situation, 1998

If they want to say I'm sleeping on the moon, that doesn't worry me.

Glenn Hoddle ruining a *Sunday Sport* exclusive, 1998

These people are going out of their way to invent stories and make this job almost an impossible job.

Glenn Hoddle refuting press stories alleging a post-match row with captain Alan Shearer, 1998

Years ago, reporters would always come back to you to check a story. Now they don't because they are afraid you will knock it down. They'd rather run with it, true or false.

Terry Venables, 1996

They can smell the blood of an Englishman, and in this case the Englishman's name is Taylor.

Graham Taylor, under pressure before England's European Championships qualifier in Poland, 1991

I get letters from Princess Di thanking me for taking her out of the headlines.

Long-suffering Graham Taylor, 1993

I'm beginning to wonder what bloody vegetable grows in Norway.

Graham Taylor after SWEDES 2 TURNIPS 1 and SPANISH 1 ONIONS 0 headlines, 1992

That nickname still sticks now. It might have been funny at the time, but once you are called something like that, anything goes.

Watford's Graham Taylor on the never-ending turnip jibes, originally instigated by the Sun, 1998

Whatever people say about me, they can never accuse me of avoiding the media. Maybe I said too much while I was in charge of England, but I never ducked the issue.

Graham Taylor, 1998

I will not let these people get to me or rattle me. They have no qualifications. They have never been anywhere or done anything in football. Why should I listen to them?

Bobby Robson under siege from certain sections of the press, 1988

At times I wondered whether there was some sort of conspiracy to undermine any chance we had of doing well.

Bobby Robson on press criticism of his England selections and tactics during the World Cup, 1990

I was just a victim of the tabloid newspaper war. I had watched this cancer spread over the eight years I had been in the job. It was ugly and damaging.

Bobby Robson stepping down from the England job, 1990

You go into a press room and there's 250 journalists from all different countries. You've got fifty tape recorders on your desk, and that's just the front row. There's five or six camera crews all filming live, so if you stumble on a word it's all on tape.

Bobby Robson, 1989

Hitler didn't tell us when he was going to send over those doodlebugs, did he?

Bobby Robson refusing media requests to announce his team in advance of the World Cup qualifier in Sweden, 1989

When I came down the tunnel after walking round, my overcoat was covered in spittle. I had Jimmy Hill sticking a microphone under my nose and asking if there was any point in us going on the summer tour. Eight days later we won 2–0 against Brazil in the Maracana!

Bobby Robson recalling the dark days in 1984 of England's home defeat by the Soviet Union, 1998

If there's a prat in the world, he's the prat.

Alex Ferguson on Jimmy Hill after the BBC pundit criticised Manchester United's Eric Cantona for appearing to stamp on John Moncur of Swindon Town, 1994

The BBC are dying for us to lose. Everyone is from Liverpool with a supporter's badge. They will be at our games every week until we lose, that mob – Bob, Barry, Hansen, the lot of them. That's what will drive us on.

Alex Ferguson pursuing his theme of BBC bias, 1994

The so-called experts, the muppets off the television, said they would rather watch paint dry than watch Southampton play, and that was after about four or five games. I got a little bit annoyed about that.

Southampton's David Jones, 1998

If I go to a match in Europe in mid-week, I come back to a stack of videos and I can hardly be bothered. What's going on in *Coronation Street* is what I want to know.

England's Graham Taylor, ground down by saturation football coverage on television, 1992

Television saturation is driving the fans away.

Cardiff City's Jimmy Scoular, 1972

I'm against any rehearsing and always refuse to do it. I've also refused to have Bob Wilson talking about managerial problems, not when I'm on anyway. He's a player and he knows nothing about management.

Brian Clough, a frequently outspoken guest on the BBC soccer panels of the 1970s

I came home once and watched a recording of a sports programme I'd been on and I thought, bloody hell, that's not me, is it? What a big-headed, dogmatic bastard. So next time I tried to calm down. It meant they got themselves a crappy interview.

Brian Clough, 1970s

Suddenly I was depicted as a champagne-swigging, cigar-smoking Jack-the-lad who could hardly move his body because it was weighted down by gold trinkets.

Birmingham's jewellery quarter, Ron Atkinson, reflecting on the surge of media interest when he took over at West Bromwich Albion, 1984

When I'm watching football on the television and the editor suddenly cuts to a shot of the coach sat on the bench, it strikes me as an absurd and irritating interruption – even if it's me!

Real Madrid's camera-shy Jorge Valdano, 1995

When we won the semi-final of the European Cup, I remember Kenneth Wolstenholme saying: 'We've made it!' We became British that night . . .

Former Celtic boss Jock Stein reliving the memories of Lisbon, 1970s

We gave the TV people every cooperation to present a serious picture of how we are trying to solve the problem of crowd behaviour. But they tried to crucify the club.

Millwall's Gordon Jago in the wake of a controversial *Panorama* programme, 1977

I don't want people to think of me as a hooligan . . . I say things others think.

Leyton Orient's John Sitton after a TV documentary about the club portrayed him as highly confrontational, 1994

It's my responsibility to select the Romanian team. Reporters have no part in the decision-making process. Although the media are entitled to their opinions, they appear to think they are all-powerful and can pull my strings like a puppet.

Romanian coach Anghel Iordanescu, 1994

Why should they be bothered with interviews at eighteen years of age? Ask any parent if they would be happy having their boy the focus of newspaper and magazine articles and personal appearances to open shops. They don't want all that.

Alex Ferguson protecting his Manchester United fledglings, 1992

We don't want anyone taking horrible little pictures through windows or hanging around the gates day and night.

Middlesbrough's Bryan Robson urging privacy for Gazza during his stay in an addiction clinic, 1998

You must be fucking joking.

Alf Ramsey, renowned for his dislike of the Scots, after being told 'Welcome to Scotland' by a Scottish journalist when the England team landed at Prestwick airport, 1967

Yes. There was a band playing outside our hotel till five o'clock this morning. We were promised a motor-cycle escort to the stadium. It never arrived. When our players went out to inspect the pitch, they were abused and jeered by the crowd. I would have thought the Mexican public would have been delighted to welcome England . . . But we are delighted to be in Mexico, and the Mexican people are a wonderful people.

The ever-diplomatic Alf Ramsey, asked whether he had anything to say to the Mexican press after a goalless draw in Mexico, 1969

This is my day off.

Alf Ramsey declining to talk to reporters on the Sunday after England won the World Cup, 1966

Are you taking the piss?

Alf Ramsey on being thanked by a journalist for press cooperation during the World Cup, 1966

9 The Sack

If you're a manager, you don't have fitted carpets.

John Barnwell, ex-Peterborough, Walsall, 1990s

There are only two types of manager: those who've been sacked and those who will be sacked in the future.

Leeds United's Howard Wilkinson, a week before he joined the list, 1996

There are only two certainties in life. People die, and football managers get the sack.

Republic of Ireland manager Eoin Hand, 1980

In the last ten months, 33 League clubs have changed managers. The directors have power without responsibility. The government should issue a health warning to managers: the only certain thing is the sack.

Johnny Giles quitting West Bromwich Albion, 1977

There have been better managers than me sacked, but now I am just a statistic – the 543rd manager to be sacked since the war.

David Pleat leaving Leicester and showing the effect of doing too many commentaries with John Motson, 1991

If you survive the first few years, then you are more equipped to survive more revolutions. But if you are knocked off early, you don't survive.

David Pleat at Luton likening soccer management to a carousel, 1994

In football, everyone believes the inevitable is that you get the sack. I am always trying to hold off the inevitable by giving hope for the future.

David Pleat, 1994

You're not a real manager unless you've been sacked.

Malcolm Allison speaking from experience, 1990s

We need to ensure the basic security of the manager's post. How often do you see managers who have poured their energies into setting up a youth policy not being allowed the time to exploit that work? If you give him a cast-iron contract, then he has a chance.

Terry Venables at Crystal Palace, 1976

I've walked the tightrope now for six seasons and I know that one day I'm going to fall off.

Charlton's Lennie Lawrence, 1989

Players get you the sack.

Sheffield United's Dave Bassett, 1991

The great thing about football management is you know when you sign a contract that the only thing missing is the date of your sacking.

Tommy Docherty, 1981

There are 92 clubs in the Football League, but there can only be one which finishes at the top of the First Division. They have succeeded, but it doesn't mean that the others have failed. If winning the Championship was the only yardstick, 91 managers would get the sack every season.

Tommy Docherty, 1970s

I've been punished for falling in love.

Tommy Docherty on being sacked from Manchester United after revealing that he was having an affair with Mary Brown, wife of club physiotherapist Laurie Brown, 1977

How's the wife?

Tommy Docherty's mischievous enquiry to 69-year-old Altrincham physio Jeff Warburton on arriving at the club, 1987

Preston. They're one of my old clubs. But then most of them are. I've had more clubs than Jack Nicklaus.

Tommy Docherty, 1979

They offered me a handshake of £10,000 to settle amicably. I told them they would have to be more amicable than that.

Tommy Docherty on his departure from Preston, 1981

When one door opens, another smashes you in the face.

Tommy Docherty, 1981

I've had to swap my Merc for a BMW, I'm down to my last 37 suits and I'm drinking non-vintage champagne.

Ron Atkinson forced to live in reduced circumstances after his sacking by Manchester United, 1986

I have been let down sadly and savagely by weak men I feel should have been stronger.

Ron Atkinson after getting the push from Sheffield Wednesday, 1998

Sheffield Wednesday have still not told me I'm not their manager.

Ron Atkinson, three months after his successor, Danny Wilson, took over at Hillsborough, 1998

Jesus was such an unpredictable man, he wanted to win everything. He was sometimes charming, one of the boys almost, but would then criticise everyone and everything. You'd be talking or eating with him, all as nice as pie, and then you'd pick up the papers the next day and could barely believe what he was saying in them.

Former Atlético Madrid manager Colin Addison recalling his 1989 sacking by club president Jesus Gil, 1996

You'd think taking a club from eighteenth to third in three months was good enough.

Ron Atkinson, smarting at his sacking by Atlético Madrid, 1989

I see Atlético just sacked another manager before the season has even started. He must have had a bad photocall.

Ron Atkinson, 1995

I can see now why Terry Venables wants to buy his own club.

Don Howe, sacked by Queens Park Rangers, 1991

Even all Dad's sackings didn't deter me.

Alan Ball, 1994

I've been punished for being enthusiastic about the game.

Roy McDonough of Ryman Leaguers Heybridge Swifts, sacked for his and his players' poor disciplinary record, 1998. Sent off 21 times in his own career, McDonough saw his Heybridge team have 6 men sent off and 33 booked during his 11 games in charge. McDonough had also been handed a nine-month ban by the FA after twice being asked to leave the dugout

How can they sack me? It's not fair.

Ruud Gullit learning of his shock sacking from Chelsea, 1998

Alex Ferguson must be having a field day. The Chelsea board have killed off the only challenge to Manchester United.

Ruud Gullit on his enforced departure from Stamford Bridge, 1998

I was arrogant. I felt like King Canute.

John Sitton speculating on why he may have got the sack from Leyton Orient, 1994

That is what I am supposed to say, but I was given only the one option.

Chester City's John Sainty reacting to a club statement which said that he had left by mutual consent, 1983

Those senior players – fellas like Giles, Bremner, Hunter, Madeley, Lorimer – they sold themselves short. They turned out to be very sensitive about criticisms and home truths. I had thrown a few barbs at them over the years and I meant every one, but I thought the slate would be wiped clean on both sides. How could I know they would be so sensitive? They hadn't conveyed much sensitivity on the field. I thought that was something Don had erased from their lives.

Brian Clough on his unhappy spell at Leeds, 1975

I think it is a very sad day for Leeds and for football.

Brian Clough on the termination of his 44-day reign at Leeds, 1974

Wales are a laughing stock, a joke.

Terry Yorath after being harshly sacked by Wales, 1993

Look at Carlos Alberto Parreira. Four years ago, he was the most important man in world football, having won the Cup with Brazil. Two World Cup final matches later, this time in charge of Saudi Arabia, he loses his job after a game in which he has a player sent off against the host nation in front of 80,000 fanatics.

Bobby Robson, once sacked by Fulham, on the increasing perils of soccer management, 1998

It's because I have asked the players to train twice a day and they wanted to train three times a week.

Saudi Arabia's Dutch coach Leo Beenhakker citing player power as the reason for his dismissal from the Middle East hot-seat, 1994

I was at home watching the Louise Woodward case on television when I turned on Ceefax and read that I had been sacked.

Queens Park Rangers' assistant manager Bruce Rioch, 1997

When the chairman asked to see me, I thought I was going to get a contract.

Mike Walker, sacked from Colchester when the team was top of Division Four, 1987

That's a home win and an away draw inside four days. We've only got one more game in November and, if we win that, I'm in grave danger of ending up as manager of the month.

If things carry on like this, if we end up in mid-table and in the FA Cup final, then they'll have to ask him not to bother coming. They'll have to sack him.

There can be few managers who have lost their job after seven consecutive victories.

With the new reward of three points, two victories can suddenly put you in the reckoning for Europe. And two defeats can put your job on the line.

I told the chairman to back me or sack me. He sacked me.

I don't understand it. We did everything right in training, but yesterday every time they came near our goal they scored. I'm very disappointed. I still think I'm a good manager.

I was given the sack at 9.30 in the morning, but I didn't leave the ground until 5.30. I loved the job, you see, and I wanted to savour the last few hours.

Where does a big-name manager get you? In Southampton's case, a load of foreign imports and the wrong end of the table.

In the end you get what you deserve, don't you? So will Souness and Southampton.

Dave Merrington, still smarting at being sacked from The Dell, 1997

Graham Turner said I was the man to succeed him. He thought he was doing me a favour, but it turned out quite the reverse.

Billy McNeill, sacked after eight months at Aston Villa,
from *Back to Paradise* (Mainstream, 1988)

I love being manager of Arsenal. They have always let me get on with doing the job, with no interference.

George Graham, 1992

Rumours of my impending resignation have proved somewhat premature.

George Graham's programme notes on the day he was sacked by Arsenal, 1995

After eight and a half years, they sacked me in two minutes.

George Graham bemoaning the manner of his exit from Highbury, 1995

To be told in ten minutes, after eighteen years at a club, is hard to accept.

Steve Gritt, dismissed by Charlton, 1995

A lot of people thought I was just a slippery Cockney boy with a few jokes. It has taken one of the biggest clubs in the world to acknowledge what I can do.

Terry Venables preening himself at Barcelona, 1987

I am not disappointed to be given what they call the sack for the first time in my life. Strangely, although I always thought such a situation would be upsetting, I find it interesting.

Terry Venables, kicked out by Barcelona, 1987

I always believe in my boys. It would be easy just to fall to pieces, but we have a lot of things to look forward to. The future looks very rosy.

Ossie Ardiles at Spurs, 1994. He didn't see out the year

I will definitely be in charge for the next two matches.

There is certainly a buzz of excitement around the Bridge . . . I'm really optimistic about our chances this season.

I will live or die by my actions. Time will tell if I make the right ones.

With this squad I feel we have got something to build on, something very strong.

I leave Maine Road with my conscience clear. The club are in a far healthier position than when I arrived, both financially as well as from a playing point of view . . . What do they want?

There is no way I will resign. I have never run away from a fight in my life and I'm not going to start now.

I didn't walk out deflated, feeling I was a failure. I walked out with my head held high and thought I had done a good job.

It's not playing the last post, is it?

I won't pack it in. They will have to shoot me to get rid of me.

I did not stick to my principles of building a side. My first priority has always been to get it right at the back, and I neglected that. The prospect of having Robbo in the side blinded me.

Peter Taylor, sacked by Derby after building his team around the mercurial talents of winger John Robertson, 1984

The chairman has told me I've got a contract with him for life.

Fulham's Bobby Campbell, shortly before getting the sack, 1980

I had dinner with Mark on Saturday night and he told me my job was safe.

Charlton's Ken Craggs, 24 hours before being sacked by chairman Mark Hulyer, 1982

There's been a lot of speculation about my position at Old Trafford, some of it going as far as to link Howard Kendall with my job. But I mean to be here, making a success of things, three years from now.

Alex Ferguson during his troubled early years at Manchester United, 1989

I know that my vultures are out there.

Wales manager Bobby Gould after the Manic Street Preachers changed the chorus of 'Everything Must Go' to 'Bobby Gould Must Go' at a Cardiff concert, 1998

If we'd lost it would have been different. They were all circling. Even now they're only resting their wings for a few weeks.

Republic of Ireland boss Mick McCarthy on critics who were calling for his head before the European Championships qualifier victory over Croatia, 1998

I told him my fingernails are bloody but I am clinging to the precipice.

Bobby Gould, hanging on, and finding time to wish Glenn Hoddle good luck, 1998

I'll tell you why I've survived these six years – because I don't get beaten too many times. If you don't succeed, it's not long before the death-rattle comes.

Tranmere Rovers' John King, 1994

It's not something I lie awake about, but I am certainly not naïve enough to believe that it can't happen to me.

Nottingham Forest's Frank Clark contemplating the sack two weeks before his departure, 1996

I want us to have won some games before it takes place, otherwise it will be somebody else spending the money.

Forest's Frank Clark on the impending takeover of the club, 1996

I felt like a turkey waiting for Christmas. As soon as the club got new owners, I was going to be out like a shot.

Frank Clark preferring to resign before he was pushed, 1996

Nice day for an execution.

Frank O'Farrell eyeing the blue sky on the morning of his sacking from Manchester United, 1972

The pressure on the players in trying to keep me in the job was too much for them.

Walsall's Tommy Coakley, 1988

When I went to tell the players this morning, they were in tears.

Steve Wicks receiving an emotional farewell from Scarborough, 1994

My heart is broken.

Ossie Ardiles' heart entering the same state as his English on being axed by Newcastle, 1992

I've been out of short trousers for a long time now and I'm not going to say this is the worst day of my life.

Fashion guru Kenny Dalglish leaving Newcastle, 1998

It was like a death in the family.

Jim Smith getting the chop from Birmingham City, 1982

I think about the sack all the time. It's my biggest worry. Having a job like this is like loving a beautiful woman and fearing to lose her. If you're sacked by a top club you can drop down a division and try again. But from Mansfield, there aren't many places lower to go.

Mansfield's Andy King baring his soul, 1994. A year later, his love affair ended

Kristine's gone shopping as usual and I've gone to the Job Centre looking for new employment. Funny ol' game, innit?

Barry Fry's answerphone message after his dismissal from Birmingham, 1996

It's sod's law. Now I've got time to improve my golf, it's the wrong time of year.

Howard Wilkinson, sacked by Leeds, 1996

I'm here to help Ian. I'm here to add my experience.

Lawrie McMenemy offering his wealth of knowledge to assist the beleaguered Ian Branfoot at Southampton, 1994. Three weeks later, Branfoot was sacked

Things were so bad I received a letter from *Reader's Digest* saying I hadn't been included in their prize draw.

John McGrath, sacked by Halifax Town, 1993

10 The Board

Michael Knighton, the chairman, has now got the manager he deserves.

Ousted Carlisle United boss Mervyn Day on Knighton's decision to assume the dual roles of chairman and manager at the club, 1997

If they look into my background, they might not find 400 League games, but they will find a football person.

Carlisle manager/chairman Michael Knighton, 1998

It may not be the job for me. I may be the first manager to sack himself.

Lincoln City's John Reames on joining the ranks of manager/chairmen, 1998

I would rather spend one day on my feet than a lifetime on my knees.

Luis Aragones walking out of Spanish club Real Betis, 1998

I'm furious, flabbergasted and bewildered. It's ludicrous what the board have done . . . it's me and the players now against the world.

Norwich City's Gary Megson after chairman Robert Chase had sold two key players in order to reduce the club's overdraft, 1996

He doesn't know a goal-line from a clothes-line.

Plain-speaking Barry Fry on Birmingham City owner David Sullivan, 1994

You wouldn't treat a dog the way I've been treated.

John Bond leaving Birmingham City, 1987

The Villa chairman, Doug Ellis, said he was right behind me. I told him I'd sooner have him in front of me where I could see him.

Tommy Docherty trying to keep an eye on Deadly Doug, 1970

Doug Ellis told me, 'Tommy, we've given you a vote of confidence.' I said, 'Thanks, chairman, I'll pack my bags and clear out now.'

Tommy Docherty leaving Villa, 1970

I found him absolutely impossible.

Billy McNeill with few fond memories of Doug Ellis during his brief tenure at Villa Park, 1987

He revels in being known as Deadly, perhaps in the misguided belief that it conjures up the image of a powerful football figure able to deal ruthlessly with whoever crosses his path.

Former Villa boss Ron Atkinson weighing in with his thoughts on chairman Doug, 1998

It wouldn't matter if it was Frankenstein and Dracula offering me a job, I just wanted the chance to prove myself.

Brighton's Steve Gritt working for reviled chairman and chief executive Bill Archer and David Bellotti, 1997

There wouldn't be a Barnet Football Club without Stan. I love him, but he's evil.

Barry Fry complimenting Barnet chairman Stan Flashman, 1991

If you didn't know him, you'd think he was an absolute ignorant pig. He is, in many ways, but he does care for the club.

Barry Fry, still struggling to express his true feelings for Stan Flashman, 1992

It's quite difficult dealing with Mr Flashman because if you speak your mind he tends to sack you. I've been sacked three times now.

Fry's assistant at Barnet, Edwin Stein, 1992

He's sacked me at least twenty times and he's meant it. But I have just got up the next morning, gone to the ground and got on with my work, and he's phoned up two or three days later as if nothing has happened. There is going to be a time when he sacks me and really means it.

Barry Fry on Stan Flashman, from *Season in the Cold* by Ian
Ridley (Kingswood Press, 1992)

I'm absolutely gutted, I'm devastated. The man is a complete and utter shit.

**Barry Fry, sacked for the final time by Flashman a
month later, 1992**

If I heard that at club level I would be worried.

**England manager Ron Greenwood on receiving a
personal vote of confidence from Dick Wragg, chairman
of the FA's international committee, 1981**

It's no good me walking out. I am not Kevin Keegan. They would not come rushing to the gates and drag me back. They would push me through them!

**Crystal Palace's Alan Smith on his volatile relationship
with chairman Ron Noades, 1994**

I don't really know if I've got any money to spend and I've no plans to see the chairman. The way things are going here, he's the one who will probably want to see me.

Alan Smith, 1994

A bigger Bentley for the chairman, I suppose.

**Alan Smith when asked what staying in the Premiership
would mean to Palace, 1995**

I remember Noades turning to me and saying: 'You'll never run the club like you've run it this year. I'm changing it all.' So within an hour and a half of winning the Championship, it had almost been taken away from me.

**Alan Smith, stunned by Ron Noades' reaction to winning
the First Division title in 1994,** from *I Think I'll Manage*
(Headline, 1996)

I had nothing to lose, quite frankly, which also bugged him, I think. I mean, the day I walked out of Palace was not a financial disaster for me, and that probably bugged him.

Alan Smith on Ron Noades, 1996

I feel I am being unfairly stampeded into a corner at a time when I should be getting support and backing from the chairman.

Peter Shilton's financial problems causing more of a chasm than a rift with his Plymouth chairman Dan McCauley, 1995

There's a seven-man board at Derby and I wouldn't give you tuppence for five of them.

Brian Clough, 1972

You could never get much sense out of the directors there. One director was a self-appointed boardroom spy who used to go round the club checking up on people to see if they were enjoying extras.

Tommy Docherty on the Derby County board, 1979

The ideal board of directors should be made up of three men: two dead and the other dying.

Tommy Docherty, 1977

He likes publicity. He wears a card round his neck saying, 'In case of heart attack, call a press conference.'

Tommy Docherty on Manchester City chairman Peter Swales, 1982

His appointment is bizarre. Why didn't Swales just go to France and get Mickey Mouse? He's a personality who would get the crowds back and give them a laugh. Football is a professional business. How can you put an amateur in a position like that?

Malcolm Allison on Peter Swales' controversial appointment of former journalist John Maddock as Manchester City's general manager, 1993

I could find a better chairman than Swales. I think he's past it. He's over the bloody hill. Hey, I didn't think he was good enough to get the job in the first place.

Brian Clough after Peter Swales had said that it was too late for him (Clough) to become England manager, 1992

When you win they shower you with gifts, and when you lose they ignore you.

Terry Venables experiencing the fickle nature of the Barcelona directors after the club's exit from the European Cup, 1986

I know that I've never had a fantastic relationship with board members . . . There's one thing no board can ever take away from me, and that's my experience, which gives me the right to think.

Outspoken Barcelona coach Johan Cruyff, 1995

Football today is too big a job to be a director's hobby.

Arsenal's Herbert Chapman, 1934

After I'd made sure my family were safe, I went to the players' lounge and told them to get out, quick. I then went back up to the boardroom where I had a slanging match with a Lincoln City director who told me to stop swearing in front of his wife. I said, 'Suit yourself. Stay here and die.'

Former Bradford City boss Terry Yorath recalling painful memories of the Valley Parade fire nine years earlier, 1994

My chairman, Robert Maxwell, they ought to let him run football.

Jim Smith, when manager of Oxford United, 1983

There are some things that baffle me about the bloke – like why he loves seeing his mug across the back pages, because Robert Redford he ain't.

Brian Clough on Maxwell, 1987

He even came in the dugout with me once. But he only lasted ten minutes before all the cursing and swearing got to him.

Jim Smith on that renowned shrinking violet Robert Maxwell, his former chairman at Oxford, 1990

I've seen him drop his trousers and stand on the bar and sing when he's had a few drinks.

Jim Smith, this time thankfully not about Maxwell but about Bill Bancroft, his chairman at Blackburn Rovers in the mid-1970s, from *Bald Eagle* (Mainstream, 1990)

Will I go out for dinner with him as I did on previous occasions? The answer is probably no.

Martin O'Neill playing hard to get with Leicester City chairman John Elsom, who had refused to allow O'Neill to talk to Leeds, 1998

I don't normally bother going up to the boardroom after a game, but I think I will after this Cup tie. It would be nice to speak with the Leeds directors at last.

Martin O'Neill before Leicester's Worthington Cup tie with Leeds, 1998

I won't be going up to the boardroom.

George Graham before taking his Tottenham team back to his old club Arsenal, 1998

The fans will remember who won the trophies, not who was on the board.

George Graham, 1998

Of course I wanted to go to Iran, but I'm staying at Brighton to do a job. I'm not saying I'm happy here.

Brian Clough falling out with the Brighton board, who had stopped him taking up an offer to manage the Iranian national side, 1974. In July he left Brighton anyway for Leeds

I'm a better man because of what happened at Leeds . . . I don't have to worry about one little twerp on a board having the power to rule my life.

Brian Clough, 1975

Could I have that in writing?

**Brian Clough on being told by his former employer,
Leeds chairman Manny Cussins, that his Nottingham
Forest team deserved a draw instead of defeat at Elland
Road, 1977**

I decide who plays. I'd rather lose in my own way in front of
80,000 spectators and a hundred million television viewers than
lose in the minister's way. And even if you lose with a team
picked by the minister, it's still the coach's fault.

**Nigeria's Dutch coach Jo Bonfrere on interference in
team selection from Nigeria's Minister of Sport, 1996**

I'm worried that Sir Jack's going to want to play.

**Wolves' Mark McGhee as 74-year-old club owner Sir
Jack Hayward left hospital after heart surgery to fly
across the Atlantic to attend the Cup semi-final with
Arsenal, 1998**

I feel I have been undermined in front of my players and
everyone else. The day I stop choosing who I buy and who I sell
is the day I am not managing a football club any more. I'm not
a mug, and I don't need a job that badly that I'll let people walk
all over me.

**Harry Redknapp in a row with the West Ham board over
the sale of Andy Impey, 1998**

I refuse to have players at the club that I don't want.

**Bobby Charlton resigning from Preston over a dispute
with the board about transfers, 1975**

If I get any hassle, I'll walk away from it.

**John Toshack accepting the Wales job, 1994.
Forty-seven days later, he quit**

I'm ready to throw in the towel. Instead of doing their job, the
directors are making statements on television and to the
newspapers.

John Toshack at Turkish club Besiktas, 1998

248

I knock every day on the boardroom door and hope for positive signs from the directors.

Ruud Gullit brandishing the begging-bowl for new players a month into his reign at Newcastle, 1998

When I joined East Stirling, with about two or three weeks to go to the start of the season, I said to the chairman: 'Could I see your player file?' . . . It was then that I discovered he only had eight players! I said: 'Mr Chairman, you know you need eleven players to start a bloody game of football?'

Alex Ferguson, from *A Year in the Life: The Manager's Diary* (Virgin, 1995)

I had to ask the directors' permission to stick a twopenny stamp on a letter.

Derby County's Tim Ward, following his sacking, 1967

The directors would tell you on a Friday night that they hadn't got enough money for the wages, so you'd do what you could to top them up. My chairman, Father Young, would put the collar on and we'd go out collecting. He'd call one or two favours in.

Notts County's Sam Allardyce remembering his first managerial job at Limerick, 1998

Someone asked me what Sam Hammam was doing on the track. He was saying: 'For God's sake, Joe, tell them not to score any more goals – I can't afford the bonus!'

Joe Kinnear enjoying a dig at club owner Sam Hammam following Wimbledon's 4–2 win at Chelsea, 1996

Sam said I could bring in two new faces, so I asked him for Jack Walker and Sir John Hall.

Joe Kinnear, 1997

Sam told us that if we don't make Wembley, he will take us to a Chekhov play every night for a week, then for another Lebanese meal. So we've got to get to Wembley now.

Joe Kinnear before Wimbledon's Coca-Cola Cup semi-final defeat against Leicester, 1997

Their chairman did no credit at all to the club. He wrote absolute filth all over the wall.

West Ham's Billy Bonds bridling at Sam Hammam's graffiti, 1993

My row with the directors has gone right to the heart of football's greatest problem. It has been about money – the need for it and the balancing of it against such assets as young players. My directors insisted we sold Ian Mellor to Norwich. They are responsible for the club and I am not going to resign.

Malcolm Allison in strife at Manchester City, 1973. Three weeks later, he left to join struggling Crystal Palace

We've never had any money. Somebody said we were going to sign a player from Huddersfield for £200,000 and the chairman fell off his chair.

Bury's Neil Warnock, 1998

The only money Forest directors cough up is when they buy a golden goal ticket.

Brian Clough, 1987

The chairman is very watchful of the purse-strings. If we get into Europe, we'll be the only club that travels to Poland and back in one day.

Oldham's Joe Royle, 1994

There are eight gentlemen in the boardroom absolutely delighted because it's as good as another home draw with a full house to us. We're going to make some money and, if we're not careful, we're going to be solvent in six months.

Exeter City's Terry Cooper after holding Norwich to a draw in the FA Cup, thus earning a lucrative replay at Carrow Road, 1990

They've been loyal to me. When I came here they said there would be no money, and they've kept their promise.

Dave Bassett on the Sheffield United board, 1993

Sir John Hall was a multi-millionaire when I came back to Newcastle. With all the players I've bought, I'm trying to make him just an ordinary millionaire.

Kevin Keegan, 1994

I'm sorry I'm not here at the moment. If you are the president of AC Milan, Barcelona or Real Madrid, I'll get back to you.

The answerphone message of Wimbledon's Joe Kinnear, 1990s

I love the work, but in the boardroom you never know what reaction you'll get – win, lose or draw.

Rochdale boss Graham Barrow, 1997

I had told the directors on Thursday that I was going – win, lose or draw.

Dumbarton's Jim Fallon resigning after a 5–0 defeat by Livingston, 1996

It's a bloody stupid colour. I think one of the directors' wives must have chosen it.

David Pleat on Luton's orange away strip, 1992

The chairman is new to football. He's having to learn what I learnt at fifteen.

Trevor Francis on QPR chairman Richard Thompson, 1989

There is no sign of the chairman, but since we have not seen him we have only lost once.

Jan Molby as Swansea's temporary upturn in fortunes coincides with the absence of chairman Doug Sharpe, 1996

I'm past the Kenny Dalglish stage. I've gone potty. I've been there and I'm coming back.

Terry Venables on his long-drawn-out battle to buy Spurs, 1991

I have deliberately not consulted Terry about the chairman. I want to keep an open mind.

George Graham on why he did not ask pal Terry Venables about his old adversary Alan Sugar before taking the Tottenham job, 1998

When I first came to Crewe in 1983 I asked the directors what they expected of me as manager. They said that if we finished fifth from bottom – in the old Fourth Division – they would give me a contract for next season.

Dario Gradi, still at Crewe, from *The Boss* (Vista, 1997)

That's how they were at Portman Road, very civilised. When we were bottom of the table they called me in and offered me a new contract.

Bobby Robson on the gentlemanly Ipswich board, from *Bobby Robson: Against the Odds* (Stanley Paul, 1990)

Mr John's idea of a boardroom crisis was when they ran short of white wine after a game.

Bobby Robson on former Ipswich chairman John Cobbold, affectionately known as 'Mr John', 1990

Not going to Goodison Park was one of the best decisions I ever made.

Bobby Robson, happy to reject overtures from Everton and stay with his Ipswich board, 1979

When the directors said to me, 'Do the things you think are right', that was good enough for me. The board meets once a month. It is a lovely, uncomplicated club.

John Lyall being introduced to the charms of Ipswich, 1990

There's so much class in our boardroom that some of them call the Queen 'mate'.

Southampton's Lawrie McMenemy, 1970s

He regularly let the players go shopping in Libya at his expense after a good result and ferried them there in his presidential plane.

David Otti, Uganda national coach in the 1970s and sole member of the Idi Amin fan club, 1996

I said to the directors, 'Be fair and honest with me over my salary and that's all I ask.' They offered £12,500 a year and I agreed. I went into the ground for the first time on 22 October 1981. In the evening I took all the players' contracts back to my hotel, went through the lot of them, and found that two players were on £150 more per week than I was. I phoned the chairman and told him he'd have my resignation in the morning because the board had been dishonest with me. I got an increase!

Bobby Gould recalling his arrival at Bristol Rovers, from *The Boss* (Vista, 1997)

I made a promise to the chairman that I would take the club out of the Second Division. I did. I took it straight into the Third.

Tommy Docherty keeping his word at Rotherham, 1968

Jim explained what powers I would have in thirty seconds: none. It took me another fifteen seconds to realise I had to go.

Tommy Docherty on his 28-day reign at Queens Park Rangers, highlighted by problems with chairman Jim Gregory, 1968

He'd had lots of problems and lots of managers. So when I got there, he put the back of his hand under his chin and said: 'I'm up to here with that managerial nonsense – you get on with it.'

Terry Venables on QPR chairman Jim Gregory, from *The Best Game in the World* (Century, 1996)

I said, 'If you pull that deal off, I'll kiss your backside.' He said, 'If I pull this one off you might have to kiss it in the middle of Piccadilly Circus.'

David Webb on an exchange with Ken Bates over the Chelsea chairman's plan to swap Mick Harford for Luton's Phil Gray, 1993. Luckily for Webb, the deal fell through

Compared to my chairman at Southend, Ken Bates is Mary Poppins.

Chelsea's David Webb, 1993

Sorry. There is only one person at this club with an ego, and it certainly isn't me. I don't need one.

I told the chairman Rome wasn't built in a day. He said, 'I know, but I wasn't on that building site!'

I was absolutely ripe for the England job in 1977. They were wary of me. I was never one for hob-nobbing in boardrooms. They had a sneaking suspicion that I might have tried to run the FA and change a few things. They were worried about that. I had a superb interview and I should have got it. I was spot on that day. They gave it to Ron to quieten things down. But I was the one for the job. They dropped a clanger.

I have never been in love with the directors at Forest or anywhere else ... unfortunately the game attracts a certain percentage of people who are nobodies in their own walk of life and want to become somebodies through football.

Football hooligans? Well, there are 92 club chairmen for a start.

I remember the Liverpool directors leaving the ground in single file, with their shoulders slumped, like a funeral procession.

When I went to see the chairman to tell him, it was like walking to the electric chair.

My nature and that of the chairman will be that we will become stronger for this.

11 The Boss

He's very fortunate to have inherited some very good players.

Malcolm Allison on his successor at Manchester City, John Bond, 1980. City hadn't won a League game all season when Allison was asked to resign in October

It's because of his behaviour, which is little changed from our time together at West Ham in the 1950s, that I can never see Malcolm being a manager in his own right.

John Bond suggesting that Allison would never amount to much without Joe Mercer at his side, 1980

If John Bond is so good, why hasn't he done anything in his previous years as a manager?

Malcolm Allison wouldn't let it lie, 1980

John Bond has blackened my name with his insinuations about the private lives of all football managers. Both my wives are upset.

Malcolm Allison, 1983

I don't regard it as putting one over on City. How can I when I know these lads so well?

Joe Mercer returning to Maine Road to rousing cheers as general manager of victorious Coventry, 1972

Gordon Milne has done a very good job at Coventry.

Malcolm Allison, barracked by Manchester City fans, unable to resist one last dig at his erstwhile partner by placing the credit for Coventry's win at the feet of team manager Gordon Milne, 1972

When Joe Mercer and I were friends, no one in football could live with us. Between us we had it all. I charged into situations like a bull, full of aggressive ambition and a contempt for anyone who might be standing in my way. And Joe came behind me, picking up the pieces, soothing the wounded and the offended with that vast charm.

Malcolm Allison on his partnership with Joe Mercer at Manchester City, from *Colours of My Life* (Everest, 1975)

I know he hates me. He's walked past me on the golf course as if I were a tree. He's the moaningest minnie I've ever known.

John Bond, then at Birmingham, sounding off about Kenny Dalglish, 1987

I don't know what will happen when he goes full-time!

Bobby Robson on the success of Kenny Dalglish as Liverpool's player/manager, 1988

If Kenny Dalglish has resigned because of the pressures of the job, the rest of us have no chance.

Leeds' Howard Wilkinson on Dalglish's departure from Liverpool, 1991

All that big-transfer stuff is just showbiz razzmatazz in many ways. You need to get your basics right. Kenny Dalglish spent seventeen million in the summer and a fat lot of good it did him.

Aston Villa's John Gregory, 1998

Kenny Dalglish has associates, but only a few friends. There's nothing wrong with that because, at the end of the day, you only need six people to carry your coffin.

Alex Ferguson, 1990s

You might as well talk to my [baby] daughter. You'll get more sense out of her.

A Kenny Dalglish aside to a journalist interviewing Alex Ferguson after an acrimonious Liverpool-Manchester United match, 1988

With a record like his in management I would have kept quiet, yet he had the audacity to tell me how I should be doing my work.

Bobby Robson rounding on one of his most vociferous critics, Alan Ball, from *Against The Odds* (Stanley Paul, 1990)

He wasn't much of a manager either.

Bobby Robson responding to yet another tabloid tirade from ex-Rotherham supremo Emlyn Hughes, 1990

He was talking out of jealousy because he's a coach who has never won anything.

Juventus coach Marcello Lippi reacting to claims by Roma's Zdenek Zeman of widespread drug-taking in Italy's Serie A, 1998

If all the managers and players acted like him, knocking each other all the time, then there very soon wouldn't be any game left.

Don Revie, stung by Brian Clough's criticism of his Leeds team, 1973

He is a genius. I just work hard.

Derby's Arthur Cox on his East Midlands neighbour Brian Clough, 1987

I have known Brian for over thirty years, and yet in one way I still don't know him. I've had plenty of kisses from him, but sometimes he can just walk past you. That's Cloughie.

Jack Charlton, 1993

The most amazing man I've ever met. I'm fascinated by him, and whenever I've talked to him, I find things he's said buzzing around in my head while I'm driving home. You find yourself telling your wife about him when you get into bed.

David Pleat on Brian Clough, from *His Way: The Brian Clough Story* by Patrick Murphy (Robson, 1993)

Bugger Cloughie. What about me? I've never won the FA Cup either, you know.

Jim Smith after his Portsmouth team beat Nottingham Forest 1–0 in the sixth round to end Brian Clough's hopes of an elusive FA Cup success for another year, 1992

I was told I would never be as good as Brian Clough, never score as many goals, nor do this or that like Brian Clough – and most of the time it was *him* telling me.

Son Nigel Clough taking over at Burton Albion, 1998

He might come to watch a game or two – so long as he doesn't start shouting from the stands.

Nigel Clough on the chances of dad Brian going for a Burton, 1998

He offered me £500 to take it easy. There were no witnesses. I said no. And when I said no, he asked me if he could approach my players. I said under no circumstances . . . After that match, I lost all respect for Revie.

Bury boss Bob Stokoe claiming that Don Revie tried to bribe him to forfeit a crucial 1962 relegation battle against Leeds, 1977

I hadn't a lucky suit like Don Revie, so I decided I'd come as one of the lads.

Sunderland boss Bob Stokoe, dressing down for the FA Cup final and mocking the superstitions of his old enemy, Don Revie, 1973

He should have been castrated for the way he left England.

Bob Stokoe on Don Revie, 1990

Radomir Antic is just an attention-grabber. He can't stand it if a couple of days go by without his picture being in the papers. And he's too fat. It must be all the beer he drinks.

Spain coach Javier Clemente cutting Atlético Madrid's Antic down to size, 1996

Johan Cruyff isn't worthy of consideration as a coach. He thinks he's a diva.

Clemente on Cruyff, 1989

He's come here from Japan and he's telling English people how to organise our football. He should keep his mouth firmly shut.

Alex Ferguson on Arsène Wenger's criticism of Manchester United's request to play their outstanding Premiership match at Newcastle after all the other fixtures had been completed, 1997

A stubborn bugger.

Brian Clough on Sir Alf Ramsey, 1970s

He was a good manager of a bad team, but a bad manager of a good one.

Malcolm Allison on Sir Alf Ramsey, 1970s

I am the shop front. He is the goods in the back.

Brian Clough on managerial partner Peter Taylor, 1973

Peter looks for and identifies the ability to play a ball, to get a ball, to hold a ball, the ability to fit into a side. Once he is convinced individuals have such talent, I can persuade them to deliver it, and I can persuade them to deliver it a second time when they are knackered.

Brian Clough on Peter Taylor, 1975

In my book Taylor is a rattlesnake. I don't want to see or hear from him again.

Brian Clough on Peter Taylor (then at Derby) over the transfer of John Robertson from Forest to Derby, 1983

We pass each other on the A52 going to work most days of the week. But if his car broke down and I saw him thumbing a lift, I wouldn't pick him up – I'd run him over.

An unforgiving Brian Clough on the split with Peter Taylor, 1983

I worshipped him until the day he took off his boots. Then the barrel-chested giant became, for me, a Tom Thumb in management.

Brian Clough on Dave Mackay, his successor at Derby County, 1976

I'm fed up with him pointing to his grey hairs and saying the England job has aged him ten years. If he doesn't like the seat at Lancaster Gate, why doesn't he go back to his orchard at Ipswich?

Brian Clough taking a swipe at Bobby Robson, 1983

I'm as bad a judge of strikers as Walter Winterbottom – he only gave me two caps.

Brian Clough, 1988

It's not the kind of experience you would wish on anyone. I can think of a lot of managers I would rather it had happened to.

Brian Clough after Nottingham Forest had tanned Bobby Campbell's Chelsea 7–0, 1991

Management is hard – especially for a lad like him brought up on five-star hotels, à la carte menus and vast sums of money.

Brian Clough expressing reservations about Trevor Francis' suitability for his first venture into management with Queens Park Rangers, 1988

He's learning about management now, isn't he? He's just got the sack.

Bobby Robson on Trevor Francis, sacked by Queens Park Rangers, 1990. Robson had earlier been critical of Francis' decision to fine midfielder Martin Allen £1,200 for missing a match in order to be present at the birth of his child

I thought they'd appoint Danny – I don't even know Terry Neill.

Bill Nicholson expressing surprise that Danny Blanchflower was not chosen to be his successor at Tottenham, 1974

Joe is right out of order for criticising us. We have a dodgy past, but everyone seems to have a go at this club.

Millwall's Keith Stevens responding to an attack from Manchester City's Joe Royle, 1998

It was more the majority rather than the minority who were giving the previous manager stick. They were very disappointed at what he was doing, and quite rightly so. I have got the same players that he had and, basically, they can all play. If you take a club as far down as he did, you are going to get trouble.

Hull City's Mark Hateley putting the boot into his predecessor Terry Dolan, 1997. A year later, Hateley-inspired Hull were bottom of the Football League

I wish him all that he wished me when I was in the job!

Manchester City's Ron Saunders on former assistant Tony Book, who succeeded him as manager when Saunders was sacked, 1974

The man spent a million and still can't beat us.

Leyton Orient's Tommy Taylor after a 2–1 win over Ron Noades' Brentford, 1998

His management style seems to be based on the chaos theory.

Wolves' Mark McGhee on his neighbour at Birmingham City, Barry Fry, 1996

The squad I inherited were short on both physical and mental strength, were under-coached and displayed practically no desire to try and appreciate tactics.

Mark McGhee having a go at his Wolves predecessor Graham Taylor, 1996

He attacked three players during the match and at the end he wanted to fight anyone in sight. It was disgraceful. If I'd done that in England, I would be banned for life.

Birmingham's Barry Fry on Ancona coach Massimo Cacciatori, who proved to be no chicken during a stormy Anglo-Italian Cup tie in Italy, 1995

He should try managing Barnet.

Barry Fry, learning of Graeme Souness's heart trouble, 1992

I hear there's a new drink in Glasgow called the Souness. One half and you're off.

Tommy Docherty on Graeme Souness's disciplinary problems as player/manager of Rangers, 1988

Graeme became a victim of his own personality. He wanted so desperately to be successful, and everything became too intense. He wanted people to think and act like he did. He expected every player to be committed in a physical way, and not everybody is.

Roy Evans on his Liverpool predecessor Graeme Souness, 1994

It's like any relationship. Sometimes it goes wrong and you simply have to work at putting it right again. There's no point trying to pretend it's perfect all the time. We don't sit here holding hands seven days a week.

Liverpool's Roy Evans on his partnership with Gerard Houllier four days before Evans left the club by mutual consent, 1998

I can see you now, John, wandering along the King's Road, jangling with jewellery, and clicking your fingers in time to the music on your walkabout headphones.

Malcolm Allison taunting 48-year-old Wearsider John Neal, newly appointed manager of Chelsea, 1981

Take Stan Cullis. Look at all that success he had when he managed Wolves. Once he was 55, no one ever spoke to him. It's the waste, the waste of knowledge.

Malcolm Allison, from *The Mavericks* (Mainstream, 1994)

I wish the FA or someone would get together fellows of vast experience like me, Tommy Docherty, Malcolm Allison, John Bond and use our expertise. We know the pitfalls. We could help young managers, and that would help the game. Get us together maybe once a month, tape it and let the questions roll in. There'd be 50 per cent rubbish and 25 per cent laughs, but an essential 25 per cent of wisdom.

Former Southampton boss Lawrie McMenemy, 1988

He kept Arsenal in the headlines by continued success and flamboyant methods. No reporter lacked help in getting a story.

Tom Whittaker on his Highbury predecessor George Allison, 1950s

Gordon Lee is passionate and fizzes like a bottle of pop.

Roy Sproson on his predecessor in the Port Vale managerial chair, 1974

When we scored our equaliser from a penalty, everyone else leapt off the bench to cheer except Jock, and it was then, when I came to my seat and patted Jock on the head, that I should have known. He just sat motionless, and I didn't read into that the meaning that I should have because my thoughts were totally absorbed in a stupid game of football.

Alex Ferguson on the minutes leading up to Jock Stein's death, from *A Light in the North: Seven Years with Aberdeen* (Mainstream, 1985)

Jock had everything. He had the knowledge, he had that nasty bit that managers must have, and he could communicate. On top of it all, he was six feet tall and sometimes he seemed to get bigger when he was talking to you.

Graeme Souness on Jock Stein, 1990s

He ruled with a rod of iron, an iron fist without a velvet glove.

Graeme Souness on Jock Stein, 1990s

John, you're immortal now.

Bill Shankly to Jock Stein after Celtic's historic European Cup triumph, 1967

They say he's tough, he's hard, he's ruthless. Rubbish, he's got a heart of gold, he loves the game, he loves his fans, he loves his players. He's like an old collie dog, he doesn't like hurting his sheep. He'll drive them. Certainly. But bite them, never.

Joe Mercer of Manchester City on Bill Shankly, 1968

He signed Alec Lindsay, who was a left-back, from Bury and the lad had two years in the reserves at Anfield until the day came for his debut. Shanks said to him: 'Now look, Alec, when you get the ball I want you to beat a couple of men and smash it into the back of the net just the same way as you did at Bury Football Club.' Alec Lindsay said: 'But boss, that wasn't me, it was Bobby Kerr.' So Shanks turned to Bob Paisley and said: 'Christ, Bob, we've signed the wrong player!'

Tommy Docherty spinning a typical Shankly tale, 1980s

Even Ian Callaghan had to bend down to get through the door after one of Shankly's team talks. It was amazing how he could build you up.

Tranmere boss Ron Yeats recalling his days at Anfield, 1974

I believe Bill Shankly died of a broken heart after he stopped managing Liverpool and saw them go on to even greater success without him. Giving your whole life to a football club is a mistake.

Johnny Giles starting his second spell in charge at West Bromwich Albion, 1984

One of my great regrets is that I got the chance to speak to Bill Shankly only the once. After I signed for Liverpool, John Toshack took me to Shanks' house to meet him. He gave me two pieces of advice: don't over-eat and don't lose your accent.

Kenny Dalglish, 1989

If Bill had one failing, it was the fact that he did not like to upset players that had done so well for him. He was a softie at heart.

Liverpool's Bob Paisley on Bill Shankly, 1980

He, Joe Fagan and Ronnie Moran give the club that homely appearance, but beneath what might seem a soft exterior there is a hard centre.

Jimmy Armfield of Leeds on Bob Paisley, 1977

He's broken this silly myth that nice guys don't win anything.

Brian Clough on the success of Bob Paisley, 1978

There's a bit of Shanks in his mannerisms. He gives one hundred per cent, and if he believes in something he'll go to the ends of the earth to achieve it.

Liverpool's Roy Evans on Kevin Keegan at Newcastle, 1994

If Kevin Keegan fell into the Tyne, he'd come up with a salmon in his mouth!

Jack Charlton, 1993

When he arrived at Pittodrie in 1975 he beat the drum to such an extent that everyone believed the team could climb Everest with their slippers on.

Aberdeen's Alex Ferguson on Ally MacLeod, from *A Light in the North* (Mainstream, 1985)

He was a man of real substance. He never bowed to the press and he never criticised his players. That's something I've never forgotten. He'd always defend his players to the death, even though he was under pressure. Unfair, but that's the way the modern media is. You could see the strength in his eyes, so nobody messed with him too much.

Alex Ferguson on his old Rangers boss Scot Symon, from *A Year in the Life: The Manager's Diary* (Virgin, 1995)

Me and Alex had a very volatile dressing-room relationship. We were playing a game at Forfar in the Aberdeenshire Senior Cup and Fergie's number two, Archie Knox, had come into the dressing-room and was tearing into the team. Behind him came Fergie, and he started shouting and yelling at this centre-forward called Stevie Cowan. As Fergie walked forward he kicked the dirty pile of kit and washing on the floor all over the place, and a pair of underpants floated through the air and landed on the head of the boy sitting next to Cowan. While Cowan was getting slaughtered, the boy next to him didn't move. He was rigid with fear, sitting there bolt upright with these underpants on his head. Alex finished slaughtering Cowan and then barked at the other lad: 'And you, get those fucking pants off your head!'

Mark McGhee on his Aberdeen mentor, Alex Ferguson, 1995

He simply likes winning.

Everton's Walter Smith on old pal Alex Ferguson, 1998

He is a man who hates to be second anywhere, and for it to happen in Manchester was quite a new experience.

Malcolm Allison on Matt Busby after City beat United en route to lifting the First Division title, 1968

I felt quite green about the managerial side of the game when Leeds gave me the job. I turned to Matt Busby for guidance. He went patiently over the ground with me and answered question after question. He demonstrated his wonderful gift for making the man who seeks his advice seem like the most important man in the world. Later, when things weren't working out too well, he put his hand on my shoulder and said, 'It'll turn out all right, son.'

If you look at Matt and ask where he might have failed, you immediately think of George Best. But could anybody have handled him? It's a shame that his talent wasn't fully used because after the age of 26 he just played around. But if Matt Busby couldn't handle him, nobody could.

Liverpool's Bob Paisley, 1980s

He was the outstanding man of them all – even Bill Shankly and Jock Stein sought his advice and experience. He was the lord of all managers. I'm just glad we won the Championship before he died.

Alex Ferguson paying tribute to the late Sir Matt Busby, 1994

Frank O'Farrell wasn't allowed to do the job because the old pros ganged up on him. Some of them, like Crerand and Willie Morgan, were very friendly with Sir Matt, golfing partners of his. It was a dressing-room full of old pros . . . and shit-stirrers.

Tommy Docherty on his predecessor at Manchester United, 1970s

How could a manager chastise players who misbehaved when they were aware that he had been involved in something like this?

Sir Matt Busby on Tommy Docherty's affair with Mary Brown, which led to his exit from Old Trafford, 1977

It would be better to be the one after the one who follows Jack.

Mick McCarthy on the difficulties of following a legend like Jack Charlton into the Republic of Ireland job, 1996

The best manager in Scotland.

National boss Craig Brown on Stenhousemuir's Terry Christie, 1995

He didn't say a lot, but what he did say wasn't airy-fairy. He was a real boss though, a real manager of the time.

Former Tottenham boss Arthur Rowe on Peter McWilliam, who managed the club for two spells (1912–27 and 1938–42), 1979

It was like finding Miss World was free and asking for a date.

Bristol Rovers' Bobby Gould on persuading Don Howe to be his coach, 1986

Nearly 62, he's like a two-year-old.

Halifax Town coach Kieran O'Regan on veteran boss George Mulhall, enjoying his third spell at The Shay, 1998

As a young player at Portsmouth, I was George Graham's legs, but I would never have dreamed that he would become a football manager, not in a month of Sundays.

Bradford City's Chris Kamara, an even more unlikely candidate for management given his disciplinary record as a player, 1997

At Preston we had an old-school manager, John McGrath. He used to think that if you drank iced water you'd get the cramps. So I had to sneak into the shower cubicles to drink iced water before a game.

Notts County's Sam Allardyce on the importance of preparation, 1998

He would take us out on to the pitch and hit the crossbar six times out of six from the eighteen-yard line, just to show us that he could play.

Doncaster boss Peter Doherty on his old Derby County manager Edward Magner, 1950s

If a club has millions they send for Ron Atkinson; if they are skint they send for Dave Bassett.

Bassett on taking over at cash-strapped Sheffield United, 1988

He's the only person I know who can talk for an hour without stopping for breath.

Ron Atkinson on Dave Bassett, 1997

They call him Big Ron because he is a big spender in the transfer market. I just call him Fat Ron.

Bristol Rovers' Malcolm Allison preparing for a Cup tie with Atkinson's Villa, 1993

The sacking of Ron Atkinson is the best thing that could happen to Manchester United, and it didn't come a day too soon . . . His downfall has been all of his own doing. I dislike him because of his flash personality. And to my mind it's that sort of attitude which has finally got him the sack.

Tommy Docherty not shedding too many tears over Big Ron's demise at Old Trafford, 1986

All I do know is that I'll never be able to achieve what Tommy did, and that is take Aston Villa into the Third Division and Manchester United into the Second Division.

Ron Atkinson, sacked by Villa, smarting at criticism from Tommy Docherty, 1994

It's perfectly fair to suggest I hate and despise the little so-and-so.

Atkinson on Docherty, 1998

I don't think I have ever seen a man who appears less able to relax in my life . . . He was a cold man, difficult to approach, and lacked a sense of humour.

Tommy Docherty on former Preston and Hull City manager Cliff Britton, 1970s

I've always wanted to know what his results have been. Wherever he's been, I have kept an eye on what he's done, probably more so than him needing to keep an eye on how I've done, because a lot of things that I've done have been written about – not all of them good either.

Stoke City's Brian Little on brother Alan, manager of York City, 1998

I take no pleasure in beating my brother.

Brian Little after Stoke's 2–0 win over York, 1998

There are certain things you can learn about coaching, but personality and leadership are essentials you are born with, and Terry is blessed with both.

Malcolm Allison on his Crystal Palace assistant and, ultimately, successor Terry Venables, 1976

The only contact you get from him is when he wants to do a deal – which is most of the time! He is the sort of bloke who comes up to you out of the blue at a dinner and asks if you will sell such and such. You say: 'OK, if the money is right,' then off he goes and that is the last you hear of it. He used to bounce off managers to get the value of players.

Jim Smith on Terry Venables, from *Bald Eagle* (Mainstream, 1990)

Jim's racing tips can be lousy, but his football ideas are excellent.

Bolton's Colin Todd on the much-travelled Jim Smith, 1997

Ossie Ardiles is not the only man with a dream, but I'd like to see him try to make his fantasies come true here.

Terry Dolan, boss of ailing Hull City, 1994

12 The Gaffes

He's literally got no right foot.

**David Pleat on United States winger Preki, who favours
his left foot, 1998**

We've got complete harmonium in the dressing-room.

Blackpool's musical boss Joe Smith, 1950s

I can't understand why Alf hasn't picked Giles for England.

**Scotland boss Willie Ormond raving about Johnny Giles,
unaware that he already had a stack of caps for the
Republic of Ireland, 1973**

Watch out for the blond at corners and free-kicks.

**Willie Ormond warning his players before Scotland's
international against a Swedish team which contained
six big blonds, 1975**

What we must do now is harmonise the defence with a view to
its new disposition.

**Craig Brown seeking vocal backing for Scotland
following the loss of Alan McLaren from his European
Championships squad, 1996**

The boys' feet have been up in the clouds since the win.

Walsall's Alan Buckley, 1983

We're halfway round the Grand National course with many
hurdles to clear. So let's all make sure we keep our feet firmly
on the ground.

**Charlton's Mike Bailey, cautious about his team's
promotion prospects, 1981**

I can count on the fingers of one hand ten games when we've caused our own downfall.

Wimbledon's Joe Kinnear, 1993

He did a lot of growing up in Hong Kong.

Rangers' Graeme Souness on 5ft 4in striker John Spencer, back at Ibrox after a year in the Far East, 1991

He has two arms and legs, same as the rest of our players, but once he's found his feet I'm convinced he'll do well.

Aberdeen's Ian Porterfield welcoming Charlie Nicholas to Pittodrie, 1988

Even when you're dead, you shouldn't lie down and let yourself be buried.

Gordon Lee on leaving Everton, 1981

It is important to have setbacks and disappointments early on in any career.

Aston Villa's Vic Crowe, 1971

I would have to have been blind or deaf not to have read the speculation.

Wolves' caretaker boss Bobby Downes, aware that his days are numbered, 1995

We don't want to get like basketball, with sin bins.

Glenn Hoddle momentarily confusing the rules of basketball and ice hockey, 1998

Once he starts to open his legs, you've got a problem.

Howard Wilkinson on speedy Aston Villa winger Tony Daley, 1992

I am a firm believer that if you score one goal, the other team have to score two to win.

Sheffield Wednesday's Howard Wilkinson, 1983

I think if they hadn't scored, we might have got a better result.

Leeds' Howard Wilkinson after a 1–1 draw at Chelsea, 1994

The first ninety minutes are the most important.

England's Bobby Robson, 1980s

We can beat anyone on our day – so long as we score.

Kilmarnock's Alex Totten, 1995

If we score more goals than they do, we will win.

Blackburn's Kenny Dalglish, 1994

We had enough chances to win this game. In fact, we did win.

Aberdeen's Alex Smith, 1991

I don't blame individuals – I blame myself.

Oldham's Joe Royle, 1983

Without picking out anyone in particular, I thought Mark Wright was tremendous.

Liverpool's Graeme Souness, 1993

He'll take some pleasure from that, Brian Carey. He and Steve Bull have been having it off all afternoon.

Ron Atkinson on a feud at Wolves v. Leicester, 1994

I have other irons in the fire, but I'm keeping them close to my chest.

John Bond after leaving Norwich City, 1980

I promise results, not promises.

John Bond at Manchester City, 1980

I just wonder what would have happened if the shirt had been on the other foot.

Norwich City's Mike Walker, upset at decisions against his team in a 3–1 defeat by Manchester United, 1993

I didn't have time to do the job justice.

Leicester City's Matt Gillies packing in his other duties as a magistrate, 1968

There's only one team going to win it now, and that's England.

Kevin Keegan two minutes before Dan Petrescu's winner for Romania in the World Cup, 1998

You, my old son, may be the only friend I have left in the world.

Scotland's Ally MacLeod patting the head of a stray dog during the ill-fated World Cup campaign in Argentina, 1978. The dog promptly bit his hand

I felt a lump in my mouth as the ball went in.

Terry Venables on a goal conceded, 1980s

No thank you, I don't want to dinner.

Fresh from elocution lessons, Ipswich's Alf Ramsey addresses a restaurant car steward on the way back from a match, 1960

Kevin, get stripped ... Not that Kevin, the other one.

A flustered Sir Alf Ramsey, always uncomfortable with substitutions, trying to get Kevin Hector on five minutes from the end of England's ill-fated World Cup qualifier with Poland, 1973. Misinterpreting the instructions, Kevin Keegan had removed his tracksuit first, so that by the time Hector finally made his international debut, there were less than two minutes left

Some of our players have got no brains, so I've given them the day off tomorrow to rest them.

Plymouth Argyle's David Kemp, 1992

There's more ice down there than sunk the *Bismarck*.

QPR's Gerry Francis complaining about the number of injured players in the Rangers' dressing-room, 1992

What I said to them at half-time would be unprintable on the radio.

Gerry Francis of Spurs following a second-half fightback at West Ham, 1995

My heart was pounding and I was feeling as sick as the proverbial donkey.

Republic of Ireland boss Mick McCarthy, 1997

The beauty of Cup football is that Jack always has a chance of beating Goliath.

Sunderland's Terry Butcher before a Coca-Cola Cup tie with Leeds, 1993

We are on the right street.

Tottenham's Christian Gross after defeat at Derby, 1998

There's a rat in the camp trying to throw a spanner in the works.

Brighton's Chris Cattlin, 1983

We can't rest on our laurels because you can soon have your feet kicked out from under you.

West Brom's Bobby Gould, 1992

I've no time for mates. I make the rules and I'm the one with his head on the line.

Chris Waddle sensing that his job could be on the block as player/manager of Burnley, 1997

You weigh up the pros and cons and try to put them in chronological order.

Dave Bassett, 1995

I'd like to think it was a case of crossing the i's and dotting the t's.

Nottingham Forest's Dave Bassett, hopeful of signing keeper Kevin Miller from Watford, 1997

I wish Glenn luck, but he is putting his head in the frying pan.

Ossie Ardiles fearing for Hoddle's future as England coach, 1996

It's a clash of the Titanics!

Chelsea's Ruud Gullit on England v. Germany at Euro 96

It's the men without the balls who should decide the play.

Ruud Gullit on the importance of running off the ball, 1996

Maradona gets tremendous elevation with his balls no matter what position he's in.

David Pleat, 1986

Stoichkov is pointing at the bench with his eyes.

David Pleat, 1996

I was very impressed by the way he took his punishment. He took it on the chin.

Bobby Robson welcoming Arsenal's Paul Davis back into the England frame after the midfielder had served a nine-match ban for smashing the jaw of Southampton's Glenn Cockerill, 1988

My heart goes out to Graeme Souness.

Brian Clough hearing that the Liverpool manager was going into hospital for heart surgery, 1992

Both our other goalkeepers were unavailable. We played him to get us out of jail.

Spurs' caretaker boss David Pleat on giving Hans Segers a surprise comeback against Southampton, 1998. Segers had recently been acquitted in court on charges of match-fixing

That number fourteen for Holland is a marvellous player ... that Johan Strauss.

Joe Mercer struggling to compose himself after his comment on Johan Cruyff, 1974

Magnifico! Or whatever they say in Paris.

Sunderland's Peter Reid, delighted with the performance of French goalkeeper Lionel Perez, 1997

I walked into the dressing-room a few minutes before kick-off and saw this strange guy standing there. I was about to chuck him out when one of the lads told me he was our substitute keeper.

Ian Ross, manager of part-timers Berwick Rangers, facing an identity crisis, 1997

Well, it wasn't easy, you know, because most of the players out there are unfamiliar to me. I kept thinking that [Pat] McGinlay was Charlie Nicholas because he looks like Nicholas – no, not Nicholas, the other one, Paul McStay.

Jack Charlton trying to check on the form of the Celtic players in his Republic of Ireland team but becoming confused by the absence of numbers on the Celtic shirts, 1993

Are you one of my players then?

Gerry Francis, two days after taking over at Queens Park Rangers, to Huddersfield's Rob Edwards, 1998

No one hands you cups on a plate.

Newcastle United assistant manager Terry McDermott, 1995

We must have had 99 per cent of the game. It was the other three per cent that cost us the match.

Chelsea's Ruud Gullit after defeat by Coventry, 1997

Index